Inf rmati n architecture

BLUEPRINTS FOR THE WEB

SECOND EDITION

Christina Wodtke and Austin Govella

New Riders

VOICES THAT MATTER™

Information Architecture: Blueprints for the Web, Second Edition

Christina Wodtke and Austin Govella

New Riders
1249 Eighth Street
Berkeley, CA 94710
510/524-2178
510/524-2221 (fax)

Find us on the Web at: www.newriders.com
To report errors, please send a note to errata@peachpit.com

New Riders is an imprint of Peachpit, a division of Pearson Education

Copyright © 2009 by Christina Wodtke and Austin Govella

PROJECT EDITOR: Michael J. Nolan
DEVELOPMENT EDITOR: Alyssa Wodtke
TECHNICAL EDITORS: Sarah Rice, Larry Cornett, Robert Hoekman Jr., Frank Ramirez, Livia Labate, Cindy McWilliams, Joshua Porter, Bryce Glass, Chris Baum, and Jorge Arango
PRODUCTION EDITOR: Becky Winter
COPY EDITOR: Marta Justak
PROOFREADER: Marta Justak
INDEXER: Julie Bess
COMPOSITOR AND BOOK DESIGNER: Maureen Forys, Happenstance Type-O-Rama

ISBN 13: 978-0-321-60080-6
ISBN 10: 0-321-60080-0

9 8 7 6 5 4 3 2 1

Printed and bound in the United States of America

For the extraordinary minds of Silicon Valley who have taught me so much, my sister Alyssa who rode this crazy ride with me twice now, and Amelie who let me write when I really, really should have been playing fire engines with her.

—Christina

For Debbi and Aiden who didn't mind Daddy disappearing (too much); for all the friends, co-workers, and colleagues who helped this happen; and for the amazing editors (especially Alyssa) who made it kick ass.

—Austin

Acknowledgements

Christina once said that the writing really happens in the editing. Austin wasn't sure, but he quickly learned how true it was. This book would not have happened or be even half as good if it weren't for Alyssa's fearless, patient, frenzied, kind, and amazing editing skills. She whipped everything into shape, herded us cats, and buffed everything to a nice shine.

Similarly, the rest of the crew worked miracles. The designers got it, Becky had the patience of a saint, and Marta's copy-editing eye caught every Lilliputian detail. Michael made the whole thing happen.

Erin Malone's beautiful photographs set the scene for each chapter. And Michael Fleming's charming illustrations bring a smile to our faces every time they appear.

We recruited a whole passel of practitioners to handle the technical editing. In addition to making sure we weren't crazy, they poked holes, made suggestions, and offered ideas that helped both of us. Fortunately for the reader, the tech editors are some of the smartest people in the business: Sarah Rice, Larry Cornett, Robert Hoekman jr, Frank Ramirez, Livia Labate, Cindy McWilliams, Joshua Porter, Bryce Glass, Chris Baum, and Jorge Arango.

We're both indebted to the wonderfully wise communities of smart people who talked, argued, and shared with us.

Thanks for the persona pics: Rahel Bailie, Erin Malone, Joshua Porter, Scott Hirsch, Bryce Glass, Allison Walker, Angie Serna, Alyssa Wodtke, Michael Fleming, Jeff Sensabaugh, and MJ Broadbent.

Contents

Chapter 3: Sock Drawers and CD Racks—Everything Must Be Organized 37
In which we learn that a lot of stuff can be a bad thing, and organization can be a good thing.

Chapter 4: A Bricklayer's View of Information Architecture 65
In which we learn to design our architecture from the bottom up.

Chapter 5: Search and Ye Shall Find

In which we study the dark arts of search engines, algorithms, and query suggestions.

Chapter 6: From A to C by Way of B

In which we design a nice path for the user to get from one place to another, surviving such perils as shopping carts and pop-up windows.

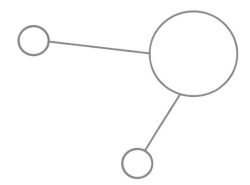

Foreword

It's hard to recall, now, the world that greeted the first edition of this book upon its publication seven years ago. The world has changed, of course, but perhaps more significantly, information architecture itself, and its place within that world, has changed even more.

At that time, some pronounced information architecture a fad, an artifact of the inflated expectations (not to mention job titles and salaries) of the late-'90s dot-com boom. And just as that boom had recently gone bust, some expected the field of information architecture to go bust right along with it.

But then something happened that took some people by surprise: As the bubble burst and the prospects of Web startups deflated, information architecture actually became more important than ever. To stay alive in an increasingly hostile competitive environment, Web sites looked for ways to deliver better experiences and become more useful and usable to their users.

They didn't need more sophisticated technology or flashier graphics. They needed better blueprints. And they turned to information architects to create them.

And it wasn't just the startups that saw the value of information architecture. As larger organizations embraced the Web, then struggled to understand it, then worked to make it deliver more value for their customers and their businesses, information architecture moved from luxury to necessity. And now, in organizations that recognize the critical strategic role that information architecture plays in the success of their Web offerings, information architects are increasingly considered vital decision makers.

Meanwhile, the profession itself has blossomed, spawning conferences, publications, professional organizations, academic programs, and books. A community of professionals and academics has emerged, sharing their ideas and insights and building the foundation for the further evolution of the practice of information architecture.

In the last few years, a new generation of Web startups has captured the imagination of the industry once more. The "Web 2.0" wave has brought with it new ideas about what the Web is really good for, and new ways to deliver great experiences. But once again, information architecture is central to delivering on the promise of this new trend. The more dynamic architectural approaches embodied by this new generation of Web products are at the heart of their success.

And information architecture itself has started to look beyond its roots on the Web. Information architects have begun to see connections between their work and work being done in fields like industrial design, environmental design, and service design. They have looked beyond the digital realm and seen new applications for the tools, methods, and principles they have developed.

So the world that greets this new, second edition of *Information Architecture: Blueprints for the Web* is quite different from the world of seven years ago. But some things really haven't changed: People still need Web sites that reflect the way they think, work, and behave. And those Web sites still need blueprints that outline a vision for the experiences they will deliver to users, and talented information architects to create that vision. And those information architects still need books like this one, to benefit from the wisdom and experience of their authors.

—*Jesse James Garrett*
  October 2008

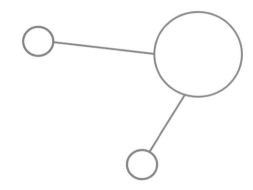

Introduction: Why Blueprint a Web Site?

Once upon a time, a very, *very* long time ago, the Internet was composed of homepages. These one-page sites introduced a company or a person, told a little about the subject, and offered a link to email the proprietor. It took only one person to write, design, and code this site, and it was easy.

Flash forward a few years, and everything we can imagine is online: million-page newspaper sites, online calendars, photo galleries, and shopping malls. Huge teams of specialists are building these sites with experienced designers, engineers, writers, and producers. With so many people devoted to producing so much information, you'd think that the result would be nothing short of a masterpiece.

So why are so many of these sites so difficult to use?

When you build a building, you make a blueprint. When you build a toaster, you create a diagram of its workings. Yet Web sites, whose complexity far exceeds a toaster's, are often thrown up hastily with barely a thought about how they will be used. A company wanting a Web site hires an engineer, a marketing guy, and a graphic designer, and says, "Go to it." It's the equivalent of hiring an electrician, a plumber, and an interior decorator, and then saying, "Build me a shopping mall." That shopping mall desperately needs an architect, and today's Web site needs an information architect.

An information architect will look at the business's needs, the end user's habits, what technology has to offer, and then create a blueprint for how to organize the Web site so that it will meet all these needs.

Who Is This Book For?

All Web sites have information architecture (IA), just as all houses have architecture. In the days of log cabins, houses did not have architects, and in the pioneer days of the Web, sites didn't have architects either. But just as someone chose where to lay those logs and where to leave a window, someone is choosing what goes in a navigation bar, or if there is one at all. Those choices can be made off-the-cuff, or they can be carefully thought through.

As professional information architects, people often come to us in pain. If they have a small site, they've muddled through designing the architecture for their site. Most of the Web was built this way.

But their site got bigger, and eventually it became kind of overwhelming. Suddenly, people from the entire company were putting up pages of documents. Perhaps they allowed their end users to put up content, too! Perhaps they plugged in a search engine, hoping that would fix the problem, but found it turned up pages they didn't know they had, but not the ones they were looking for. The lack of planning resulted in a lack of finding.

This is fun for Christina and Austin, and for most information architects. We tend to like big messy nightmare problems that we can tidy up. So we make a nice living by taking a lot of disorganized information and making it useful for people.

But the fact is that budgets are shrinking while Web sites are getting bigger and bigger, and sometimes there isn't any money to hire a professional information architect. In fact, more than sometimes. Often. So now what?

You are going to do it. You might be the project or product manager, the designer, the engineer, or the marketing guy. You're not really sure why this site organization problem landed on your desk; heck, you're looking around to see if there is another desk you can slide it onto. But as your hope for getting someone else to do it fades, you realize it has to be done. And this is the book we wrote for you. Not for Johnny-IA, but for every person who got stuck with the hard job of figuring out where to put the home link.

Yes, It's a Short Book

And the best part is—you don't have to read it in order! Feel free to flip to the section that addresses what you are working on. Got to put in a search engine? Chapter 5! About to add tagging? Chapter 4! Budgets aren't the only things shrinking—timelines are, too. The Web isn't slowed by packaging and shipping the way software can be. Because you can get things on the Web very quickly, everyone thinks you should put something up tomorrow. However, information architecture is actually a hairy profession. There is a lot to learn, and the problems are complex. One information architect I know likes to say, "It *is* rocket science." So you've got hard problems, no time, and no money.

Sounds like a typical Web project to me.

Our goal for this book is for you to learn rocket science in a day without blowing anyone up. We're not going to tell you everything about information architecture. There are a lot of good books if you decide that IA is your cup of tea and want to go further. But we'll try to give you enough information so you can make a better Web site without having to hold off the project until you've finished graduate school.

A wise man once said, "The best is the enemy of the good."[1] Trying to be perfect will both make you crazy and make you miss your launch date. This book is full of stuff to make your Web site better, not perfect.

We've also put up a Web site at `http://www.blueprintsfortheweb.com`, and we'll be putting up additional resources there. If there is a neat new book or a good article, we'll point you to it.

Plus, we're going to put up the chapters we cut from this book so you can see another short book up there, too. In case you just gotta know more.

Why a Second Edition?

When Christina wrote this book in 2000, two things had happened to the Web: the dot-com crash and the widespread acceptance of the Web as a part of every single company's business practice. And two things hadn't happened: search wasn't much help when you were looking for things, and social networks didn't exist. Christina wrote a book that knew that information architecture was critical to this new world of business online, but wasn't enough of a psychic to see how IA would grow and change to meet the new challenges of a much bigger, more dynamic Web. After seven years, some parts of the book were looking a bit embarrassing. Search had gone from hit-or-miss to almost psychic-like accuracy in finding anything online, and more than ever people expected miracles when they typed a word into a search box. Moreover, where once there were just a few user forums, now everything had comments, ratings, and community participation, and millions *more* pages were added to the Internet. Suddenly, everyone who could type was participating in the creation of the content of the Internet (and many who didn't need to type—video, photos, and MP3s got a lot more common).

More than ever before, you needed a book that helped you make sure your site visitors were finding what *they* needed, and more than ever, this book was only part of the story of how to do so. A third thing had changed—Christina is a mom now, with even less time than before. Happily, Austin signed on to lend a hand in writing an updated

---

1 Voltaire, who also said, "The best way to be boring is to leave nothing out."

version. We now have got sections on tagging, social and community architecture, and a pragmatic look at search, as well as updated sections on interaction and interface design.

How to Read This Book

With your eyes.

Okay, seriously, we tried to do two things to make this book helpful. First, if you read it from start to finish, it should set up your brain to create a site that helps people find what they want. IA is first and foremost about *findability*.[2] We do it step-by-step, taking you through the basic principles and then through techniques that grow more and more complex.

But let's say your timeline is really, really short—in that case, you can flip to a chapter and get an overview of any given subject, from search to metadata. Each chapter mixes an overview, lots of examples, principles to help you design more effectively, and techniques to a better design. If we are missing anything, drop us a note on our site. We'd love to hear from you!

---

2 Term coined by Peter Morville to describe the quality of a system or object that makes it easy for people to find it when they need it. It was made to be the sister of usability: after all, you can't use it if you can't find it, right?

"A blueprint is good
thinking written down.
You have to do the
good thinking part
first and the writing
down second."

1

First Principles

*Some rules of thumb, and
some thumbing of rules.*

A blueprint is good thinking written down. You have to do the good thinking part first and the writing down second.

One of the many secrets of good thinking is to learn from those who have suffered before you. Over time, design, architecture, software engineering, and usability have developed many good rules of thumb to help us avoid making the same dumb mistakes our predecessors did.

As you create your own Web sites, you'll add your own rules to this list. But let's begin with these eight principles.

Principle #1: Design for Wayfinding

A few years back, we read an interesting study[1] that showed that women navigate through the world using landmarks (turn right at the Quickie Mart, turn left at the white house) and men navigate with their sense of direction and space (go five miles east, then two miles north).

On the Web, everyone is a woman. You cannot use your sense of direction; it's a physical attribute, and physically you haven't moved an inch from your monitor, no matter how many Web sites you've visited.

To ensure that people can return to items of interest and that they can find new ones, information architects (IAs) can borrow from a discipline used in architecture called *wayfinding*.

---

1 Georg Grön, Arthur P. Wunderlich, Manfred Spitzer, Reinhard Tomczak, and Matthias W. Riepe, "Brain Activation During Human Navigation: Gender-Different Neural Networks as Substrate of Performance," *Nature Neuroscience 3*, no. 4 (April 2000): 404–408. Or in English rather than scientist-ese: "Study: Sex Affects Navigation. Men Find Their Way More Easily in Unfamiliar Settings." Available Online at http://www.nature.com/neuro/journal/v3/n4/abs/nn0400_404.html.

Wayfinding lets people know four things:

1. Where they are.

2. Where the things are that they're looking for.

3. How they can get to those things they seek.

4. Where they have already looked.

Wayfinding is typically employed in disorienting places like malls, airports, and subways to help people get from one point to another.[2]

Wayfinding doesn't do this just with signs. Architects also use architectural cues and interior design choices. Think of an airport; some of its features include

- Wide main corridors that not only let lots of people through, but also let them know the path to stay on (**Figure 1.1**).

- Small corridors hidden in corners provide access to employee areas. The design is finished with an "Employees Only" sign, but if the design is good, you will never find yourself facing that sign.

FIGURE 1.1 Even if you've never been to Heathrow Airport, it's pretty obvious where you're supposed to go.

---

2 Now don't take this too far! Your users always know where they are; they are sitting in front of a computer screen. Unlike the real world, they aren't that lost. They might be peeved that they can't find the camcorder they're looking for, but they aren't going to starve to death and get eaten by bears.

On Amazon, the main section of the page is devoted to customers, who are the bulk of Amazon's visitors. Down along the side is a small link, Associates Program, which is for people who sell items for Amazon. A normal book buyer would never accidentally click the Associates link in **Figure 1.2**.

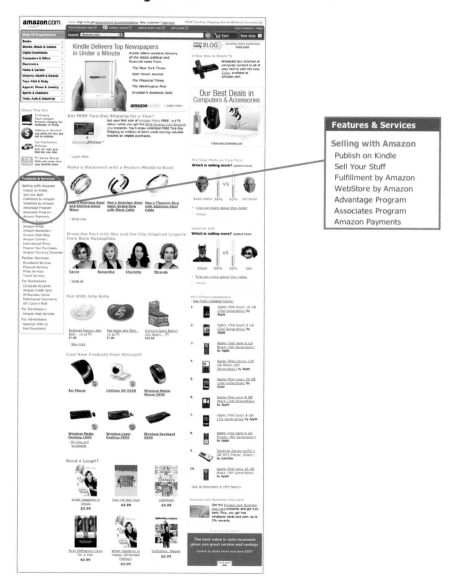

FIGURE 1.2 On Amazon, the normal customer would never accidentally click the Associates link, Amazon's version of an "employees only" entrance.

1. Tell visitors where they are.

It's time to use the big "You are here!" sign, as well as subtle design clues to indicate location. On the Web, this sign translates to

- Logos reminding you whose site you are on.

- Breadcrumbs[3] or a visual indicator telling you where you are in the system (see **Figure 1.3**).

- Clear page titles telling you what page you're on.

FIGURE 1.3 *Businessweek* uses red to draw a breadcrumb along your path. Right now you are clearly in Managing > Books. They keep the alternatives open to you, so you can easily find other sections of interest.

2. Tell visitors where the things are that they're looking for.

As you design your navigation system, ask yourself, "What do the bulk of the visitors coming to my site want?" And ask yourself a follow-up question: "What do I want my visitors to be able to find easily?" Once identified, you want to keep these items in front of your site's visitors as they travel throughout the site.

A software site, for example, usually needs to offer product information, downloads, and support. It's useful to allow users to always find their way easily to these key places. Although this can be done a number of ways, global navigation is the most common.

---

3 Breadcrumb is the term for the navigation that lets you move up and down a hierarchically organized collection of stuff. You probably first saw it on Yahoo! when you were researching Jane Fonda's breathtaking performance in *Klute* and followed this trail:

Home > Entertainment > Movies and Film > Titles > Drama > Suspense

And you found *Klute* just like Hansel and Gretel following breadcrumbs to their parents' home. It's a useful tool that allows users to widen their search.

Global navigation is a set of navigation tools that are consistent throughout a Web site. Let's look at the global navigation for three hotels: Omni Hotels, Holiday Inn, and Park Lane Guest Suites. Park Lane is a tiny bed and breakfast in Austin, Texas. Holiday Inn is a large chain of mid-priced hotels, and Omni is a smaller chain of higher-priced hotels. All three sport prominent links to Reservations (**Figure 1.4**): it's the one thing they all want you to find. It doesn't matter if you're a big company or a small one—if you have rooms to reserve, you had better put reservations right in front of your potential customer, or you're in trouble.

FIGURE 1.4 Even though these three companies offer very different accommodations in different places, all three have a prominent link to Reservations, the one thing the bulk of their visitors are looking for.

3. How do they get to those things they seek?

"How to get there" is achieved with intelligent navigation design. In good navigation design, links look clickable. They have clear labels that set expectations of what lies beneath. And they're grouped with similar options so they gain meaning through context. If you have a link to Macintosh, it means something different when it's next to a link titled London Fog Trench Coat or Jonathan Apples or IBM Think Pad. Navigation can be tricky. We have a big section on navigation in Chapter 8, The Tao of Navigation.

4. Where have they already looked?

In the beginning, there was the link, and it was good. And yea, kind and powerful Tim Berners-Lee[4] said, "Let that link be wise in the ways of the past and present, and show that it hath been clicked." And it was called the "visited link," and it was good. But this displeased the designers of the earth-tones and the sky-blues, and they grew angry and used images and did designate the link *not* show a different color if it were clicked, and the people of the Web despaired, and they kept looking in the same section, even though they had looked there three times already.

Do we have to say more? It's just randomly cruel *not* to let people know where they have been.

---

4   Inventor of the Internet. Did you really think it was Al Gore? http://www.w3.org/People/Berners-Lee/

Principle #2: Set Expectations and Provide Feedback

On the Web, you don't know what to expect when you click a link, submit a form, or push a button. It's the designer's job to set expectations for every action and clearly present results of those actions. There are many ways you can keep people in the loop.

Let folks know it hasn't happened until it's happened

If your users are in the middle of a process that has several steps, it's good to let folks know nothing's happened until it's happened. The Snapfish Web site allows users to store, edit, and print their personal photos. The tool for cropping keeps a small image of the original photo in the corner of the page while you edit. This procedure assures you that your original photo is still intact, and you can start over at any time (see **Figure 1.5**). Photos are precious to people, and this provides the level of comfort needed to allow people to edit without being afraid.

FIGURE 1.5 On the bottom-right, Snapfish shows a small version of the original photo, so you can be assured your changes haven't gone through yet.

Remind people where they are in the process

You can also remind people where they are in the process. Drugstore.com's shopping bag is always on the left side of the page, letting you know how much you've spent and what you've selected to buy (see **Figure 1.6**).

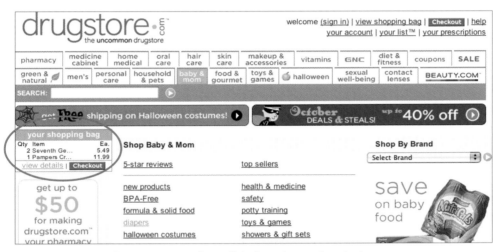

FIGURE 1.6 On the left, Drugstore.com shows all the items in your shopping bag.

Occasionally, the user has to wait for a process that takes a bit of time. To let people know it isn't their computer that's running sluggishly, you can display a message letting folks know what's going on.

Animation is important here because movement provides a sense of activity. A still screen is worrisome… Has my computer died? Have I lost the connection? Is their server down?

Expedia animates a series of small dots to let you know it is searching for flights (**Figure 1.7**). Users can't tell how long the search will take, but at least they know everything is working.

Similarly, Web applications can often take a while to load. Picnik, an online photo editor, handles potential user anxiety by displaying a status bar that slowly fills while the animation loads (see **Figure 1.8**). The friendly status messages are a bonus.

Expedia is searching for flights on
selected travel dates:
Fri 3/20/2009 — Sun 3/22/2009

FIGURE 1.7 If we could only animate paper, then you'd see that this line of dots is flickering, letting the user know the process hasn't stalled.

FIGURE 1.8 As the Picnik photo editing application downloads, the status bar slowly fills with green.

Principle #3: Design Ergonomically

When you're designing in digital spaces, remember an oft forgotten fact—human beings have bodies, and these bodies vary widely. In the real world, it's easier to remember. Herman Miller, the furniture company, went to the bank when its designers applied that knowledge to the humble office chair, and created a seat that could be adjusted endlessly: the Aeron. Herman Miller designers Bill Stumpf and Don Chadwick have ergonomics in their DNA, and brought sitting in front of a computer to a new pinnacle of comfort by designing the Aeron chair, which comes in a variety of sizes to reflect the variety of sizes our bodies come in. It can be adjusted so the lumbar support actually supports the lumbar and even sports a lightweight mesh to keep you cool as you burn the midnight oil.

But tall and short doesn't mean much on the Web. On the Web, the only body parts you engage are hands, eyes, and ears.

Hands

When designing for hands, consider such things as scrolling distance, and scrolling frequency. Think about designing shortcuts for people with repetitive stress injury (RSI). When Razorfish Germany redesigned the Audi site,[5] the company did extensive testing of navigation on the right side of the screen with potential Web site visitors (see **Figure 1.9**).

FIGURE 1.9 The Audi site, sporting racy, right-sided navigation!

This was an innovation because almost all Web sites had navigation on the top or left side of the screen at that time. In user testing, Razorfish discovered that not only did users not mind the change, but the right-side toolbar provided easier access to the scrollbar for faster navigation. The change made it easier to concentrate on the content.

---

5 "Challenging the Status Quo: Audi Redesigned," James Kalbach tells the story of how a Web design firm, Razorfish Germany, redesigned the Audi Web site to be as innovative as the product they sell (see http://www.boxesandarrows. com/archives/002695.php).

On a warm August evening, Cederholm and Luke Dorny crowd that had just finished walked across the street to most of the casual and cur name recognition and a sm minute of their time. Even

Such a person walked up t conversation with a questi soon turned into hard core validation, and strict adher figured these topics were s matters at 10PM in a art ga provide a best setting. Still his focus on the visitor and his reputation for being a r

Hard of hearing in a crowd the guy became irate and h conversation turned into a that Mr. Bulletproof did no seriously as he should. And for-word) that considering the gospel too askew for tl

It was at this point that Do between the two and mast minute later Dan quietly ba just been through a minor and his new friend were or (knowing Dorny that mean

The results can be sta written report for bus focus on what Service wanted the analysts to technology providers

Rather than producir wastebasket, C2 sent t tall male doll dressed "Talk" button was pus ServiceSource," the fig revenues and earning

Months after ServiceS the "action figures" st

Other design-thinking automaker, asked Jur refurbish its retail spa showrooms. Modeled guided tours and tou samples on Saturn mo of fabric and leather i

FIGURE 1.10 Your users need to be able to read your content. On the left, Airbag Industries, a design blog, uses small type that can be hard to read. On the right, The New York Times uses large, easy-to-read type.

Eyes

When designing for eyes, consider blindness, color blindness, nearsightedness, and farsightedness.[6] Airbag Industries, a small California design concern uses small, elegant type on its blog—so small, it's hard to read if you don't see very well. Of course, this is a personal blog about personal stuff, so it's okay if it's not the easiest Web site in the world to read. In contrast, The New York Times uses large, easy-to-read type for its articles since for the Gray Lady, it's very, very important that everybody, young and old, nearsighted and far, can read their news (**Figure 1.10**).

When designing your site, you'll want to ask yourself who will need to read your content. Teenagers with perfect eyesight? Or people in their forties and fifties — those lovely years when reading glasses and bifocals go on the shopping list?

Ears

When designing for ears, remember not only deafness, but also people who may be listening in public spaces. Who hasn't been in a quiet office when suddenly loud music floods the room from a nearby cubicle? Background music on your site or a catchy audio track for a video sounds like a good idea in a design brainstorm, but

6 To learn more about attending to the needs of the blind, the color-blind, and the girls who wear glasses, please check out the wonderful Americans with Disabilities Act Web site at http://www.ada.gov (though, no, they can't help with the "seldom make passes" part).

it will annoy people surfing at work or at the coffee shop. MySpace offers catchy music for the ads on its homepage, but the music is off by default (**Figure 1.11**).

The body and the world the body inhabits matter—even in the digital realm.

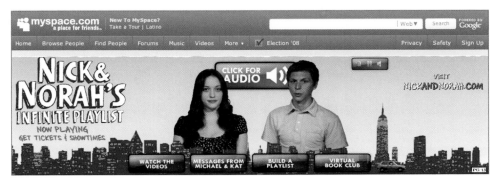

FIGURE 1.11 Ads on the MySpace homepage use animation and sound to drive the message home, but they have the good sense to leave the audio off by default. Interested users can turn the audio on at any time.

Principle #4: Be Consistent; Consider Standards

Your Web site is probably not the first Web site your visitors have ever been to. This means that when people type your URL into their browser window, they already have some expectations of what you will give them.

For example, watching online video in "full screen mode" has emerged as something of a convention, so designers have started adding full-screen buttons to online video players. Before designing a site, take a tour of competing and related Web sites. Look for best practices patterns you can adopt.

Do be thoughtful, though. You don't need to slavishly copy what other sites are doing. Rather, try to see why they've done what they've done. Is it a best practice? A common practice? An idle whim?

In these three examples, Hulu, Fancast, and YouTube, you'll see that they all have full-screen options. Why do Hulu (**Figure 1.12**) and Fancast (**Figure 1.13**) place full-screen at the top right? Why doesn't YouTube label its icon? Hulu and Fancast also offer tiny, pop-out screens. Why doesn't YouTube do that (**Figure 1.14**)? These variations may have come through experimentation, or the designers may simply be reinventing the wheel. The nice thing is, if you are doing a video site, you can test their variations to discover which one works the best.

FIGURE 1.12 On the Hulu video player, full screen is at the top-right corner. To open a new window, they say, "Pop out."

FIGURE 1.13 On the Fancast video player, full screen is also at the top-right corner, but to open a new window, they say, "Tiny."

FIGURE 1.14 YouTube uses an unlabeled icon for full screen. Unlike Fancast and Hulu, it's at the bottom-right corner. And they don't offer any option for opening a new window.

Your repeat visitors also have expectations. Did you call the help section Customer Support on the homepage? Then don't call it Help on interior pages or confusion ensues. Consistent labeling and design also give an air of professionalism; it doesn't look like you have 30 interns running around building Web pages without talking to anyone.

As you design, keep track of the conventions that arise with your site and break them with caution. You also need to keep a running style guide of your own decisions to ensure that your design is consistent.

Principle #5: Provide Error Support— Prevent, Protect, and Inform

Life is hard. People make mistakes. People then feel stupid. To avoid contributing to this sad state of the world, design defensively.[7] Try to keep errors to a minimum by doing the following:

- **Preventing.** Use clear, brief, conventional language in your instructions and dialogue. Live365 prevents errors by telling users exactly what kind of user name and password they should choose (**Figure 1.15**).

---

7 If there's one book you should read about providing error support, it would be *Defensive Design* by 37Signals. Published in 2002, the experts at 37Signals devote 200 pages to helping you prevent errors and help your customers recover when errors do happen.

- **Protecting.** Save user-entered information. Nothing is more frustrating than writing a long email and then losing it. Google's Gmail automatically saves the email you're writing as a draft (see **Figure 1.16**). Gmail also offers a Save Draft feature so savvy users can protect themselves by saving any time they want.

- **Informing.** If an error occurs, tell users exactly what's happened, use a nonjudgmental tone, and try to help them recover. For example, Expedia.com explains why the search was not successful and helps users avoid further errors by providing a drop-down list of potential choices (see **Figure 1.17**).

Sign Up Now!
New Member

Live365 will never share your e-mail address or personal information with anyone. Privacy Policy

*E-mail Address:		(A confirmation e-mail will be sent here.)
*Choose a **Username**:		(5-18 characters, no spaces)
*Choose a **Password**:		(4-18 characters, no spaces)
*Re-type Password:		

FIGURE 1.15 Live365 lets people who are joining their service know what rules they have for choosing a password.

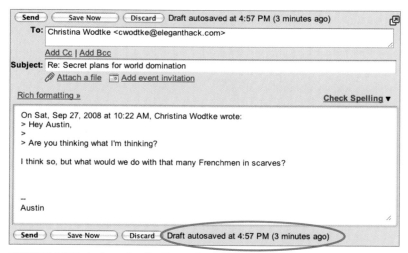

FIGURE 1.16 Notice how Gmail tells you the draft was "autosaved at 4:57." And if you don't trust the autosave (or it's not working), Gmail offers a friendly button to Save Now.

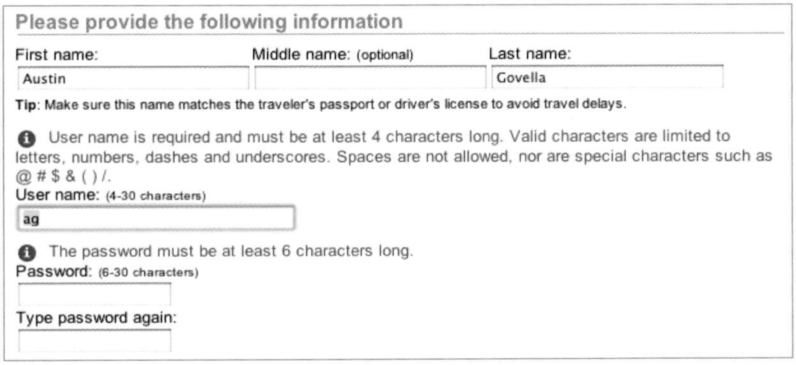

Please provide the following information

First name: Middle name: (optional)   Last name:

Austin   Govella

Tip: Make sure this name matches the traveler's passport or driver's license to avoid travel delays.

🛈 User name is required and must be at least 4 characters long. Valid characters are limited to letters, numbers, dashes and underscores. Spaces are not allowed, nor are special characters such as @ # $ & ( ) /.
User name: (4-30 characters)

ag

🛈 The password must be at least 6 characters long.
Password: (6-30 characters)

Type password again:

FIGURE 1.17 There is a lot right with Expedia's error messaging: it is polite, the errors are shown in red next to the area that needs correction making them easy to spot, and advice is given on how to correct the problem.

Principle #6: Rely on Recognition Rather than on Recall

Most humans have dicey memories. Not only do we forget to pick up bread from the store, but we also have trouble remembering long phone numbers, the address of our dentist, or that word for when you think you've seen something but you haven't. Research has told us even more about human memory capabilities: familiar items are easier to remember than unfamiliar, short words easier than long, and it's easier to remember in no particular order than in a particular order.[8]

Unlike humans, computers are pretty terrific at remembering long strings of characters. So why make people remember something if the computer can do it for them?

Yahoo! Maps takes advantage of this by storing the last address you typed into their search box and then displaying it in a drop-down in the Directions tool (see **Figure 1.18**). Not only does that save lazybones from having to type, and reduces errors caused by typos, but it saves users from having to drag out their address books to look up the information.

---

8 A. D. Baddeley, "The Magical Number Seven: Still Magic After All These Years?" *Psychological Review* 101 (1994): 353–356.

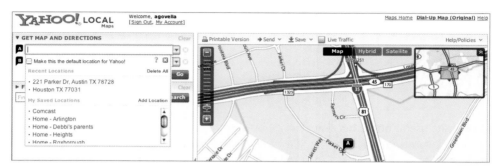

FIGURE 1.18 Yahoo! Maps stores the last address you typed into the search box, and shows it in a drop-down when you go to search for a location. It also lets you store other addresses you may use a lot.

Relying on recognition also means you should always look for ways to keep information in front of the visitors' eyes. Dreamhost is a company that provides hosting for Web sites. They offer a control panel where customers can manage their Web sites. The control panel is the place where Web site owners should be able to manage their Web sites. Let's say you want to check your log files to see how many people are coming to your site. Where is that link? Is it under Domains? Goodies? Users? Nope, it's under Status (see **Figure 1.19**).

Admittedly, the labels are a big part of the problem. The label Status doesn't suggest Site Statistics, and it fails as a memory trigger. But rather than struggling to find a label that will work, why not simply display the links? Showing all the links avoids forcing users into this game of hide-and-seek. Although listing all the links will cause the page to scroll, scrolling is much faster for users to do than clicking each option, then clicking the Back button, and then clicking another option as they try to find where the log files are hidden.

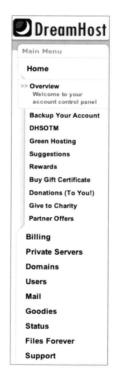

FIGURE 1.19 In DreamHost's control panel, where should you look for your log files? Dream-Host hides your Web site's log files under Status.

Anytime that you can take the burden off the user's poor overtaxed memory and place it on the computer, you are making your site just a bit more valuable to your customers.

Principle #7: Provide for People of Varying Skill Levels

A Web site user is only a beginner for a short time. By about their third visit to a site, they've become an intermediate. They stay this way for a very long time, perhaps never advancing to expert; they don't need to. Intermediate use means they can accomplish nearly everything they want and they have no desire to learn anything beyond that. Experts are even less common. Experts continue to learn how a Web site or piece of software works until they use the power features. Yet we design simple sites for beginners and then build shortcuts and special features for experts. We're spending all our time designing for beginners and experts, the least common users.

It's time to consider "the user" as a real person in motion through time, constantly changing and learning. Your design should assist users in moving to a level of accomplishment that is satisfactory. You don't need them to become experts—just design the interface to help move people to a place where they are happier with their results.

Flickr is a great example of a site that caters to intermediate users (see **Figure 1.20**).

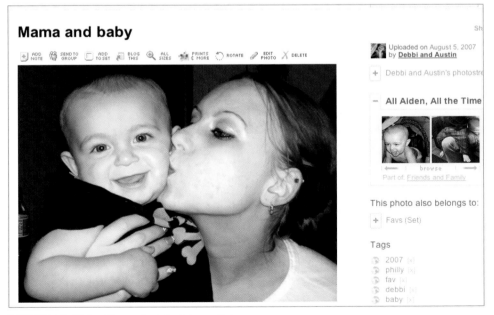

FIGURE 1.20 Flickr offers gadgets for intermediate users.

The site looks like a typical photo site. After looking at a few photos, you start to notice the gadgets. You play. Intermediates quickly learn how to add tags and Share This. Experts eventually learn how to annotate photos by adding a Note. But those experts are few and far between. And, fortunately, the special features never get in the way of the typical photo viewer, which is the role most of us will stay in.

Principle #8: Provide Contextual Help and Documentation

Help is pretty poor, pretty consistently. Your DVD manual has been translated from Swedish into English by someone who speaks neither well. Your software manual was written by an engineer who wanted to knock it out so he could get back to coding. When you need help while writing, you find yourself stalked by a menacing paper clip in MS Word. The Help section on a Web site—well, you've probably never looked at it because how could it possibly help? Every other time you looked at a manual, it just confused things.

Meanwhile the kind of "help" people do think might actually help, such as phone assistance, is expensive for the company and often annoying to the caller. "Press 1 for Spanish, press 2 for Chinese, press 3 for French, press 4 for Laplander…"

People doing any kind of vaguely complex task will inevitably require help and resist asking for it. What you can do as a designer is offer the right help at the right moment in the most unobtrusive way possible. Place information in clearly labeled locations, rather than grouping it all under the generic and menacing Help.

Figure 1.21 shows the page you see when you first sign in to Aviary, a suite of Web applications. A new user may be uncertain how to begin; but Aviary has anticipated this problem and wisely listed some options.

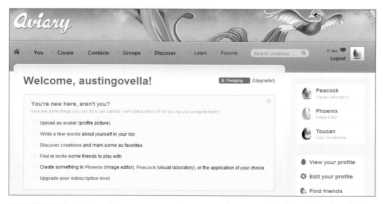

FIGURE 1.21 Aviary gives new users tips on getting started when they sign in for the first time, right when they need it most.

Aviary teaches you how to use the site right when you first sign in, when you most likely need some guidance. Aviary's help is relevant and meaningful.

This Chapter Will Self-Destruct in Five Seconds

Remember what we said about memory? About it being dicey? You do remember, right?

These principles are best used if you can manage to get them off the paper and into your head. Because when you're in a project, you're going to be hit with so much information that your brain is going to want to make some room. And what we've explained in this chapter could go up in a puff of smoke.

We guess it would be easier to remember if we said, "Just put seven links on a page and all will be fine." But it wouldn't be fine. Humans are just too complicated. Beware of easy-to-get, easy-to-remember answers.

"Information may
want to be free,
but people like
to get paid."

2

Balancing Acts—
Users, Technology,
and Business

*In which we discover that businesses
like to make money, engineers like to
make code, users like to make good,
and many other shocking facts.*

I nformation architects are often in the design group, but information architecture is a task that can end up in anyone's lap. A product manager may have to decide how to manage the influx of thousands of pieces of user-generated content, a marketing manager may have to figure out how to deal with creative assets, and an engineer may be stuck with sorting out the relevance of a search algorithm. Even though most Web companies don't have a dedicated IA, somebody has to make sure the Web site make sense to the people who use it.

To do so, the IA (or whoever is playing that part) must understand the various forces at play in the creation of a Web site. Misjudging the business goals, underestimating the technical complexity, or lacking empathy with the desired user base is dangerous to the success of the effort. While there are dozens of other forces at work in Web site creation—from marketing to graphic design—the business, technology, and user goals need to be balanced while the Web site is being mapped out.

Because information architecture is so often a distributed task, let's take a look at these three areas. Feel free to skip any areas in which you are already an expert.

- Who are your users? (understand your base)
- Why does your business need you to make a Web site? (understand the business)
- What are your materials? (understand the technology)

Who Are Your Users?

You have to know who your end user is going to be. You can't say that your audience is anyone on the Web and hope to make something effective (unless you are Google, and they had to resort to black magic[1]). However, you can determine what actions your potential users will want to perform, how they will approach accomplishing those tasks, and then how you can help them succeed. When your users succeed, your company will succeed.

Be a rolling suitcase

In the beginning, only flight attendants had rolling suitcases. They had them because someone who understood the flight attendant's job designed the suitcases for a very specific set of needs. Flight attendants needed to dash from flight to flight. They had to stay fresh for the long flight's exertions, so they didn't want to get tired carrying a heavy bag. Many flight attendants were quite petite, so carrying a big bag could be tough. And finally were changing flights so often, they really needed to carry all their essentials on the plane—they never knew when their job would send them to Tokyo when their bags were already on their way to Paris.

Does this sound familiar? Ordinary people go through the same pains when they fly. We want to carry all our valuables onto the plane with us. We need them to fit in the overhead compartment. We get tired of carrying bags in the long lines to the ticket counter or while dashing from Terminal C to Terminal F. And our bags often seem to be determined to head for Paris when we are en route to Tokyo.

---

1 Search Algorithms. More on that in Chapter 5, Search and Ye Shall Find.

A travel-savvy designer met a very specific need for a particular group extremely well, and ultimately he met the needs of flyers everywhere. It's your job to do the same. Understand that core audience: who are they? What are their unique needs? Then meet those needs perfectly by practicing user-centered design.

User-centered design is pretty simple.[2] You want to get into the heads of your typical users and apply that knowledge to your design decisions. There are five basic steps:

1. Discover who the target user is.

2. Talk to the target user.

3. Design the site for the target user.

4. Test a prototype of the site with the target user.

5. Test the final site with the target user.

The secret to making a site that people love is involving them throughout the process. Guessing what people want and then building a site for them is expensive because if you guess wrong, you have to do it all over again. But an informed guess—which is tested and then refined—may look more expensive in the project plan, but saves the big bucks when you get fewer customer calls (and makes big money with happier customers).

Our Five Steps

1. Discover who the target user is.

The very first question you must ask is, "Who is this site for?" A lot of times it can be hard to answer this question usefully. Some people will say, "Everyone on the Web." Others will say, "Anyone who loves X (where X is the product category)," or, "Anyone who loves books!" or, "Anyone who loves fishcakes!" This is a place where your marketing department can help you get started. The marketers have probably done a fair amount of research into the demographics and, hopefully, even the psychographics of the Web site's users. You should also interview the business owners to ask which users they would like to reach and what user behavior is the most valuable. Set up some hour-long, one-on-one interviews with a couple of people from each department and try to get as much information about the potential user base as possible. Listen carefully to what your coworkers tell you about the users and try to spot information that will help you choose which potential users will be the best to interview.

---

2 Admittedly, it's complex enough that there have been tons and tons of books written about it and gigabytes of blog posts. Do a quick search for user-centered design on your favorite search engine, and you'll see. We'll give you the "user-centered design for idiots" version!

For example, your conversation might go like this:

You: *Tell me about the people you think will come to the site once it's live.*

Jill, *marketing associate: Well, our demographics are 25–35 in the bargain-hunter category and 35–50 in the prestige-buyer category.*

You: *What's the difference between the bargain buyer and the prestige buyer?*

Jill *(getting excited): Well, bargain hunters care a lot about sales. They also like packages… you know—buy one, get one free, and so on. The prestige buyer cares about her image. She wants the product to reflect who she is and what her lifestyle is.*

You *(thinking to yourself): Okay, I need to find some people who buy based on price and some who care deeply about brands.*

You: *What else can you tell me about the shoppers?*

Note that in this conversation, rather than just collecting demographics, we're really looking for behavior that helps us design a better product. While knowing that the audience is older might lead to some design decisions, like larger font sizes, in general, it's not very telling. However, knowing that price is a key decision factor can influence dozens of your decisions, from what weight to give price in your search algorithm to what navigation to show on browse pages and even to what elements are bigger on the product page.

2. Talk to the target user.

Now that you've discovered who those potential users are, you need to go talk to them. If you are doing a redesign, you are lucky. You can reach your current users through a variety of ways:

- Ask for volunteers in your newsletter (if you have one)
- Ask for volunteers on your site
- Contact people via customer service

If you don't yet have a customer base, you may need to hire a recruiter who specializes in finding people to talk to—try doing a search for "market research recruiting." If you can't afford a recruiter, you may have to get creative. Try posting on bulletin boards, going to malls, or grabbing people off the street. Just be certain that the people you are speaking to are similar to the ones using the site. If you grab a schoolteacher off the street, and you are building a Web site for stock traders, you may get less-than-useful feedback.

Secondly, be careful how you take in your feedback. Often, people will say things like, "I wish the button was bigger," when they mean, "It's too hard to check out." Or "Can you make that red?" when they mean, "It took too long to find what I wanted." Ideally, the best thing you can do is to follow your users while they do tasks in the environment where they usually perform those tasks. For example, watch someone try to book a ticket online at home or at work. At home they may be dealing with kids asking for cookies while the time runs out on a search; at work you'll see how music playing on a Web site makes them suddenly the most popular person in the cube farm.

So when you talk to them, ask them questions like, "What are you trying to do?" and, "What did you expect here?" and try to avoid, "Where do you think that link should go?" You may still get requests for the "hold this search while I feed the husband" button, but take that with a grain of salt and focus on the challenges people have while they try to get things done.

3. Design the site for the target user.

There are a lot of techniques to make sure you keep your end users in mind as you design. We can't cover them all, but we cover a few we've found particularly effective in Chapter 6, From A to C by Way of B.

4. Test a prototype of the site with the target user.

Prototyping is a way to get feedback without spending hours and hours coding a site. In fact, the site doesn't even have to have a final visual design. You can test a rough layout of the site. It's just a way to see if you've gotten the basic concepts right. Frequently, site prototypes are done with paper, and sometimes with digital mockups that have been image-mapped to allow for some interaction. The important thing is not to take time making sophisticated interaction with robust code. All you want at this stage is to see if you've got the core concepts right. A drawing on paper that the user can "mouse" over with his finger will tell you a lot, and doesn't cost a dime in engineering time.

One trick is called "rapid prototyping,"[3] and it takes its cues from agile programming. If one or two of your users falter over an element and you see something obviously wrong (or perhaps not obvious until your user tripped on it), you can change the prototype quickly. Then with the next user, you can see if your change made things better, and then with the user after that, become more certain about the change. Some researchers get very caught up on scientific methods and will get nervous about this approach, but you don't always need eight or more users to tell you that you made a dumb mistake. Tweaking swiftly gets you to a better baseline design that can be more formally evaluated later.

5. Test the final site with your target user.

You still can be wrong up to the bitter end. Be certain once the code is written and the visual design is in place that you return to the users and test again, and budget enough time to make fixes for the inevitable issues you'll discover. Surprisingly, small things can make a big difference. For example, one designer we worked with put a colored background behind a sidebar so the users would see it. But no users in our studies ever noticed it. When we pointed out the sidebar to one user, she said, "Oh, I thought it was an ad so I didn't read it!" The colored background had the opposite effect from what had been intended. A solid, formal testing process at this final stage is the equivalent of a solid, formal QA process: a usability bug can cost you just as much as a technology bug.

Why Does Your Business Need You to Make a Web Site?

While information may want to be free, people like to be paid. Most businesses exist to make money. You may find yourself in a meeting, arguing with business development or marketing and saying, "no one wants to pay for that," or, "no one wants to give their personal information," or, "no one likes to fill out forms." No one likes to pay for groceries, either, but somehow we find ourselves doing it week in and week out.

Business analysts love to boil everything down to supply and demand: all business is driven by the fact that one person wants something and the other person has it. For example, the business has a piece of content, and the user wants it. Conversely, the user has personal information, and the business wants it. Or perhaps the business wants the user to see advertising, or even give them money in exchange for their tasty content. The finesse comes in when we start trying to find the delicate balance between the user's desire and the user's price point.[4] If you were in a bazaar, the fair exchange would be settled by

---

3 There's actually a nice technical name for this method: Rapid Iterative Testing and Evaluation (RITE). We think "rapid prototyping" sounds more friendly.

4 George Bernard Shaw once asked a woman if she would go to bed with a man for 50,000 pounds. She said that she thought that she would. Shaw then asked whether she would do it for two pounds.
"What do you think I am?" she said.
"We've already established what you are," he replied. "Now we're merely haggling over the price."

haggling. On the Web, it often comes in a similar form, albeit slower, in which the business puts up a price they suspect is too high (five-page registration form) or too low (advertising is free) and then measures and adjusts as the market reacts. It's a scary process, because users are answering the opening offer by walking away or by flocking in droves and crashing the servers. But with luck and some experimentation (and vigorous analysis), sites find the correct price point. Rather than taking the near-socialist view that many user-centered designers fall into, try thinking about what a fair market price is for the things the business wants from the user. Work with business to balance avarice and altruism.

It's critical to know what your business model is. Without this information, you have no idea which actions of the user are valuable and which are not. And without knowing that, you are likely to spend many hours working on an aspect of the Web site that delivers no value, compared with only a few hours on one that does. This is not usually a fatal mistake in a large corporation (although sometimes it's a firing offense), but in a start-up it can literally kill the company.

The table below has a few common Internet business models listed; see if you recognize yours. The job of the information architect (as well as others on the design team) is to deliver the high-value user behavior to support the business needs. This list is not meant to be definitive. Internet business models constantly change and adapt. Also, a company may combine several different models as part of its overall Internet business strategy; for example, a content-driven business may blend advertising with a subscription model. Still, this chart may help you think about how your company is able to write you a paycheck every two weeks.

Type of Model	Description	Users must
Marketplace Model	Marketplaces bring buyers and sellers together and facilitate transactions. They can play a role in business-to-business (B2B), business-to-consumer (B2C), or consumer-to-consumer (C2C) markets. Usually, a marketplace charges a fee or commission for each transaction it enables.	Be able to find merchandise they are seeing, connect with seller, exchange payment
	Services Broker—Offers a full range of services covering the transaction process, from market assessment to negotiation and fulfillment. Example: **Orbitz**	
	Auction Broker—Conducts auctions for sellers (individuals or merchants). Broker charges the seller a listing fee and commission scaled with the value of the transaction. Example: **eBay**	
	Transaction Broker—Provides a third-party payment mechanism for buyers and sellers to settle a transaction. Example: **PayPal**	

Type of Model	Description	Users must
Advertising Model	The Web advertising model is an update of the one we're familiar with from broadcast TV. The Web "broadcaster" provides content and services (like email, IM, blogs) mixed with advertising messages. The advertising model works best when the volume of viewer traffic is large or highly specialized. Classifieds—List items for sale or wanted for purchase. Listing fees are common, but there also may be a membership fee. Example: **Craigslist, Match.com** Targeted Advertising—Content-based sites that are free to access but require users to register and provide demographic data. Registration allows inter-session tracking of user surfing habits and thereby generates data of potential value in targeted advertising campaigns. Example: **NYTimes** Query-based Paid Placement—Sells favorable link positioning (for example, sponsored links) or advertising keyed to particular search terms in a user query, such as (Yahoo!-owned) Overture's trademark "pay-for-performance" model. Examples: **Google, Overture** Content-Matched Advertising—Pioneered by Google, it extends the precision of search advertising to the rest of the Web. Google identifies the meaning of a Web page and then automatically delivers relevant ads when a user visits that page. Example: **Google**	Notice advertising, interact with it, share their information demographic information in order to provide a higher CTR and better targetting
Affiliate Model	The affiliate model allows brokers and merchants the capability to garner more traffic by offering financial incentives (in the form of a percentage of revenue) to affiliated partner sites. It is a pay-for-performance model—if an affiliate does not generate sales, it represents no cost to the merchant. Revenue Sharing—Offers a percent-of-sale commission based on a user click-through in which the user subsequently purchases a product. Examples: **Barnes & Noble, Amazon.com**	Be able to incorporate the parent site's promotional material into their site, despite varying technical abilities

Type of Model	Description	Users must
Community Model	The viability of the community model is based on user loyalty. Revenue can be based on the sale of ancillary products and services or voluntary contributions; or revenue may be tied to contextual advertising and subscriptions for premium services. The Internet is inherently suited to community business models, and today this is one of the more fertile areas of development, as seen in the rise of social networking. Open Source—Software developed collaboratively by a global community of programmers who share code openly. Instead of licensing code for a fee, open source relies on revenue generated from related services like systems integration, product support, tutorials, and user documentation. Examples: **Red Hat**, **OpenX** Open Content—Openly accessible content developed collaboratively by a global community of contributors who work voluntarily and often donate money for infrastructure. Example: **Wikipedia**, **Freebase** Social Networking Services—Sites that provide individuals with the ability to connect to other individuals along a defined common interest (professional, hobby, romance). Social networking services can provide opportunities for contextual advertising and subscriptions for premium services. Example: **Facebook**, **MySpace**, **LinkedIn**	Create an identity, connect with other users, build a reputation, create and share content
Subscription Model	Users are charged a periodic—daily, monthly, or annual—fee to subscribe to a service. It is not uncommon for sites to combine free content with "premium" (for example, subscriber- or member-only) content. Subscription fees are incurred irrespective of actual usage rates. Subscription and advertising models are frequently combined. Content Services—Provide text, audio, or video content to users who subscribe for a fee to gain access to the service. Example: **Netflix**, **Rhapsody** Software as a Service—Many services that would have typically been provided via shrink-wrap software installed on the desktop are now provided online for a subscription. Example: **Basecamp**, **Mint**, **Flickr** Internet Services Providers—Offer network connectivity and related services on a monthly subscription.	Able to evaluate the offering, subscribe and unsubscribe to offering, realize value offered

What Are Your Materials?

1. Know your code.

It doesn't matter if you are an artist or an information architect, you have to know the materials with which you're working. In art school, most painters will learn to stretch their own canvases and mix pigments. While they rarely continue this practice into their professional life, it gives them a deeper understanding of the strengths and weaknesses of the materials.

It's pretty much the same with the Web—just replace "canvas and paint" with "data and code." You really don't have to know how to roll your own perl or java to be able to design a good Web site. Conversely, having built a page or two by hand in HTML will make a big difference in your understanding of what is possible. Redoing your blog templates will force you to gain an understanding of template-driven design and that's even better. If you design your own database, you will be a force to be reckoned with.

But if you are dyslexic or disinclined, you can make up for a lack of coding chops by spending as much time as possible with the engineer you'll be working with, to assure yourself that the solutions you're coming up with can be done in the real world. More than one designer has spent hours coming up with an amazing navigation system, only to discover it's based on a piece of data not in the system. D'oh! Moreover your engineer may come up with a solution more elegant than the one you've thought up, due to his insight into the possibilities inherent in code. Collaboration trumps dictatorships, especially on multidisciplinary teams.[5]

2. Know your delivery mechanism.

When IA was born, it was pretty much a Web site-only deal, viewed in browsers on computers. Since then data has become a critical component of almost all applications, and applications are not only on computers but also on smart phones, kiosks, TVs, and other devices as well. Sometimes you get the pleasure of customizing the interface to a unique device, while other times you have to try to design a structure that's robust enough to be reinterpreted by a soccer mom browsing for directions on her iPhone on the freeway. Yep, you heard me, make that interface easy, or she may kill you.

Any mobile device is an obvious case of a challenging delivery system (small screen, difficult to use while driving) that can be improved with good IA, but it's not the only one.

---

5 Highly recommended reading: *Understanding Engineers: Feasibility* by Charles Miller. His explanation of the engineer's favorite phrase "non-trivial" alone makes it worthwhile.

http://fishbowl.pastiche.org/2007/07/17/understanding_engineers_feasibility/

Information architecture is finding many new homes in need of solutions for findability problems. For example, think about the complexity of a feature-heavy software program such as Microsoft Word. Is spellcheck under Edit or Tools? This is essentially an information architecture problem.

We now find movies on phones, TVs, and even in the local supermarket. IA has to adjust to unforeseen challenges.

iTunes is the best-known example representing an entire suite of emerging data management tools living on a variety of devices (**Figure 2.1**). Ordinary people who have never considered metadata or classification are designing playlists and inventing genres left and right in order to find music and movies on their iPods. Those same people apply their new classification chops to their bookmarks on Delicious and then their photos on Flickr. Then they take those photos, resize them, crop them, sepia tone them, and reclassify them. Once upon a time, information architecture and interaction design could ignore each other. But now the peanut butter is in the chocolate,[6] and it's here to stay. As you design content, consider the interaction. As you design interaction, consider the content.

3. Know your content.

We've (lightly) covered code and distribution, so now let's talk data. A critical aspect of knowing your materials is an understanding of the nature of the content of the Web site. For example, if you are building a Web site for a music store, it's important to know the genres of music and the musicians. Imagine you are browsing through your local used CD store, and you come across Britney Spears in the Heavy Metal section. Britney is a pop princess, and no self-respecting metal-head would put her in the Heavy Metal section.

---

6 Apologies to our foreign readers. We're referring to an old advertisement for Reese's Peanut Butter Cups, available at a sweet shop near you, thanks to the wonder of globalization.

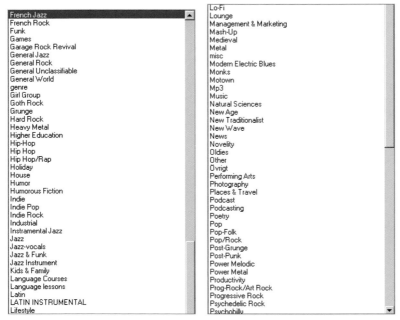

FIGURE 2.1 When everyone is a classification expert, there are as many genres as there are people! Who can say if it's goth-rock or post-grunge? Only the user of iTunes knows for sure.

Since Britney is clearly misclassified, you'll start to wonder what else is wrong here and worry that you will have to look through every section in hopes of finding that rare Ozzy Osbourne album you were seeking—it could be in Bluegrass for all you know. You may walk out and try the store next door instead of spending the next several hours searching.

To effectively classify the music on your music site, you have two choices:

- You can attempt to become an expert.
- You can work with people who are already experts.

If the subject area is huge, it's simpler to hire a subject matter expert (SME) to review your classification work than to give up sleep for several weeks trying to learn everything about the world of music. If the subject area is relatively small, though, it may be worth learning its language and conventions.

To learn the subject area, you can do the following:

- **Interview subject matter experts.** The guy down at the used record store really isn't doing much between 10 A.M. and 11 A.M. and would probably chat with you in return for a cup of coffee delivered to the counter.

- **Read books and magazines about the area.** Granted, it's slow, but paying extra attention to introductions, overviews, indexes, and tables of contents can help get you grounded and speaking the language. You can probably skim the rest.

- **Conduct a landscape analysis.** If you have direct competitors, you might want to look at how they handle their content. But if a lot of different kinds of Web sites are working with the same type of content and issues related to that content as you are, you could get greater insight by broadening your research.

If you were designing a music store's site, one of the questions you'd have to answer is, "How do I organize the music so people can find the songs and albums they want so they can then purchase them?" You might start by looking at a bunch of different music Web sites: commerce sites, research sites, radio sites—maybe even fan sites. You would look for any place that might have solved the same problem you now face: how to organize and present music.

Suppose that you are researching jazz in particular. There are a lot of good places to get ideas about how to organize jazz music (see **Figures 2.2** and **2.3**).

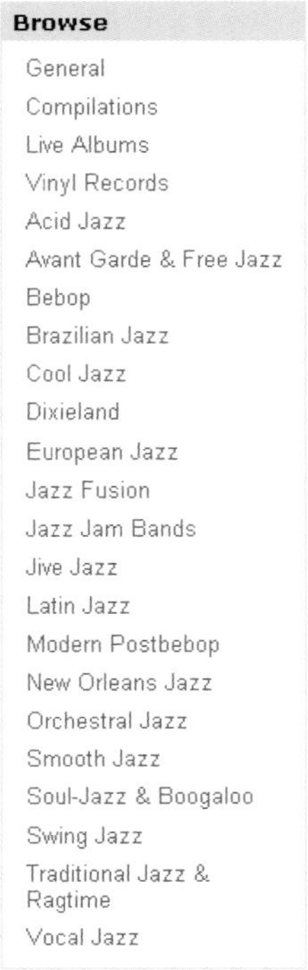

Browse

General
Compilations
Live Albums
Vinyl Records
Acid Jazz
Avant Garde & Free Jazz
Bebop
Brazilian Jazz
Cool Jazz
Dixieland
European Jazz
Jazz Fusion
Jazz Jam Bands
Jive Jazz
Latin Jazz
Modern Postbebop
New Orleans Jazz
Orchestral Jazz
Smooth Jazz
Soul-Jazz & Boogaloo
Swing Jazz
Traditional Jazz & Ragtime
Vocal Jazz

FIGURE 2.2 Amazon has a very stable, well-tested set of genres and subgenres, and because of their traffic, users are likely to be familiar with their terms. Why not start here?

By stretching your search beyond the typical competitive analysis, you can gain a deeper understanding of the content you'll be working with. Try taking it even further: pick up catalogs for music, visit physical music stores, and maybe even look into ticket companies' organizational schemes.

As well as looking at how the various sites label and organize their material, it is useful to look at features they offer, what type of content they show, and how they display it. This will give you a hint as to what others have found that works. You should not be afraid to learn from other people and build from their knowledge. True innovation comes from understanding what's been done in the past, why it works and why it doesn't, and then seeking a solution. After all, BMW doesn't reinvent the wheel every time it designs a new car, and it still manages to come up with some interesting vehicles.

Pandora has eschewed traditional genre classification in favor of the "Music Genome Project." What creative classification possibilities are opened up with a more flexible classification system? Pandora uses the Music Genome Project to power their recommendation engine, delivering you the song you've never heard before but instantly love.

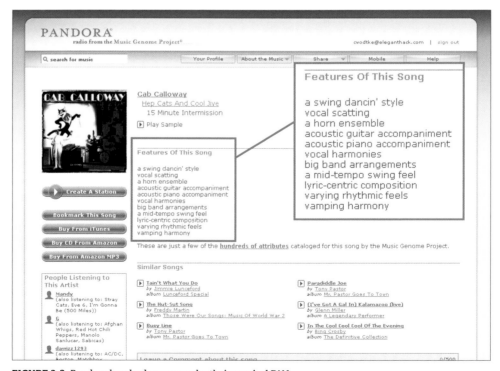

FIGURE 2.3 Pandora breaks down songs by their musical DNA.

Landscape analysis is not a substitute for user research, however. User research can be a big help in understanding why things work and why they don't. After you've done a landscape analysis, you'll probably have a huge list of questions about the choices others have made. To get answers, you need to talk to (and watch!) the potential end user.

Once you have this knowledge in place, you can move on to building cathedrals on the Web...one brick at a time.

Children organize things for fun. On the left, Amelie groups all of the shiny ornaments together on the Christmas tree (photo by Christina Wodtke). On the right, Alice organizes sugar packets to facilitate task flow (photo by Cindy Chastain).

3

Sock Drawers and CD Racks—Everything Must Be Organized

In which we learn that a lot of stuff can be a bad thing, and organization can be a good thing.

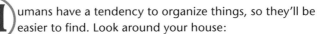

Humans have a tendency to organize things, so they'll be easier to find. Look around your house:

- You've got a sock drawer, an underwear drawer, and a t-shirt area so you can find your clothes when you get dressed.

- You have a silverware organizer that separates spoons from forks to make it easy to set the table.

- You alphabetize your CD collection in a CD rack so you can quickly find that band you're looking for.

It's a simple fact: when you have a certain amount of stuff, you have to organize it. Otherwise, you can't find anything.

May I Help You?

People visit a Web site for three main reasons:

- They're looking for something.

- They're trying to accomplish a task.

- They have five minutes before their next meeting and want to kill some time.

Too many site creators think their audience is made up of visitors who want to kill time. They also tend to think those visitors have two hours instead of five minutes. Too many site creators think the visitor is dying to be entertained (even if they are coming to a tax-preparation site), so they festoon the place with animated GIFs and zooming navigation.

Sites exist that are made just to entertain—for example Cartoon Network, Hulu, E!online, and so on. But the bulk of the Web consists of informational Web sites whose purpose is to inform, educate, or persuade.

Let's say you're not the Cartoon Network—you aren't here to entertain. Your site has tons of information, and people come to your site to find something, accomplish a task, or perhaps a combination of both. You want to help them.

As a site designer, your job is to design an experience that allows people to successfully complete their quest—whether it's to find the right driver for their printer, write a paper on the Industrial Revolution, or do a bit of shopping.

When someone visits a Web page, they ask themselves these four questions:

- Am I in the right place?
- Do they have what I'm looking for?
- Do they have anything better (if this isn't what I want)?
- What do I do now?

If you're in charge of the information architecture, it's your job to answer these four questions on every page of your site. Design-wise, this means you have to do four things:

- Assure visitors they're in the right place.
- Make it easy for visitors to find what they're looking for.
- Make sure that visitors know what their options are.
- Let them save it, buy it, find something new…

It doesn't matter what visitors are trying to do on your site. You have to answer these questions, all the time, no matter what.

Question #1: Am I in the Right Place?

When on a quest, people want to know if they are looking in the right spot.

Let's say Austin is shopping for a scarf. If he types in your URL, he wants to know if he's on a site that sells scarves.

Take a look at **Figure 3.1**, Gap's homepage. Is Austin at a site that sells scarves? Maybe. Compare this to **Figure 3.2**. Nordstrom's homepage offers a glimpse at the range of items you can buy there: clothing for men, women, kids, as well as shoes and accessories. Accessories sounds promising for a scarf hunter. Gap's categories are a little less revealing. Their range of offerings is limited to types of people looking for things: men, women, pregnant women, and kids. Luckily for Austin, the models on the homepage are all wintered up. They're not wearing scarves, but they're wearing winter clothes, and scarves are winter clothes.

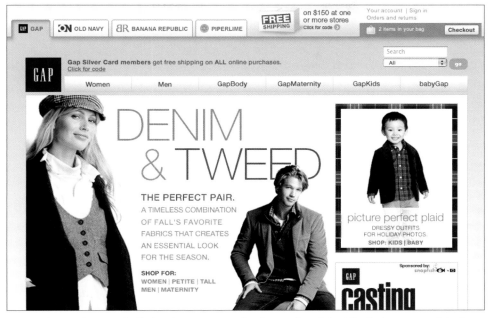

FIGURE 3.1 Gap's range of offerings is pretty general and pretty broad. Luckily, the homepage ad depicts winter clothes.

FIGURE 3.2 Nordstrom's range of offerings is a little more specific.

Your organization scheme is the first thing your visitors will look at when they come to your Web site. Whether you want it to or not, your organization scheme will do two things:

1. Orient people. It tells visitors, "This is a Web site for X."

2. Tell them where to go. It shows your visitors, "This is the stuff you can explore/ buy/watch/read/touch/share."

To be successful, your organization scheme needs to show people the full range of your offerings.

Yahoo! is still the best example of this (see **Figure 3.3**). On the left side, their home-page clearly lets users know about Yahoo!'s top services. Search dominates the top of the page. News is front and center, and personalized services like Mail, Messenger, and Local are on the right. The Yahoo! homepage says, "It's all here," and then tells you where to click.

FIGURE 3.3 The Yahoo! homepage.

Back at Gap and Nordstrom (**Figure 3.4**), you can see the range of their offerings once you select a section. In this case, Austin selected Men.

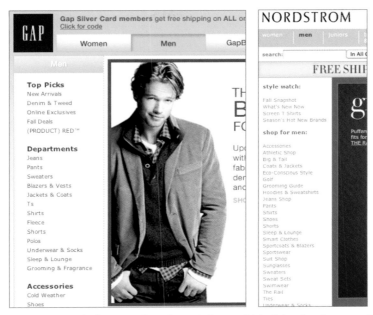

FIGURE 3.4 Both The Gap and Nordstrom's do a good job of showing the range of their offerings once you choose a section like Men.

Every page is your homepage

The wonderful thing about search engines is that people no longer have to bother with navigating from your homepage; they can go directly to any page they want from a results set on Google. The flip side of this convenience is that every page on your site needs to answer the question, "Am I in the right place?"

If you search for "iPod," you get a link to the iPod page on Apple's Web site. You skip right past the Apple.com homepage (see **Figure 3.5**). Are you in the right place? Similarly, if you're searching for information on "design thinking," you find a blog post on Luke Wroblewski's site (**Figure 3.6**). Does this page talk about design thinking?

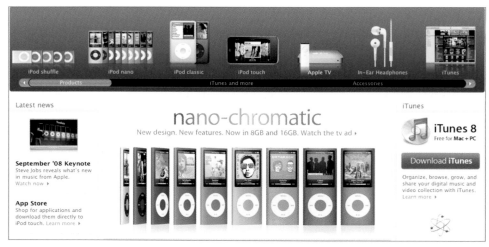

FIGURE 3.5 Apple's page for the iPod pretty clearly answers the question, "Am I in the right place?"

FIGURE 3.6 The page title on Luke W.'s site is also pretty clear about reassuring visitors they're in the right place.

Question #2: Do They Have What I'm Looking For?

After a user has satisfied herself that she's on the right site, the next question becomes, "Where on the site are they hiding what I want?" She may use your navigation system to figure out where to go.

Building architects call this *wayfinding*, the hints and clues we use to figure out where we are and where we're going. On the Web, there are four key elements of wayfinding to keep in mind.

1. Familiar organization systems.

Using familiar organization systems is equivalent to using familiar street signs to help drivers navigate through a town. For example, stop signs should be red and octagonal. If they were teal and triangular, they could be misread or ignored.

If you are building an online grocery store, don't divide it into sandwich making and salad making (even though it might be kind of nifty[1]). People shopping for groceries are used to bakery, dairy, and produce in an organization scheme.

Nathan Shedroff[2] collected a list of common organization systems most people are familiar with. He says you can organize things by alphabet (an employee directory), location (a map), time (a calendar), continuum (top-rated), numbers (zip codes), categories (newspapers organize articles by local, world, business, and so on), or randomness (iTunes shuffle).

Organization System	Example
Alphabets	Artists in a music store, phone books
Locations	Maps, mechanical diagrams
Time	Calendars, history
Continuums	Ratings (1–5 stars), scales
Numbers	Dewey Decimal System, grocery stores (aisle numbers)
Categories	Music genres, blog categories,
Randomness	iTunes shuffle

TABLE 3.1 Organization Systems and Examples

If you use an organization system people are used to, then they won't have to learn it, and your site will be easier to use. iTunes uses its own organization scheme but also offers its users familiar ways of organizing music, such as by artist name, album name, or release date (**Figure 3.7**).

---

1 However, salad making and sandwich making might not only be a cool way to organize, it might be a helpful one for those people who do like eating sandwiches a lot. Although you don't want to give up the traditional organization systems that most folks have learned, you may want to supplement them with alternatives. Skip ahead to the "You Really Can Be in Two Places at Once" section in this chapter to find out how.

2 Nathan Shedroff's excellent article, "Information Interaction Design," is packed with tons of useful information about design, the Web, information architecture, and interaction design http://www.nathan.com/thoughts/unified/index.html.

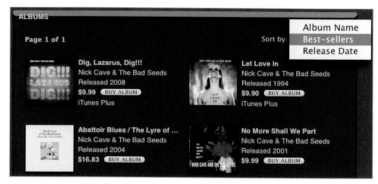

FIGURE 3.7 By default, the iTunes store organizes an artist's work by best-sellers, but they also let you organize by album name or release date.

On the Nordstrom and Gap Web sites, Austin was looking for a scarf for a man, so he clicked Men. Organizing the site by Men, Women, and others is a system we're familiar with from the real world. That's how department stores are organized.

2. Obvious labels.

Repeat after me, "A label is not a place to promote your brand. It's a signpost to help people find stuff." If you have a greeting card site, Naughty Humor may not be as in tune with your brand image as Snickers and Snorts, but as a label it will keep the grandmas out and draw the college kids in.

Imagine what would happen if a stop sign in Santa Cruz, CA read "Be Cool" or "Chill Dude." It might match the city's groovy, laid-back attitude, but it would not necessarily promote coming to a full stop.

Gap's and Nordstrom's Web sites, where we were looking for a scarf under Men, both use very clear and obvious labels. If we're looking for scarves, Nordstrom offers the promising option, Accessories. Gap does one better by offering Winter Accessories.

3. Navigation that looks like navigation.

If we had a dollar for every person we've watched in usability testing moving a mouse back and forth across a page trying to figure out what to click, we'd run Bill Gates out of business. If it's a link, make it look like a link. Make it a button, underline it, or make the text a different color. Text for reading and text for clicking should look different from each other.

4. "You are here" and "You were there" signs.

Let people know where they are on the site. Let them know where they came from. Let them know how to get back.

As a shopper moves through a Web site, he may easily get confused. "Was the green scarf in Men's Wear, or was it in Seasonal/Winter?" "Am I in Men's Wear or Winter?" As a designer, you can alleviate this in several ways, from using breadcrumbs to changing the look of the navigation bar to providing feedback about the shopper's location.

Your visitors will use these four ways of finding elements to orient themselves and understand where to click next.

Question #3: Do They Have Anything Better?

Whether or not your visitors have found what they're looking for on your site, they'll always ask themselves if you have anything better. Is what they're looking at *really* what they want?

There are a few common approaches to handling this question.

Navigation and breadcrumbs

Highlighting where the user is in the site, as well as showing nearby content, is a good way to answer whether you have anything better. On Gap's Web site, they highlight what section Austin's in (Men > Accessories > Scarves) and also let him know about related categories (Hats & Gloves). Austin may think, "I don't know. Maybe after seeing the scarf, what I really want is a hat with good ear flaps." At Gap's site, he's only a click away (**Figure 3.8**).

"See also" options

"See also" choices are a common convention on most retail sites and a useful way to provide users with shortcuts to related items (in contrast to related categories). On Nordstrom's site (**Figure 3.9**), they've listed a couple of "see also" options on the right. If Austin doesn't like this scarf, there are two more scarves right there.

FIGURE 3.8 The Gap places local navigation on the left so you always know where you are and what's nearby.

FIGURE 3.9 Nordstrom's product detail page offers related "see also" items on the right-hand side.

A "see also" navigation tool is most effective if it offers shortcuts to a range of related items and shortcuts to related categories. Look at how Business Week designed its article page (**Figure 3.10**). Just in case this isn't the article you're looking for, they immediately offer a list of related articles. And at the top right, they link to their most popular articles.

FIGURE 3.10 Business Week makes both related and most popular articles easy to find in case you're looking for something better than the article you're currently reading.

In a Web application, a related item is a related task. **Figure 3.11** shows a close-up of a page from MySpace's profile editor. Typically, you're adding or removing an interest. But if that's not all you want to do, MySpace makes it easy to also edit your details, schools, as well as making even your groups and comments easily accessible. MySpace keeps related tasks close at hand in case that's the "something better" you're looking for.

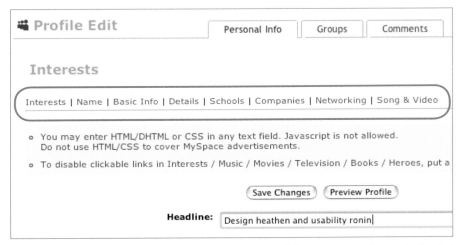

FIGURE 3.11 MySpace's profile editor keeps related profile editing tasks nearby in case that's what you're really looking for.

Question #4: What Do I Do Now?

Your users were looking for something, and they found it. Congratulations if they have made it this far. Now they're wondering: "What do I do now?"

When people do find something they like, you should provide options for the next obvious action. Ask yourself, what do our visitors *want* to do with what they've found? What's the next step?

An online store is pretty straightforward: people want to buy what they've finally found. Amazon is a good example. In **Figure 3.12**, you can see Add to Shopping Cart is the most prominent action on the page. (Amazon answers, "Do you have anything better?" with the link to 31 new and used.) But suppose you're just looking? The answer to, "What do I do now?" can also be answered by adding the item to a shopping list, your wish list, or to a wedding or baby registry.

FIGURE 3.12 Amazon's product page provides several next steps for shoppers and browsers. Notice the step they'd like you to take—buying it from them—has a stronger visual callout than the secondary steps like selling and saving to lists.

What's next once you've read a news article? In **Figure 3.13**, Business Week offers options to comment, email, or print the story, order a reprint, save a link, or share the story on Digg. What's next if you're looking for a movie? Fancast bets that you probably want to view the trailer, buy tickets, rate the movie, or share it with your friends (**Figure 3.14**).

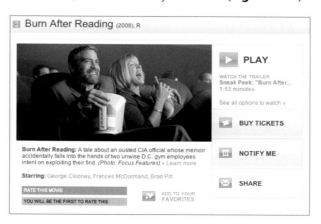

FIGURE 3.13 Business Week's tools give visitors the obvious "next step" for when they're done reading an article.

FIGURE 3.14 If you're looking for a movie, Fancast bets that you want to watch the trailer, buy tickets, add a rating, or share it with friends.

No find should be a dead-end, but the next step isn't always the same. Fancast knows there are different reasons for finding information about TV shows, movies, and people (like actors, directors, and others). If you're seeking a new TV show, maybe you want to watch the latest episode; if it's a show that's in syndication, maybe you want to know when it's on; if it's an old movie, maybe you're looking for the DVD (see **Figure 3.15**).

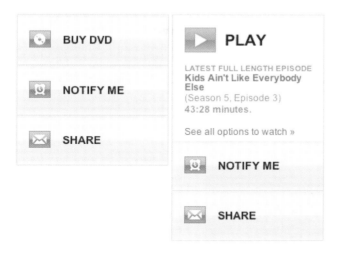

FIGURE 3.15 Fancast offers different "next steps" based on the item you're looking for. On the left, we see the options for a movie that's not on TV or in theaters (buy it on DVD). On the right are the options for a new TV show (watch the latest episode).

Helping users take that next step is what moves your site from useful to indispensable. Visitors are always using your site because it helps them fulfill some personal goal. Use your "next steps" to help them get closer.

Organization for the Masses

If you want people to be able to find what they are looking for, you must organize the contents of your Web site based on how people think about those contents. The organization of a clothing store should reflect how people think clothing is organized. The labels on the site should reflect the words people use to describe clothes. And the layout of the site should support the way people accomplish the task of shopping. This is true whether you are designing the organization of a technical support site or a music video Web site. The site must reflect the reality of its visitors, or it will confuse them.

There are four good ways to learn how people think about your content:

1. Observe others.

Go to a physical store. Visit a library. Visit your competitors' stores. If video stores and other movie sites all have an Action/Adventure category, you can bet people coming to your movie review site will expect to find a section like this one.

2. Study the enemy.

Visit your competitors' sites. How do they organize their information? Compare several organization schemes. Where are the similarities? The differences? Try to figure out why your competitors made the choices they did. Is it entropy or insight? You can even run usability testing on their site to discover what parts of their organization work and what parts don't.

This video store has sorted movies by director for those cineastes who want to follow a specific oeuvre.

3. Visit your search logs.

Suppose that you do run a movie review site, and you notice people are searching for Steven Spielberg a lot. You may want to group together all the reviews about him in one place for those diehard fans.

4. Do a card sort.

Do a card sort with some of your potential users. What's a card sort? Well, you're in luck, because that's what we're doing next.

Doing a Card Sort—An Exercise in Organization

A card sort is a simple exercise in putting like objects together.[3] You can try it right now:

What a mess—recipes from the back of packages, newspaper clippings, photocopies of family recipes, and even proper recipes on recipe cards.

1. Go get your recipe file. (If you don't have one, use your CDs or a pile of photos—anything you have a lot of and can spread all over your living room floor.)

2. Dump all the recipes out of the box and onto the floor.

3. Mix them up well, as if you were about to play poker with them.

4. Now start grouping them. As you see some things that are like others, put them together.

5. Finally, when you are done, get a few sticky notes, and name each pile.

---

3 There's a technical term for this, "affinitization." That means you sort things by what they have in common, their affinity for one another. This can also be called "chunking," but affinitization sounds so much cooler.

How nice! All the recipes are organized and each group has a name.

Now you've got an organization scheme.

You've got a scheme you can use, but can anyone else? It's time for user testing. Ask a friend to come over. Don't show him your organization scheme (hide the sticky notes). Have him do the same exercise. (Make sure you shuffle those cards well.) See where his choices are different from yours. Ask him to explain why. Try to learn the logic behind his choices so that you can incorporate it into your design.

Next invite your mom over, your grandmother, and maybe a friend who eats only at restaurants, and ask them to do the same exercise. This can be a bit time consuming, but it's invaluable insight and will save you twice the time because you won't have to redo your site later.

Now compare how everyone organized the recipes. What choices were made? Did one friend organize by course, another by ingredient? Or were they all the same? Were there any special categories, such as Extra Hot or Grandma's Specialties? The recipes are starting to fall into place.

You'll learn that people who use recipes differently also organize them differently, as do people of different generations and cultures.[4] To make this exercise as valuable (and swift) as possible, determine who will be using your organization scheme first and do a card sort only with those folks.

Now you need to resolve the results.

Look for the dominant organization scheme. Are most of your categories based on ingredients? Courses? The originating culture? Typically, one will emerge.

Adjust your organization scheme for consistency. Suppose those sticky notes say Breakfast, Appetizers, Italian, Main Course, Side Dishes, Tofu, Drinks, Chronicle Food Section,[5] and Dessert. Of all these items, a dominant theme exists—Courses. Take another look at Italian. Could those items fit under Appetizer, Main Course, or Dessert?

Set aside the odd categories that don't match. Pay very close attention to those odd categories created by more than one person: perhaps mom, grandmother, and you each created an "Aunt Sarah" category. It's an indicator that there is something special about this item. (Aunt Sarah sure could cook.) You can use this category as Featured Items on the front page or create unique shortcuts to them.

If there is only one oddball, you probably don't want to display it in your main organization scheme. If there are many, you should consider what they could mean for your design. Sometimes oddball categories suggest important criteria for how people search for an item. Thinking about the Aunt Sarah categories may lead you to realize that a tried-and-true recipe is an important factor to someone selecting a recipe. You might create a special section for Family Favorites, or you might keep your category scheme consistent and decide to add a rating system or a feedback area instead. Your categorization scheme doesn't have to do all the work.

Now look over everything.

Do the labels match? Is there more than one piece of content in each category? Is one category too big, needing to be divided into subcategories? When you are done refining, you have what you need—a taxonomy.

A taxonomy is a hierarchal organization scheme, and on the Web it's very useful for browsing (**Figure 3.16**).

If you do your work right, no one will ever notice your taxonomy. They'll just glide along effortlessly to their dream scarf or to a recipe for chicken à la king.

---

4 How things are used and the culture of your users always drive how things are organized. If you can isolate how things will be used and by whom, then you're halfway to awesome.

5 We're big fans of the very clip-able recipes printed weekly in the *San Francisco Chronicle*. Check out *The San Francisco Chronicle Cookbook*. Yum!

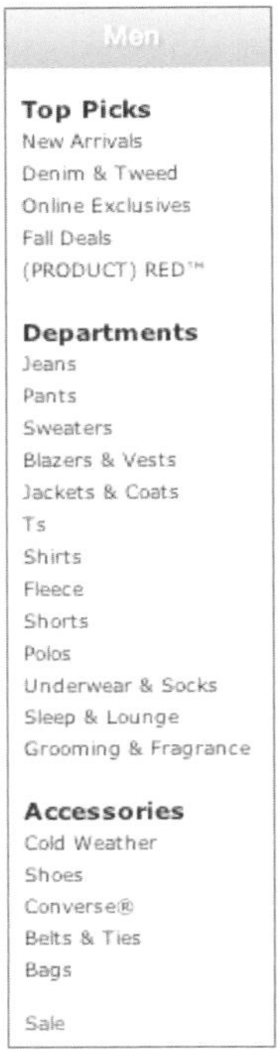

FIGURE 3.16 Gap's taxonomy for men's clothing.

You Really Can Be in Two Places at Once

"But some of my stuff could go into more than one category!" "But half my users wanted organization by course, and the other half wanted organization by ingredients!"

In the real world, you can't be in more than one place at one time. There is a crazy concept called "shelf space," and it appears to be limited. The grocery store can't have a bakery aisle and a sandwich aisle, and have bread in both. There isn't enough space—or bread. However, on the Web, it's another story.

Table 3.2 shows a section of the taxonomy from allrecipes.com for its bread collection.

As you can see by studying **Table 3.3**, allrecipes mixes several kinds of classifications. This means some bread recipes can be in more than one category. For example, you might find a hot cross bun recipe[6] under Breakfast Pastries, Holiday Breads, Yeast Breads, Fruit Breads, and Rolls and Buns. This is okay. It may make purists itch, but it gets people to the bread recipe they need.

---

6 Growing up in Iowa, Christina's Easter morning breakfast always consisted of decorated eggs (after they were found) and hot cross buns. If you haven't had the pleasure of eating a hot cross bun, let us inform you they are sweet and fluffy with little bits of candied fruit inside and a frosting cross on top.

General	Quick	Yeast
Bread machine	Quick bread	Yeast bread
Non-bread machine	Banana bread	Bagels
Breakfast pastries	Biscuits and scones	Challah
Holiday bread	Cornbread	Flat bread
	Fruit bread	Rolls and buns
	Muffins	Rye bread
	Popovers and Yorkshire puddings	Sourdough bread and starters
	Zucchini bread	White bread
		Whole grain bread

TABLE 3.2 allrecipes.com Taxonomy

Type of Classification	Items in Classification
Key Ingredients	Corn bread, fruit bread
Method	Bread machine, non-bread machine
Course	Breakfast pastries
Special Type	Bagels, challah
Time	Holiday bread

TABLE 3.3 allrecipes.com Taxonomy Classification Types

Epicurious is another recipe site that uses different types of organization schemes based on the different facets of the recipes. Unlike Allrecipes, Epicurious clearly labels the different schemes (see **Figure 3.17**). Clearly labeling the facets has several advantages. The headers help keep the page orderly and keep the visitor from feeling overwhelmed by the choices offered. Epicurious also sets the expectation in the searcher that there are different ways to find recipes.

recipe category

- Chef Recipe
- Epicurious TV
- Kid-Friendly
- Quick & Easy
- Wine Pairing

dietary consideration

- Healthy
- Low Fat
- Vegetarian
- High Fiber
- Low Sodium
- Wheat/Gluten Free
- Kosher
- Low/No Sugar
- Low Cal
- Raw
- Low Carb
- Vegan

cuisine

- African
- Chinese
- Greek
- Jewish
- Scandinavian
- Vietnamese
- American
- Eastern European/Russian
- Indian
- Mediterranean
- Southern/Soul Food
- Asian
- English/Scottish
- Irish
- Mexican
- Southwestern
- Cajun/Creole
- French
- Italian
- Middle Eastern
- Spanish/Portuguese
- Central/South American
- German
- Japanese
- Moroccan
- Thai

meal / course

- Appetizer
- Dinner
- Side
- Breakfast
- First Course
- Snack
- Brunch
- Hors d'Oeuvre
- Buffet
- Lunch
- Dessert
- Main Course

type of dish

- Bread
- Cranberry Sauce
- Salad
- Vegetable
- Cake
- Cupcake
- Sandwich
- Candy
- Marinade
- Sauce
- Condiment/Spread
- Muffin
- Soup/Stew
- Cookie
- Pie/Tart
- Stuffing/Dressing

season / occasion

- Christmas
- Grilling
- Rosh Hashanah/Yom Kippur
- Valentine's Day
- Cocktail Party
- Halloween
- Spring
- Wedding
- Easter
- Hanukkah
- Summer
- Winter
- Fall
- New Year's Eve
- Super Bowl
- Fourth of July
- Passover
- Thanksgiving

preparation method

- Bake
- Freeze
- No Cook
- Steam
- Braise
- Fry
- Poach
- Stew
- Brine
- Grill/Barbecue
- Roast
- Stir-Fry
- Broil
- Marinate
- Sauté
- Chill
- Microwave
- Slow Cook

main ingredient

- Bean
- Chocolate
- Fish
- Lamb
- Pepper
- Shellfish
- Yogurt
- Beef
- Citrus
- Fruit
- Mushroom
- Pork
- Tea
- Berry
- Coffee
- Game
- Nut
- Potato
- Tomato
- Cheese
- Duck
- Ginger
- Olive
- Poultry
- Turkey
- Chicken
- Egg
- Herb
- Pasta
- Rice/Grain
- Vegetable

FIGURE 3.17 Epicurious has more than 80,000 recipes. Good organization is not optional if the site is to be useful.

Faceted Classification

Recently, we went looking on Epicurious.com for a Bûche dë Noel. This is a special choc-olaty Christmas cake they make in France. Because we knew it was French, we clicked French under the cuisine header, and followed this route:

Browse > French > Chocolate > Dessert

After a couple pages of results, we found "Bûche dë Noel with Marzipan Mushrooms." However, if we hadn't known it was French, but only that it was a chocolatey baked cake, we could have followed this route:

Browse > Dessert > Chocolate > Bake

This is called a faceted classification. Each item has multiple characteristics: the cake is cake, is baked, is French, and is chocolatey. A person can find this item by looking in Cakes, Chocolate, Baked Goods, or in French Cooking (**Figure 3.18**). This greatly increases a seeker's chance of finding what she is looking for. Faceted classification is pretty nifty, but it can also be very tricky to execute well. First, it's much easier to do if your content is fairly homogenous.

FIGURE 3.18 Browsing French > Chocolate > Dessert eventually bring us to Bûche dë Noel, a French dessert packed with chocolate. Exactly what we were looking for.

Determining the facets of recipes is relatively easy. But how would you handle all of cooking? It would include equipment, history, regions, ingredients, chefs, and so on, and then each aspect would have its own facets. Let's look at equipment for a moment; what are the facets of a pan?

Some common ones might be shape, material, brand, and use. Now let's add in knives. The facets still work, more or less. There are other important selection criteria, such as edge: serrated versus non-serrated. And then what if we throw in knife sets. Or move outward to cookbooks. A cookbook has completely

different important characteristics than a pan—author, cuisine, key ingredients, and so on. The bigger the domain you are trying to describe, the more potential facet types it has.

This is time-consuming to document and tricky to present in navigation. So tread cautiously—it gets complex quickly.

Even homogenous content can have pitfalls. For example, say you want to help users who want to be sure they have a comprehensive view of your content. Suppose they want to see every recipe for tomato soup. They may become anxious because it will be hard to know when they've seen them all—especially when they see the same recipe cropping up in several categories. For example, they might see gazpacho in Cold Soups and Summer Meals. Searchers may wonder if they are treading the same ground, how many recipes they still have to discover, and—because human memory is fallible—which recipes they are truly seeing again and which are merely familiar. "Are those two different recipes for gazpacho or the same recipe twice?"

This is yet another time when it's important to know who your user is. If most of your users come to your site for something specific, you may want to choose one schema, with several facets that will provide access to any single item. If you know your users are browsers who visit many sections of the site, you may want to use another schema with only one or two facets so it's easy to browse.

You also need to know your content. If you do not have a lot of content, an extensive and complex classification scheme can result in a lot of clicks that lead users to the same darn thing—users can feel that they were tricked into thinking there is more on the site than there really is. Labels are the tip of the iceberg.

If your site has a lot to offer a visitor, you want to make that clear as soon as the visitor arrives. Sure, you can do that by having a million links and pictures on your front page, but that's just as likely to confuse the visitor.

Instead of bludgeoning the visitor over the head with your site's wealth, take a hint from icebergs. Icebergs are 90 percent underwater. Only the tip shows, but a sailor can spot that tip and know there's a lot more than meets the eye. As the information architect, your job is to design a tip that will suggest the size of the iceberg beneath. How much of the taxonomy should be above the water? How much do you have to show to let people know they've found the right place?

Suppose you are researching digital cameras, and you check Consumer Reports for reviews. Consumer Reports has navigation across the top (**Figure 3.19**). Each option is like an iceberg tip: Electronics will probably have reviews of digital cameras.

To improve their iceberg tips, Consumer Reports also exposes some of their taxonomy in the left column. While Electronics in the global navigation *might* take you to digital camera reviews, Electronics > Cameras and photography will definitely take you there.

In each of these cases, the site designers chose excellent labels for their tips of the review iceberg. Appliances and Electronics are generic but very common labels for large groups of a certain type of merchandise, and they are used widely in American stores. This is when Consumer Report's choice to reveal more of the iceberg really shines. Electronics could be anything, but showing subcategories such as Cameras, Televisions, and Phones suggests both a wealth of items, as well as what sort of items can be found under this label.

FIGURE 3.19 Notice the Cars, Appliances, Electronics, and other navigation across the top.

Naming a label

So what about the label itself? Cars could have been called Autos, Vehicles, or Horseless Carriages. This is the place for some ugly arguments.[7]

---

7 Christina remembers her greeting card days. She and the copy writer were going at each other's throats over whether a category should be called Office Humor or Around the Water Cooler.

I'd like to say labels are decided like this (in order of importance):

- What the user will understand
- Common conventions in the domain
- The company's brand

But more often it's like this:

- How much space there is on the navigation widget
- How bored the writer/designer is with current labels
- The company's brand

A good label is so obvious, it's dull as dirt. A good label doesn't make you pause (and it never makes you think). A good label is merely the thing you click to get to the good stuff. It may take you hours to come up with something that looks effortless. When it looks like you came up with the label in two seconds, you probably have the right one.

Here are several online greeting card companies, and each has a different label for their "I don't have a reason, but I am sending you a card, anyhow" category:

Company	Label
American Greetings	Just Because
Yahoo!	Wishes and thoughts
Egreetings	Keep in touch
Hallmark	Just a note

Which ones made you want to click through to see what it was? Which was dead obvious? Which seemed to fit the company's brand (Yahoo! as utilitarian, American Greetings as old-fashioned, Egreetings as cutting edge, Hallmark as *the* greeting card company)? Which fits on a button? What would you label it?

Stuffing the Stuff

It's a cloudy Sunday afternoon, and you're about to organize your closet. How will you do it?

- By type? Shirts, slacks, jackets
- By color? White, yellow, red, blue
- By sets that go together? To make getting dressed easier

These categorization choices are trivial. They make your life easier, sure. But no one else is affected by them. As you go to design organization schemes for others and as you organize larger and larger sets of content, the decisions become more difficult, and your decisions require deeper thought.

Categorization has consequences

A mislabeled section on a medical reference site can keep a physician from finding new research to save someone's life. A badly organized university site can discourage a poor student who may think there's no financial aid to be had. A confusing online store results in lost sales. Ultimately, if your visitors can't find what they need on your site, then your site isn't doing its job.

Categorization provides context

Buying a knife from a Hunting category, an Accessories category, or a Cooking category tells you a lot about what sort of knife you will be getting.

Categorization is shaped by context

We're foodies, so we have a very different perception of sweet peas than a suburban gardener would. We think of them sizzling in a frying pan and put them in a Side Dish category. The gardener pictures them adding color to the flowerbed and puts them in an Annual Flowers category.

Each categorizer brings his or her life knowledge and prejudices to the process. The Dewey decimal system's Religion category has nine subsections, seven of which are on Christianity. The rest of the world's religions are lumped into one sub-section: Other. Language has nine subsections; seven of them cover European languages. Looking at the Dewey decimal system will tell you in which part of the world John Dewey grew up.

200	Religion
210	Natural theology
220	The Bible
230	Christian theology
240	Christian moral and devotional theology
250	Christian orders and local church
260	Christian social theology
270	Christian church history
280	Christian denominations and sects
290	Other and comparative religions

On an investment site, a separate section for women can be interpreted to mean the institution thinks women are not good with money and need extra special help. Or that section can be welcomed as helping equalize a male-driven domain. You aren't just organizing—you are sending a message.

As you go forward into the categorization process, recognize that it takes thought and care. Your reward is a successful site where people find what they are looking for— without pausing for thought.

Of course, one of the easiest ways to make things easy to find is to use metadata, and that's where we go next.

"All big projects go easier if you break them down into little pieces."

4

A Bricklayer's View of Information Architecture

In which we learn to design our architecture from the bottom up.

Yes, there is too much stuff on the Web. There's even too much stuff on just your Web site! Yes, it needs to be organized. But how? If you're like us, you're feeling like you're facing spring-cleaning and all you can do is sit on the couch and stare at the mess.

All big projects go easier if you break them down into little pieces. Building a house seems like an impossible task (especially to someone who can't even face cleaning one), and designing an architecture for your content is similarly daunting. But like building a house, you take it one step at a time. Gather your materials and tools. Build the infrastructure. Add the bricks and mortar. Curtains and chairs will come later.

Getting Meta

Metadata is information about information. Although that sounds a bit existential, it's actually a very practical tool for information architecture (IA). Metadata is the basis of all organizational systems, from search to a faceted navigation system[1] on a shopping site. It is the brick of the IA house, and it can be arranged into a wide variety of retrieval systems, depending on what you need. Information can come in many forms—an article, an e-book, a photograph, or a catalog. Some information isn't made of words—for example, a Flash movie, a sound in MP3 format, or a photograph. When there are very few words inherent in the information, as with photos and music, metadata helps find it.

---

1   Facets are things like shop by size, shop by price, shop by brand...more about that later!

Metadata is an effective way to ensure that all these items are found by those seeking them. Metadata is all the information about each item. For instance, in a song's case, it might be the following: "Brown Sugar, version 2, outtake, written by Mick Jagger and Keith Richards, performed by The Rolling Stones, album: Itchy Fingers, bootleg, length 3:50, genre: rock and roll, blues" and so on…

Three major types of metadata are used nowadays:

- **Intrinsic.** Metadata about the thing's composition. Is it an MS Word document, a JPEG, a 20Kb file, or a zip file?

- **Administrative.** Metadata about the way the thing will be handled. Is it a temporary thing, or does it need to be archived? Who is the editor? Has it been approved for publication?

- **Descriptive.** Metadata about the nature of the thing. This is the most important for our purposes and the most commonly used on the Web. Is it fiction or fact? Is it an article? What's the subject? What are related subjects?

Beauregard the dog's metadata

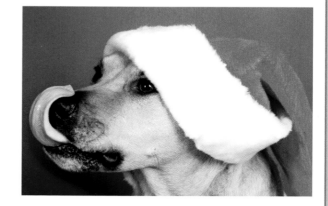

Intrinsic:
20KB
JPEG

Administrative:
Photographer: Noel Franus
Use: Christmas card

Descriptive: Dog, puppy, canine, Golden Labrador Retriever, gold lab, Santa hat, Santa Claus, St. Nicholas, Christmas, Xmas, photograph, Noel's dog, cute, sentimental, cuddly

Metadata doesn't always fall neatly into these categories. Look at Noel's Christmas card featuring Beauregard the dog. The term "Christmas card" could fall into any one of three categories:

- **Intrinsic.** Because that's what the thing *is*.

- **Administrative.** Because that's what the item's *purpose* is.

- **Descriptive.** Because that's how you would *describe* it.

In this case, you might want to put "Christmas card" in all three categories.

If you work on Web sites, you may have already run into metadata in the form of HTML meta tags. A peek at Dean and DeLuca's source file (where they keep the HTML) shows this descriptive metadata in the meta tag:

```
<meta name="description" content="Dean and DeLuca gourmet food stores.
Offering a wide selection of California wines, custom gift baskets, cakes,
cheeses, hard to find spices, coffee, caviar, truffles, holiday and seasonal
foods." />
<meta name="keywords" content="dean; deluca; gift; gourmet; food; online;
store; caviar; cheese; steak; coffee; holiday; artisan cheeses; artisan
cheese; spices; california; napa valley; baskets; corporate sales; olive oil;
vinegar; chocolate; seafood; shellfish; wine; herbs; cooks tools; cookware;
cake; cakes; wines; cookies; pies; truffles; seasonal; bakery; salmon; shrimp;
lobster; gifts; balsamic" />
```

On Kansas City Steaks, you see another line beyond description and keywords:

```
<meta name="developer" content="Digital Evolution Group, LLC">
```

And on HomeBistro.com, we see this administrative metadata:

```
<meta name="ROBOTS" content="ALL">
<meta name="revisit" content="15 days">
<meta name="robots" content="index,follow">
```

Metadata hidden away in the source code is primarily for search engines. Dean and DeLuca is telling the search engines that "crawl" their page that they sell food. Home Bistro is inviting search engines to come back every 15 days to look for new content. But this is all terribly geeky. Let's break it down.

The New York Public Library has been collecting photographs since the invention of the camera. They have thousands upon thousands of images saved on 57 terabytes of storage. Suppose that you remembered a photo you saw at the NYPL site that you particularly liked and wanted to see again. Metadata could help you find it in the sea of photos. The particular photo shown in **Figure 4.1** currently has intrinsic metadata, which you see when you right-click it and look at its properties. You can tell from the Properties screen that the following information is true:

- It's a JPEG, one of the popular formats for pictures on the Web.

- It's 303.29 kilobytes, which isn't terribly large.

- It's 609 x 760 pixels, which is about the size of a piece of paper.

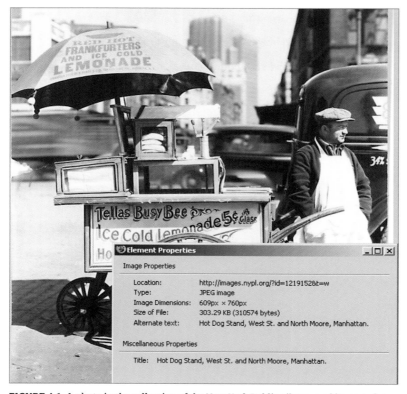

FIGURE 4.1 A photo in the collection of the New York Public Library and its metadata.

But by looking at this info, would any of it really help you find this picture again? Maybe if you had known you'd want to find it, you would have written down the ID number or the URL. But what if, like so many things in life, you didn't know you wanted it until you missed it?

You might remember that it was taken by someone named Beatrice Abbott. Or that it was taken in 1936. This is administrative metadata and includes not only the author/ creator of the information, but the date created, the date published, and so on—everything about how the item/information was managed. But what do you really remember from the picture (**Figure 4.2**)? A guy selling hot dogs in New York City? This is the third kind of metadata: descriptive. It is probably the most important information for searching and browsing, because we are humans, not machines, and we tend to remember things that interest us as humans, such as stories and images.

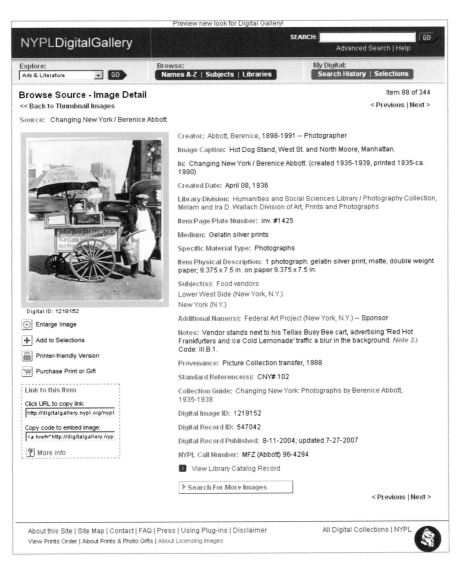

FIGURE 4.2 Properties of hot dog stand, West St. and North Moore, Manhattan.

Storytelling for "findability"

In History class, we were forced to remember dates and places. But that's not what sticks; what sticks in our heads are the stories we heard. To most of us, Napoleon isn't the ruler of France born on Aug 15, 1769 (date of birth). He isn't the 5'6" emperor (size). He's a guy with his hand in his coat, wearing a sideways hat, writing love letters to Josephine while conquering large portions of Europe. The hard facts fade, and the romantic details stay with us. We can use this human foible to assist us in improving "findability." *Findability* is a term popularized by Peter Morville.[2] It is the capability of an object to be found through searching or browsing. We like this term because it makes clear that the onus is on the object to be found, rather than on the user to attempt to craft an effective search query. On the Web, users just don't want to be bothered. A recent look at the most popular searches at Yahoo! and Google showed that 80 percent of searches were one- and two-word queries.[3] Those one or two words have to somehow be enough to turn up the object the user is looking for, and effective metadata is a good way to stretch that word faaaarther.

When you craft a collection of descriptive metadata, you draw upon the stories people tell about the object. These are the details people remember. When you did the card sort in Chapter 3, Sock Drawers and CD Racks—Everything Must Be Organized, you listened to people talk about the objects they were sorting: "Aunt Sarah's apple crisp was always so crunchy on top. I don't know how she did it." Now it's time to use those stories to select effective metadata.

To find the photo of the "new york hotdog guy," a user could search for 1219152, the image's ID number. But she probably wouldn't. It's a number in a world where we have to remember phone numbers, ATM codes, and passwords. Our brains just don't have room for more random data. A user could search for "Bernice Abbott," the photographer, or Changing New York, the series name. These are much more probable search terms, and names are easier to remember than numbers. But the user might get pages of results, as shown in **Figure 4.3**. Imagine scanning through 29 pages of results! It's much more likely that a user would search for "Hot Dog Vendor." It's descriptive, and it is born from, and intrinsic to, the story the photo tells.

These photos were not created with stories. The photographer may have provided a caption or a title, but that was a scant clue as to the nature of the photo. But the library, whose mission is to select, collect, preserve, and make accessible "the accumulated wisdom of the world, without distinction as to income, religion, nationality, or other human condition," makes sure everyone can find it by adding in the alternative text we saw earlier in the properties. Subjects include "food vendors" and "lower west side" and notes, "Vendor stands next to his Tellas Busy Bee cart, advertising 'Red Hot Frankfurters and Ice Cold Lemonade' traffic a blur in the background." These elements make up a complete story that matches the story users tell when they search (see **Figure 4.4**).

---

2 Author of *Information Architecture for the World Wide Web* (O'Reilly, 1998) and CEO of Semantic Studios, an information architecture consulting firm.

3 Google Zeitgeist (http://www.google.com/press/zeitgeist.html) and Yahoo!'s Buzz (http://buzz.yahoo.com) are fun and insightful ways to see what people are searching for at any given time.

FIGURE 4.3 A search for Beatrice Abbott will bring up all her photos held in the collection.

The New York Public Library may need to fulfill its mission, but for-profit sites have even more skin in the game. They can't gamble on text searches that may turn up more blanks than successes. The library might disappoint us, but if a for-profit company did, it would go out of business.

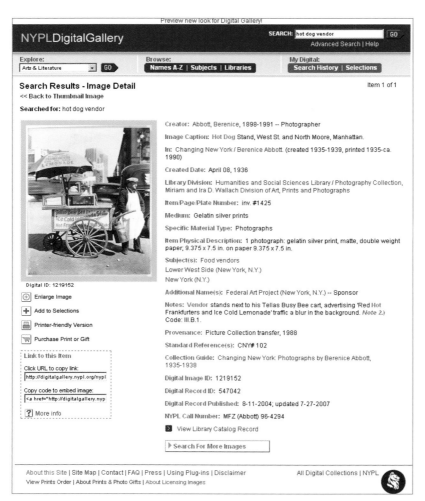

FIGURE 4.4 A successful search calls on text in both the title and the notes field.

Hand-crafted metadata for your finding pleasure

iStockphoto, a Web site with hundreds of pieces of stock photography, makes extensive use of handcrafted metadata. Their business model depends on users finding a photograph desirable enough to pay for. If their users can't find the photo, that means no profit for their company.

Next to each photo, iStockphoto displays a long list of keywords links to all the photos that have been marked with those same keywords (**Figure 4.5**). In case you want to look for the following items, you can search for:

- A different image of excess (descriptive)

- A different photo by the photographer (administrative)

- Another photo with the same color profile (intrinsic)

FIGURE 4.5 A vision of excess, photographed by Nuno Silva in the very artistic square format.

Each of these photos was looked at by a human who thought carefully about the image and chose keywords (metadata) that designers would be likely to use for their search process. The IA sat looking at the photo and thought: "Woman, sitting, she's drunk, she's living a life of excess, maybe she's an alcoholic, she's in her twenties, maybe thirty, but that's pushing it," and so on. The IA told herself a dozen little stories about the picture and picked the most powerful and most likely to be searched for terms to improve the photo's findability. Then she used them to create not only a more effective search, but also a more browsable structure. If a creative director trying to find an effective image for a design is dissatisfied with this picture, it's easy enough to follow another keyword that captures what he's looking for. More photographs are just a click away (see **Figures 4.6**, **4.7**, and **4.8**).

FIGURE 4.6 Another image of excess.

FIGURE 4.7 Another photo by Nuno Silva.

FIGURE 4.8 Another photo with the same color profile (palette).

The items in the following table (**Table 4.1**) are more likely to be found by those seeking them if metadata is added by hand.

Object	Description	Potential Keywords	Descriptive Metadata	Intrinsic Metadata	Administrative Metadata
Photo: Santorini church	A church on the Greek Island of Santorini, in the city of Fira	Church, chapel, path, Greece, Greek, Santorini, cliff, sea, ocean, blue, white, Mediterranean	File type: JPEG Image File proportions: 1600×1200 px File Size: 1814KB	Created: 4/20/202 Modified: 4/21/2002	Photographer: Christina Wodtke Used in: Greek picture book 2002
Original Song: "Ain't nobody here but us chickens"	Song riffs on the old defense for being caught at mischief. "Ain't nobody here but us chickens" in a lounge lizard style.	Jazz, lounge lizard, male vocalist, Mark Murphy, naughty, improvisation, lounge music, humor, groovy, upbeat, party music	File type: MP3 File size: 2234KB	Tempo: slow	Sung by: Mark Murphy Written by: (A.Kramer/ J.Whitney) Produced by: David Bram and Mark Murphy Licensing: 32 Records Recorded at: 96Kbps Used on: The Best of Jazz Juice
Product: Ice grips	Like tire chains for the feet, these easy-to-wear grips enable the wearer to stride confidently through snow and ice.	Shoe accessories, boot accessories, cold weather gear, ice gear, no-slip, slip, ice, snow, snow shoes, snow boots, tire chains, metal, rubber, weaving	Manufacturer: Hammacher Schlemmer	Stock: in stock	Created: 2002

TABLE 4.1 Metadata Types Example

Object	Description	Potential Keywords	Descriptive Metadata	Intrinsic Metadata	Admin-istrative Metadata
Tutorial for Adobe InDesign	Place a native Adobe Photo-shop file with transparency intact, apply editable drop shadows to objects and text, and blend colors between vec-tor and bitmap graphics for interesting effects.	Adobe, InDesign, transparency, drop shadow, text, vector manipulation, tutorial, learn-ing, elearn-ing, online learning, flash movie	Flash tutorial. Use transpar-ency effects in layouts	Flash movie Windows: 2.6MB Flash movie Macintosh: 3.6MB	Supporting: InDesign 2.0 Retire: Fall 2003
Web site: COMMON GROUND: A pattern language for human-computer inter-face design	Research paper explain-ing the use of patterns for designing interactive systems.	Design, Web site-design, interaction design, inter-active, pattern language, Christopher Alexander, content pre-sentation, nav-igation design, HTML	283KB	www.mit. edu/~jtidwell/ common_ ground.html	Author: Jenifer Tidwell Last modified: May 17, 1999 Copyright: 1999

TABLE 4.1 Metadata Types Example *(continued)*

Many things require a conscious addition of handcrafted metadata, such as animation and films, products in a catalog, newspaper columns, magazine articles, and research papers. "Not articles," you say. "They are made up of text already. Can't you just search on the text?"

Let's take this short newspaper column by a fictional columnist: "Bonds hit another dinger today. Giants fans went mad! Dogs and kids were swimming out after a token of his record-breaking year. Barry is hitting .863 this season, and it looks like a trip to the Series is inevitable for our boys."

Suppose that you were searching to find out if the San Francisco team had hit any home runs lately. This article would probably not come up. Heck, you can't even tell if it's about baseball! But add some descriptive metadata: "San Francisco Giants, home run, World

Series chances, Barry Bonds, baseball." And now a search will quite likely give you this column in its results.

One language for all

Another way to make the search more effective would be to create a controlled vocabulary. Many moons ago, Christina waited tables. One day her manager came down to tell the wait staff that from now on they were to refer to their customers as "guests." They also were to refer to courses as "first course" and "second course." Their chef, who was French, found the American use of "entrée" for the main course annoying. This was Christina's first experience with a controlled vocabulary.

English is a complex, flexible, and powerful language. Steve Martin once said, "Boy, those French, they have a different word for everything!" But really, it's the English language that is full of mischief. You can begin your meal with:

- A starter
- A first course
- An appetizer

Or terms we've borrowed from other languages:

- Hors d'oeuvres
- An amuse-gueule[4]

---

4 This is French for "little tiny bit of nothing that we tease you with at the beginning of the meal." Imagine a quarter teaspoon of caviar with two croutons on a small white plate.

Moreover, a Western restaurant could call this first course "grazing" or a sports bar "warm-ups." You can see where it might lead to some confusion. At the restaurant, if Christina asked the guests if they would like a first course, they would look at her funny and say, "Huh?" She would say, "An appetizer? Hors d'oeuvres? A nibble?" But on the Web, no one can hear you scream. And so we realize we need to create a controlled vocabulary.

Controlled vocabulary

A controlled vocabulary is simply what it sounds like—a way to control the meaning of the vocabulary used, as well as a way to keep track of the related terms. In Christina's restaurant, they had the preferred term, "first course," and all the terms their patrons might use, "starter, first course, hors d'oeuvres, appetizer," neatly tucked into their heads. So if a patron wanted an appetizer of smoked salmon, they would write on the check "first course: smoked salmon." They also kept track of related concepts: "Madam, would you care for an aperitif?" Or the more casual, "Can I get you a drink while you're looking at the menu?"

A computer tends to be as inflexible as a French chef. Let's say you're thinking of making some cured salmon for brunch. If you search for "salmon," the computer will give you results featuring the word salmon and you'll probably find what you're looking for. But if you type "fish" or "gravlax," your guests will go hungry unless the designer of the search has created some type of controlled vocabulary. There are many kinds of controlled vocabulary, from the simple one made of equivalence relationships that says, "yes, gravlax and cured salmon are the same," to a complex thesaurus that says, "gravlax is a type of salmon that is the same as cured salmon and is an ingredient for bagels and lox." Next, let's dig a little deeper.

Equivalence relationships

The simplest type of controlled vocabulary is a list of equivalence relationships: cured salmon and gravlax are the same for the purposes of a search. **Table 4.2** shows an example. The relationships can be as simple as two words for the same thing: cat and kittycat. These are synonyms. They also can be different spellings or acronyms for the same thing. Lion is lyon; SPCA is Society for Prevention of Cruelty to Animals. These are variants. The words can be slightly different, but for the purposes of search, you may choose to treat them the same: cat and kitten. Perhaps you have a greeting card site and someone wants a card with a picture of a kitten, but you have only one card with a cat on it. It's better to offer up the cat than to show the user a "no results found."

It's a lot like the index in the back of a book. You look up "moon" in a book on the solar system, and it says, "See satellites." For the purpose of that book, satellite and moon are the same. Another book (a thicker one, perhaps) might differentiate them. The key is to consider what people are searching for and what words they use, and then to get them to the content you have.

Preferred term	Variants
Smoked salmon	Fish, gravlax, lox, cured salmon, smoked fish, preserved fish, nova

TABLE 4.2 Equivalence Relationship Example

Hierarchical relationships

A more complex type of controlled vocabulary is a taxonomy. It shows hierarchical relationships, as well as equivalence relationships. It is useful not only for searches, but also for
effective browse hierarchies and for tying the two together. **Table 4.3** shows an example.

Preferred Term	Variants	Parent (Broader Term)	Children (Narrower Term)
Smoked salmon	Gravlox, lox, cured salmon	Fish, smoked fish, cured meats, preserved fish,	Smoked salmon flatbread with crème fraise, linguini with smoked salmon and asparagus

TABLE 4.3 Hierarchical Relationships Example

You can see a taxonomy in action on Yahoo! A search for "coffee mug" brings up a number of results (**Figure 4.9**).

www.yahoo.com

FIGURE 4.9 Results of search on Yahoo! for "coffee mug."

Take a closer look. Each result is accompanied not only by the title, description, and link, but also with a link to Yahoo!'s famous hierarchy. A searcher who is looking for a tchotchke to put a company logo on can click: Promotional Items > Mugs and find companies that offer that service or find a mug collector to see other collections. The categories also provide context for the searcher; for example, the mug collector is not going to click the second result after noticing it's in the *Punk and Hardcore Artists* section.

Associative relationships

The Taj Mahal of controlled vocabularies is a thesaurus. You may remember using the thesaurus in grade school. It was a way to make yourself look smarter. Instead of writing "she said," you could use a thesaurus and write "she yelled, spoke, whispered, insinuated, articulated, uttered, insisted," and so on.[5]

Thesauri have come back into our everyday life via the Web. More than a tool to get more and better words, thesauri are used to create a Web of interconnected words to help people find the things they just don't have. A thesaurus shows not only hierarchical relationships but also associative ones.

As you can see in **Table 4.4**, organizing metadata into a controlled vocabulary is a somewhat subjective exercise. On a different Web site, Jewish cuisine might be the parent and preserved fish the associated term. It depends on the type of Web site it is and who the visitors are.

Preferred Term	Variants	Related Terms	Parent	Siblings	Children	Associated Terms
Smoked salmon	Gravlax, lox, Cured salmon	Preserved fish	Smoke trout, bacalao, salt-cured sardines, pickled anchovies	Smokes salmon flat-bread with crème fraise, linguini with smoked salmon and asparagus	Jewish cuisine, kosher foods	Crème fraise, bagels, capers, dill, crackers, fish knife, caviar

TABLE 4.4 The Beginnings of a Thesaurus

Associated terms are those terms that belong together but are not the same, nor are they broader or narrower terms. They just kind of go together. For example, if **Table 4.4** were for a thesaurus for a recipe site, it might prove useful to list ingredients commonly

---

5 Of course, later on we all learned that we should save our $10 words for the dialogue and just leave "said" alone. And the thesaurus became a paperweight.

combined with the main term (crème fraise, bagels, capers, dill, and cream cheese). On a gourmet food store site, it might be useful to list other purchases someone might want to make (crackers, fish knife, and caviar). These are terms associated with smoked salmon, but no one would confuse them for being the same. All these types of controlled vocabulary are aimed at getting people to what they are seeking, no matter what crazy thing they type into the search box. Let's see it in action.

Everybody spels difernt

Well, some of us certainly spell differently.

Figures 4.10 and **4.11** show the results of a recent attempt to find different kinds of gourmet *chedder*. According to this search, Zabar's doesn't have chedder. Except they do…only they call it by the proper spelling, *cheddar,* and ask you to use that instead. Yahoo!, however, recognizes the wide variety of spelling humans manage to invent, and although "chedder" works rather well, they also prompt you to try "cheddar."

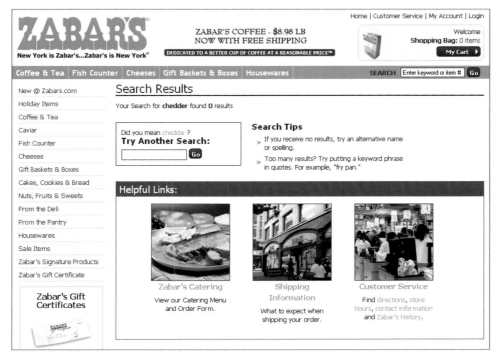

FIGURE 4.10 Search for chedder on Zabar's.

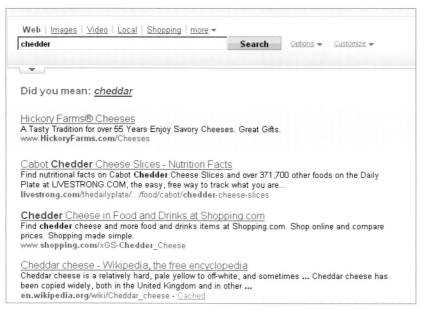

FIGURE 4.11 Search for chedder on Yahoo!

Let's try reverse engineering[6] Zabar's. We didn't make the site, and we don't know anyone who did, but by playing with it, we can make a good guess at how it works. So, if we were unwilling to believe Zabar's didn't sell cheddar, we might search for "cheese" instead. Which turns up quite a lot of cheese, including cheddar. The Zabar's controlled vocabulary includes hierarchical information that shows that cheddar is a subset of several parents: "Semi-firm cheese," "English Cheese," and even rates its own special "cheddar" collection under "All cheeses A-Z" (**Figure 4.12**).

When sites have multiple parents like this, it's called *faceted classification*. The facets can include any quality shared by a number of items, including price, weight, and color; or in this case, brand, origin, and firmness. We're surprised they don't include strength of smell, but we don't work at Zabar's. Facets are useful when users want to narrow down a larger selection of items to find the perfect thing. Ecommerce sites use them quite a bit.[7]

---

6 When engineers or five-year-olds want to understand how something works, they take it apart. When five-year-olds do it, it's called mayhem. When engineers do it, they usually go on to reassemble it—and then build their own, perhaps even better. This is called reverse engineering. It's a great way to understand how things work. Study the product, take it apart, reassemble it, and then try to build your own.

7 Learn more about faceted classification at Christina's magazine, Boxes and Arrows:
http://www.boxesandarrows.com/view/ranganathan_for_ias
http://www.boxesandarrows.com/view/all_about_facets_controlled_vocabularies

FIGURE 4.12 The wonderful world of cheese.

If we continue on to the Keen's Farmhouse Cheddar page, we see the thesaurus being used to seduce the buyer into making more purchases (**Figure 4.13**). By examining the *You May Also Like* section, you can guess the parent of Keen's Farmhouse—English cheese—even though that bit of metadata isn't listed. English cheese is featured heavily in a selection of related items, which includes the following:

- A sibling sharing a parent brand, Colston Bassett Stilton, also from Neal's Yard

- A sibling sharing a parent origin, Shopshire Blue, which is a non-cheddar English cheese; stinky but tasty

- An associated item, Pumpernickel, which isn't cheese at all, but makes eating good

Visitors seeking a good English cheddar might be better able to find what they want, but they also might be nudged gently into purchasing a few items they didn't know they wanted. The thesaurus suspected they might, as we see in **Table 4.5**, and Zabar's goes to the bank. Now if they would only understand our little spelling problem, theirs would be the perfect site.

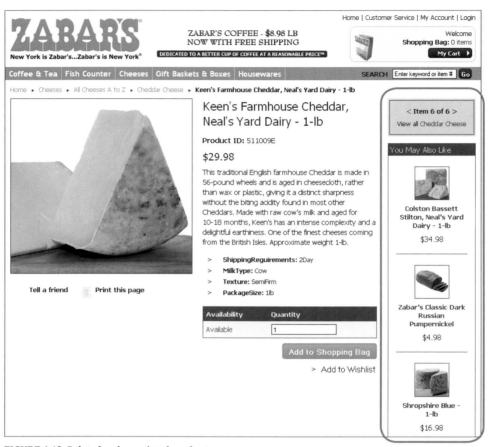

FIGURE 4.13 Related and associated products.

Preferred Term	Variants	Related Terms	Associated Terms	Parent(s)	Children	Cousins
Cheddar	chedar, Chedder, cheder	English Cheese, Semi-Firm Cheese	Keen's Farmhouse Cheddar	Colson Basset	Stilton, Shopshire Blue, Cabbott's Extra Sharp Vintage Cheddar	Pumpernickle

TABLE 4.5 The thesaurus entries for cheddar

Building a controlled vocabulary

Sold! Controlled vocabularies are the answer. Er, where do they come from? Building a controlled vocabulary is quite a bit of work. Many valuable things are. We can lay out the basic steps here, but you might want to buy a thicker book before you dig in too deeply.

1. Gather content.

Your first question needs to be, "What exactly is it that I want to organize?" The most effective way we've found to do this is a content inventory. A *content inventory* is a tally of everything that exists on the site and everything you expect to be added to the site.

Suppose that you are creating an MP3 site. You want to account for all the MP3s currently available on the site, as well as any music reviews, interviews with artists, and other supporting material (such as MP3 player information) available for download from the site. You also want to be aware of what's coming up next. Perhaps the site plans to add MPEGs of music videos that users can watch. But maybe it's slated for next year, and no one really knows what they'll be. You'll want to note that music videos are coming, but you can't organize what you don't know. And the odds that you would duplicate your work when they came in are high.

If you have the time and you want to use this opportunity to cull some content, you may want to do a content audit as well—in which you not only have to account for every piece of content, but you also have to evaluate each one on criteria such as redundancy, timeliness, and usefulness. When you are done, you should have a picture of what's there, what will be there, and what's actually valuable.

2. Gather terms from as many sources as possible.

It's time to go fishing for metadata. You can start with the content itself if the content contains words, picking out terms that are unique to the subject. You can also turn to existing thesauri. There are a lot of them already out in the world. You may not always be able to use them "as is" because each thesaurus is designed for a specific use, but they may help you better understand the domain you are trying to describe and help you find relevant terms.

Some thesauri that you can borrow from!

Getty Art and Architecture Thesaurus (http://www.getty.edu/research/tools/vocabulary/aat/index.html)— Searchable database and research tool of concepts related to art, architecture, and material culture. Includes styles and periods, agents, built works, materials and techniques, and more.

The Astronomy Thesaurus (http://www.mso.anu.edu.au/research/library/thesaurus/)—Astronomy terms in English, French, German, Spanish, and Italian; all terms cross-referenced.

Legislative Indexing Vocabulary (LIV) (http://www.loc.gov/lexico/servlet/lexico?usr=pub&op=sessioncheck&db=LIV)—Developed for use with legislative and public policy subject matter.

Thesaurus for Graphic Materials I: Subject Terms (TGM I) (http://www.loc.gov/rr/print/tgm1/)—Consisting of terms and cross references for indexing visual materials.

Maths Thesaurus (http://thesaurus.maths.org/)—Definitions of common mathematical terms, along with broader, narrower, and related concepts.

NASA Thesaurus (http://www.sti.nasa.gov/thesfrm1.htm)—National Aeronautics and Space Administration Thesaurus. Extensive coverage of scientific terms.

National Monuments Record Thesauri (http://thesaurus.english-heritage.org.uk/)—Cultural heritage data by English Heritage. Hierarchical and alphabetical listings of a variety of thesauri.

You can interview subject matter experts, and you can hold card sorts to find out how the searchers think of the terminology. You want to find key concepts and group the terms around them—a solo card sort is an effective way to do this. These key concepts, or "entry terms," should include synonyms and abbreviations, acronyms, and alternate spellings for all the important concepts gathered from your content inventory. **Table 4.6** shows an example.

Preferred Term	Synonyms	Abbreviations	Acronyms	Alternative Spellings
Rock music	Rock and Roll	Rock	R&R	Rawk

TABLE 4.6 Entry Terms Example

3. Define preferred terms.

The *preferred terms* are a tool to internally control vocabulary and keep everyone on the same page, as well as a way to inform your labeling process. In **Table 4.4**, any of the terms could be acceptable preferred terms. When choosing one, you want to consider the audience first. If the MP3 site specialized in 1950s music, it might be a good thing to use the full term "Rock and Roll." If it's Jake's Rawking Out Site, "Rawk" might be just the ticket. The difference between "Rock music" and "Rock" is negligible. If you find yourself choosing between these, it's safest to choose the least ambiguous term, or perhaps the one that fits best in your navigation bar.

As you make these decisions, be sure to note the rules that develop from your choices. A classification system is a living thing; as new content comes in, you will want to keep it organized consistently with the rest.

4. Link synonyms and near synonyms.

Comb through your terms. Link all the relationships that you haven't connected already. Dig for common misspellings. (Search reports are great for this.) Make tough calls. (Are World Music and Global Beats really two different concepts?) Bring your preferred terms down to the core collection of unique concepts.

5. Group preferred terms by subject.

Card sort! You're beginning to see that IAs shuffle cards more often than a Las Vegas dealer does. It's time to pull out those preferred terms and organize them into like groups. Rock, Hip-Hop, Rap, and Techno are kind of alike. Jazz, Bebop, and Fusion belong together—somehow.

This is also a good place to bring in potential end users of the site for a card sort, to see how they think of the genre. Or, if you feel confident that you understand the user's mental model from an earlier card sort, you can continue and test later with a more finished hierarchy. Testing is always a matter of timing, time, and money. It has to happen; the question is where in the process it will help you the most.

Nonetheless, get those terms into related piles.

6. Identify broader and narrower terms.

You now need to determine where each term fits in the hierarchy. Look at your piles. Perhaps you decide Hip-Hop, Rap, and Techno are all subsets of Rock. Maybe Hip-Hop is a subset of Rap. Looking at Hip-Hop and Techno, maybe you decide these are aspects of Club Music. You can start to form a hierarchy. You may even discover you have multiple potential hierarchies. This is where it can get scary, and it's important to take a step back and look at your scope. Your users may benefit from having a faceted classification scheme in which they can browse through many types of hierarchies, such as Rock, Dance Music, Upbeat Music, Music by Artist, and so on. But the business may not be able to afford to spend that kind of time, or the infrastructure (the technology your site is running on) may not be able to handle this wide variety of information. If the site is Virgin Records World Wide, maybe facets are just the ticket. If the site is Jake's Rawking Out Site, it may not be an option. Of course, there are many levels in between.

Artists are notoriously hard to classify because they move from genre to genre as their artistic whims hit. Country artist last week, rock star this week! You can see how iTunes deals with this in **Figure 4.14**. It presents a range of types of rock and puts the artist anywhere that might fit. So The Allman Brothers appear in both Southern Rock and Best of the '70s, as well as rating their own special callout in Legends. Balance the user's mental model of the content with the nature of the content you have, factor in how much time you have to make your thesaurus, and try to choose the best compromise. You may end up with a genre-based site but still link artist names so that The Allman Brothers' fans can find all their music. Then you might decide to skip mood and event-based organization. Or you may do it all.

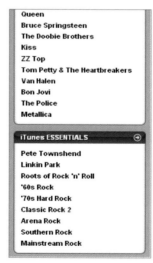

FIGURE 4.14 iTunes' rock subgenres.

7. Perform associative linking.

Now is the time for the frosting on the cake. Or rather, the candy bar at the checkout line. With each preferred term, ask yourself, "Where might the user want to go next?"

But be restrained—choose only the most obvious and important relationships:

- Cheese leads to crackers.

- A Beck CD leads to concert tickets.

- A hammer leads to nails.

- A driver download leads to support documentation.

Use your understanding of the content's relationships, the business drivers, and the user's desires and task behavior. Carefully design a place for the user to go next.

8. Document your choices and the rationale behind them.

This is the most boring step, and it's also the one everyone skips. Don't. Carefully, and with an eye to your successors (or your own forgetful self), write down what you've done in a way anyone can use.

As you are designing a controlled vocabulary, it is best to move slowly and thoughtfully (as with so many things) and create a draft you can improve and build on, rather than trying to get it right straight out of the gate (and usually at top speed). Do your best with an eye to the next version. A controlled vocabulary (just like a Web site—and unlike a book) is an ever-changing thing.

Now you have the solid beginnings of a thesaurus. Remember, though, that the thesaurus is the Taj Mahal of controlled vocabularies, and sometimes all you need is a bus shelter. You don't necessarily have to go through all the steps previously described. You may have a simple Web site that needs only synonyms defined or perhaps a simple taxonomy. As your Web site grows, so will your controlled vocabulary, and the day may come when you find a full-blown thesaurus is just the ticket.

Social classification

Information architecture is much concerned with classification (as you may have noticed), and when social classification came along, there was quite an uproar. Many IAs even thought they might lose their jobs to this new messy but scalable approach. But it turns out that you don't get a useful classification scheme from your users without some preparation, any more than you get a cathedral if you point a bunch of villagers at a pile of stones and say, "Go for it." You need a way to encourage useful participation, and then rules for how to take that participation and create a findability system.

Tagging

Tags are keywords made public. For a long time, librarians, scientists, engineers, and other individuals interested in order and retrieval have not only placed things in categories, but also attached keywords to them so they could be found via searches. Delicious was the first site to allow people to add keywords to an object, whether they were official owners of that object or not. They were called *tags* rather than keywords because, like New York taggers, you were making your mark on someone else's property. The other new thing Delicious did that no one else had was choosing to bookmark sites publicly.

Why was something as simple as defaulting to sharing bookmarks publicly useful? Delicious aggregated the most popular Web sites and tags across all their users, making their front page into a guide to the newest cool stuff on a variety of topics. If you didn't care about the topics populating the front page that day, you could use tags to narrow in on your personal interests.

If you care about health and productivity, for example, you can see that 280 people thought this lifehacker site was useful. If you are more interested in analytics, Delicious can recommend cli.gs article on short urls.

Tagging turned out to have another valuable function. In a world where user-generated content was increasingly more popular, tagging was the only way to create a scalable classification system. YouTube, Flickr, Slideshare, and other sites made up entirely from content provided by the users have no choice but to rely on classifications provided by the users.

Finally, tagging turned out to be useful in another way to end-users: personal organization. The tag "toread" emerged as a popular choice on Delicious. Flickr has over 4,000 photos tagged with "toprint." Tagging not only improves retrieval, but it also stands in for missing "save" functionality. Its flexible nature can teach a site what users really want to do.

The combination of a scalable flexible classification system with tagging's ability to aggregate, save, and even recommend new items made it a choice for Web 2.0 Web sites everywhere, and even some Web pioneers looking to stay relevant. Blended with traditional classification approaches, it can be even more useful.

For example, Etsy, a site where people sell their personal craft efforts, uses tags as well as categories to make it easy to find fun gifts. A close look shows it's not as free form as you might think. While the descriptive metadata falls into the messy "tagging" bucket, the site designers decided to add another bucket for intrinsic metadata and called it "materials." It's still tagging, in that the users of the site add the keywords, not the administrators of the site. But the choice of what goes in that bucket is shaped by the name of the bucket. In **Figure 4.15,** you can see the stars were made with paper, origami, and love.

FIGURE 4.15 The tags on the origami pastel stars also suggest ways to use them.

Buzzillions does the same in their Review Snapshot (**Figure 4.16**) by creating categories for the tags, including pros, cons, and best uses. These shape the feedback requested of users and help users think of a longer, richer set of tags.

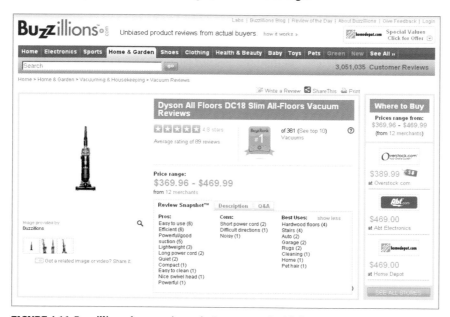

FIGURE 4.16 Buzzillions shows reviews of a Dyson tagged with "easy to use" and "nice swivel head."

You can use these tags to narrow choices when searching. Because tags are most effective when they are standardized (fewer synonyms, fewer spelling errors), Buzzillions *encourages* standardization by suggesting previously used tags (**Figure 4.17**). They don't enforce. They don't hire IAs to come in later and create a vocabulary. They simply hope with a little nudge in a good direction, and by virtue of human laziness, we'll click rather than type, and the resulting taxonomy will be more useful than free-form tagging.

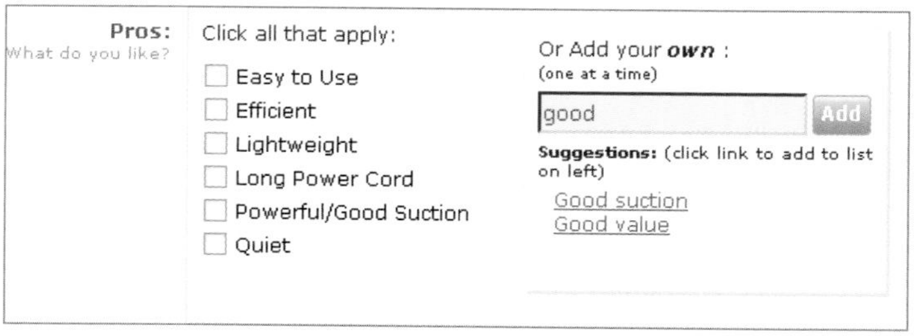

FIGURE 4.17 Buzzillions gives you easy click boxes next to previously used tags, making it easy to add your input.

Types of tags

Like metadata, there are many different types of tags. If you can teach your system to recognize them, you can start to develop semi-structured classification systems that make retrieval easier.

Figure 4.18 shows the surprising things users may use to tag items in your database. Some are more useful to your business than others, but all are useful to the community growing and starting to express itself.

Tag Type	Example
Descriptive	Massachusetts, city, Cambridge, architecture, U, building, night, ma, skyline, sky
Resource	Book, video, podcast, photo, illustration
Ownership/source	NYTimes, austingovella (author), boxesandarrows,
Opinion	Lame, tooshort, dontwasteyourhardearnedmoney
Self-reference	Me, mine, sawlive, ownit
Task organizing	Todo, toread, toprint
Play and performance	Squaredcircle, akavogonpoetry, defectivebydesign

FIGURE 4.18 Gene Smith's Tag Type table from his excellent book, *Tagging*, with some new examples from your fearless authors.

It's tempting to try to control tagging, but with community features (see Chapter 9, Architecting Social Spaces), it's typically better to encourage desired behavior rather than to try to throttle undesirable behavior. AkaVogonPoetry is a reference to *The Hitchhiker's Guide to the Galaxy* in which Vogon Poetry is so bad that it induces physical agony, spasms, and nausea.[8] This is a far better label to attach to unloved works of art than the seven words you can't say on television, and thus Amazon lets it lie, along with Defectivebydesign, the tag of choice for all who hate DRM (digital right management). However, when you show a few tags to suggest for an object, you may want to suggest more of them from the descriptive category and fewer from the opinion one.

---

8 "Vogon poetry is, of course, the third worst in the Universe.

The second worst is that of the Azagoths of Kria. During a recitation by their Poet Master Grunthos the Flatulent of his poem "Ode To A Small Lump of Green Putty I Found In My Armpit One Midsummer Morning" four of his audience died of internal haemorrhaging, and the President of the Mid-Galactic Arts Nobbling Council survived by gnawing one of his own legs off. Grunthos is reported to have been "disappointed" by the poem's reception, and was about to embark on a reading of his twelve-book epic entitled My Favourite Bathtime Gurgles when his own major intestine, in a desperate attempt to save life and civilization, leapt straight up through his neck and throttled his brain.

The very worst poetry of all perished along with its creator Paula Nancy Millstone Jennings of Greenbridge, Essex, England in the destruction of the planet Earth." Douglas Adams, *Hitchhiker's Guide to the Galaxy*. Important reading for IAs everywhere.

Challenges in tagging systems

"Woohoo!" you say. Let's use tagging for everything! Well, not so fast, cowboy. As we saw in Vogon Poetry, those crazy users may not always be on your side. Let's discuss some of the challenges found in tagging.

The cold-start problem

When Amazon first introduced tagging on its site, almost nobody used it. The few who did took the label "tags" literally and added their name to products, tagging in the style of the New York taggers we mentioned earlier. Tagging is far from widely accepted, and not everyone knows what to do when they have an empty form field with the word "tags" on it. Moreover, when you don't have any tags in your system as examples, people may have trouble thinking up what to say about a given object.

Here are some solutions:

- Try using a label that is more meaningful to people, like "materials," "topics," "keywords," or whatever is appropriate to the content of your site.

- Include a short instruction about how to tag objects next to the tagging field (see **Figure 4.19**).

- Create initial tags by identifying unusual words in descriptions. Your engineer should be able to identify unusual terms via a program and show them as tags. This will give people an idea of what tagging is and what it's good for.

- Get workers in your company to tag items as well, to create initial examples and activity. And if you can't explain to them how to do it, you'll have a hard time explaining it to your users.

The obvious tag problem

While suggestion tools may help with the "blank sheet of paper" problem, they also can create an unfortunate feedback loop in which the same tags are used over and over again. A variety of tags are useful for making items more findable. So how do you get people to put in more tags?

- Make it easy to add a lot of tags. That's a key reason many tagging systems use a single form field with comma-separated tags—you can just brain dump.

- Suggest a large number of tags, including less popular ones.

- Review popular tags and blacklist excessively generic ones from the suggestion tool.

Tags Customers Associate with This Product (What's this?)
Click on a tag to find related items, discussions, and people.

Check the boxes next to the tags you consider relevant or enter your own tags in the field below.

☐ harry potter (1354)   ☐ magic (537)   ☐ fantasy series (212)
☐ harry potter books (820)   ☐ wizard (404)   ☐ harry potter and the deathly
☐ jk rowling (750)   ☐ book (271)   hallows (171)
☐ fantasy (667)   ☐ deathly hallows (236)   ☐ fiction (166)

                                                          › **See all 703 tags...**

Your tags: | fant | (Add)
(Press the

fantasy	72300 usages
fantasy series	5184 usages
fantasy adventure	3241 usages
fantasy rpg	2755 usages
final fantasy	2692 usages
fantasy romance	2595 usages
fantastic	1158 usages
fantasy fiction	798 usages
fantasy art	750 usages
fantasy book	744 usages
fantasy movie	662 usages
fantastic four	586 usages
favorite fantasy	293 usages
fantagraphics	284 usages
final fantasy vii	254 usages
fantasy novel	225 usages
fantasy favorites	217 usages
fantasy movies	160 usages
fantasy erotica	155 usages
fantastic adventure	130 usages

FIGURE 4.19 Amazon offers a view of tags you might want to use.

The duplicate tag problem

Take a look at **Figure 4.20**. Among Flickr's most popular tags of all time we see photo, photos, and photography. If these were aggregated together, this tag would probably be one of the most popular in the system. Right now, if you search for "photo," you won't get items tagged with photos or photography. It's possible these items are sufficiently different to deserve unique tags but unlikely. In your system, you may well want people looking for "boots" to find hiking boots, no matter what the tag. You can take on the hassle of designing a synonym ring (seen in Chapter 5, Search and Ye Shall Find), or you can encourage uses to create their own.

- Suggest related terms.
- Allow users to suggest related terms.
- Create tools to let users connect tags easily with each other.

All time most popular tags

africa amsterdam animals architecture art august australia baby band barcelona beach berlin bird birthday black blackandwhite blue boston bw california cameraphone camping canada canon car cat chicago china christmas church city clouds color concert cute dance day de dog england europe family festival film florida flower flowers food football france friends fun garden geotagged germany girl girls graffiti green halloween hawaii hiking holiday home house india ireland island italia italy japan july june kids la lake landscape light live london macro may me mexico mountain mountains museum music nature new newyork newyorkcity night nikon nyc ocean paris park party people photo photography photos portrait red river rock rome san sanfrancisco scotland sea seattle show sky snow spain spring street summer sun sunset taiwan texas thailand tokyo toronto tour travel tree trees trip uk urban usa vacation vancouver washington water wedding white winter yellow york zoo

FIGURE 4.20 Flickr's most popular tags.

The gamed tag problem

In Cory Doctorow's hilarious essay, "Metacrap,"[9] he points out that,

> "Metadata exists in a competitive world. Suppliers compete to sell their goods, cranks compete to convey their crackpot theories (mea culpa), artists compete for audience. Attention spans and wallets may not be zero-sum, but they're damned close.
>
> That's why:

- A search for any commonly referenced term at a search engine like Altavista will often turn up at least one porn link in the first 10 results.

- Your mailbox is full of spam with subject lines like, "Re: The information you requested."

- Publisher's Clearing House sends out advertisements that holler, "You may already be a winner!"

- Press-releases have gargantuan lists of empty buzzwords attached to them."

---

9 Hilarious if you are an IA, certainly. Required reading if you are considering tagging.
   http://www.well.com/~doctorow/metacrap.htm

We'll leave a discussion of whether or not people who fill your life with metacrap are going to hell to another forum. But people are going to do what *they* want in your system, and not always what *you* want.

Solutions to this one are tricky. You can limit the number of tags any one person can attach to an item, but this reduces the overall effectiveness of the system. You can open up tagging to anyone beyond just the provider of the content in hopes that the aggregate of all tags will be better than the "expert" view, but this opens you up to inappropriate tags. You can monitor, but this offsets some of the value you have gotten by outsourcing your classification to your audience with increased support costs. You can ask your audience to monitor, wiki-style, but this can be difficult when the providers are competing, such as in an ecommerce situation. What if rival manufacturers of shoes removed the "shoe" tag from each other's products?

To address all of these problems, you have to look at your audience, your community, your content, and your staffing. Context is king, and the solution you pick must reflect the outcome you are trying to bring about.

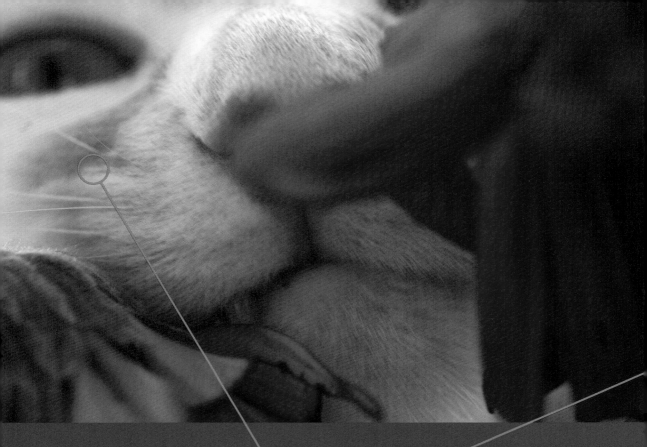

"What is this thing called search?
This funny thing called search?
Just who can solve its mystery?
Why should it make a fool of me?"[1]

5

Search and
Ye Shall Find

*In which we study the
dark arts of search
engines, algorithms,
and query suggestions.*

(I) think we all know what search is. It's the magic box. You put in a word or two, search reads your mind and tells you what you were wondering about. Like the iPod shuffle, which seems to instinctively know what song you want to hear next, it understands you better than your mother and father, and it's hard to believe it's made by humans.[2]

Search was born around the same time computers were; it's utterly intrinsic to the digital experience. It has two core values by which it is judged: recall and precision. Recall is how good it is at finding absolutely everything you were searching for, and precision is how good it is at organizing these results by how relevant they are to your query.

For example, imagine you are in the local Borders store, trying to find more books your child's favorite author, but you can't recall the author's name, just the main word in the title of her favorite book. So you type in "fuchsia." (Or perhaps you typed in "fucia." We'll get into spelling errors later.) This bookstore does have thousands of items "fuchsia" related (once you realized fuchsia was spelled with an hs); however, their search engine is only searching this particular store's inventory, so you don't find what you are looking for. This would be a problem of recall, if the book were in another branch of the store or in the warehouse. If the first thing they showed you was a fuchsia-colored notebook, then a gardening book, then some-where on the fourth page of results the book *The Fuchsia is Now,* then that would be a problem of precision. The two are interrelated; take a look at **Figure 5.1**. As Amazon's recall ability produces larger

---

1 Paraphrased from, "What is this thing called love?" Apologies to Cole Porter, who wrote it.

2 Arthur C Clark said, "Any sufficiently advanced technology is indistinguishable from magic," and we think search now qualifies. But not the iPod shuffle, which can be explained mostly by humans finding patterns in things even when there aren't any. It really is random, or at least was at this writing.

result sets as they move into selling more and more different things, it gets harder and harder to know what you mean by "Fuchsia." The author? The flower? The cute little pink booties? Within a narrow context, like children's books, it's relatively straightforward to be precise. Or, if you had typed in *The Fuchsia is Now* in the first place, precision would be a breeze. Sadly for search designers everywhere, my query, misspelled and all, was the norm, not the exception.

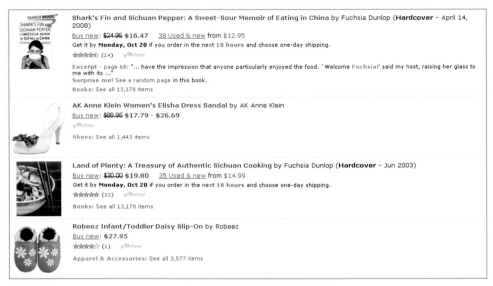

FIGURE 5.1 Amazon offers authors, high heels, and booties in exchange for the word "Fuchsia."

The Meat and Potatoes of Search

It doesn't hurt to have a basic idea of what a search engine is doing when it matches your query to the documents in its index. We'll try to make it very basic indeed. Let's pretend that you are either foolhardy or very well-funded, and you've decided you will build your own search engine rather than sensibly buying a license or using an open source one like Lucene. We'll pretend this over-funded start-up is a recipe site (because the Web needs more of those!).

Okay, first, we need a table of contents. Since this is a new site, we only have two recipes.

```
<docs>
<doc id="0" href=http://example.com/corn />
<doc id="1" href=http://example.com/parmchips />
</docs>
```

For every unique document (usually signified by a URL), the search engine makes a posting that records what word was found in each document.

```
<postings>
<posting doc="0" word="Cook" />
<posting doc="0" word="corn" />
<posting doc="0" word="in" />
<posting doc="0" word="the" />
<posting doc="0" word="husk" />
</postings>
```

And in your second document, it looks like this:

```
<postings>
<posting doc="1" word="Cook" />
<posting doc="1" word="grated" />
<posting doc="1" word="Parmesan" />
<posting doc="1" word="until" />
<posting doc="1" word="crispy" />
</postings>
```

Next, you make a word list of all the words found in your documents.[3]

```
<words>
<word w="Cook" />
<word w="Parmesan" />
<word w="corn" />
<word w="crispy" />
<word w="grated" />
<word w="husk" />
<word w="in" />
<posting w="the" />
<word w="until" />
</words>
```

Then you make an index that lists which words were found in which documents.

```
<index>
<word w="Cook">        <posting doc="0"/> <posting doc="1"/> </word>
<word w=" Parmesan ">  <posting doc="1"/> </word>
<word w="corn ">       <posting doc="0"/> </word>
<word w="crispy ">     <posting doc="1"/> </word>
<word w="grated ">     <posting doc="1"/> </word>
<word w="husk ">       <posting doc="0"/> </word>
<word w="in ">         <posting doc="0"/> </word>
<posting w="the" />    <posting doc="0"/> </word>
<word w=" until ">     <posting doc="1"/> </word>
</index>
```

---

3 The word list is in strict alphabetical order, capitalized words before lowercase. In your search engine, you *do* have to organize your word list so the computer can look up entries quickly. Your engineers should have a good idea of how to do it, but this is favored by those using binary search.

If you want phrases, you can add in the word order (referred to below as wnum for word number) to your postings. For example, if you want your users to find "sheep milk cheese," your search engine could look for places where those words not only all appear in the document, but also appear in that order.

```
<index>
  ...
<word w="sheep">
<posting doc="1" wnum="3" />
</word>
  ...
<word w="milk">
<posting doc="1" wnum="4"/>
</word>
  ...
<word w="cheese">
<posting doc="1" wnum="5"/>
</word>
  ...

</index>
```

In order to make up for the loss in performance[4] you take when you add word order, you might decide to ignore "stop words,"[5] such as "the," "and," "a," and "to." The 26 most common words account for one-third of words used in language. Each word you put in your index requires you to create, store, and search a posting. In a system that has billions of postings, ignoring these words can lead to a massive saving in speed. Of course, this comes at a cost. Consider the phrase "to be or not to be" composed entirely of stop words, or the band "the the." They couldn't be found at all!

Now if you want to improve your recall, you should consider how you can introduce a controlled vocabulary, as explained in Chapter 3, Sock Drawers and CD Racks, in order to find all the pages about a given concept. This is extra-helpful when you have only a few thousand pages in a specific context. For example, on a recipe site, it's good to know that salmorejo and gazpacho are essentially the same thing, just as on a business site it's good to know that IBM and International Business Machines are the same, in order to make sure when people do a search, they always find *something*.

Finally, you get to work on *precision*. You start layering relevance judgments over the index, creating an algorithm. You could decide that a multiword query was a better match for a document that had the words in the query in the same order as the query, for example. You might say a document had more relevance if the query term were

---

4 This means it gets real slow.

5 Hans Peter Luhn, one of the pioneers in information retrieval, is credited with coining the phrase, but neither Wikipedia nor we know why he chose the phrase "stop words." Stop searching for them? Stop in the name of love?

found in the title of the document rather than in the body of the document, or if it were in the URL, or if it had certain tags around it like <h1>.[6] If a word is in the top-level heading, it's a good bet the page is about that word.

You could say that a document that many people linked to was a better choice than one that only a few people linked to. You could choose to give prominence to a page that, when people linked to it, they did so by linking a phrase that included the query term. And so on, so pretty soon you have your own version of Google Pagerank. You could also value internal metadata over this external metadata. For example, if the editors said one recipe was, "salmorejo, a Spanish soup," and an outside blogger linked to a different recipe with the phrase, "gazpacho, a Spanish soup," which recipe is a more relevant result when someone searches for "Spanish soup?" There can only be one first result, and that one will get the lion's share of the clicks and determine what your users think of your competence.

Often, search design is considered sufficiently complex that it is left to search engineers, as everyone else runs away screaming. But as you can see, search is made up of critical decisions that require both business and end-user insight to shape it. Adding the ability to detect phrases, for example, is hugely useful. Without it, a search for "new york" would turn up documents for new shoes and York, England. Yet because it adds so much data to the index and slows computations down, many crude search engines have been built without it. Search relevancy design is a delicate balance between the three crucial goals for search: fast, easy, and magic. Getting rid of phrase detection is trading easy for fast. Even if you opt for a pre-made open source engine like Solr in which decisions like phrase detection are already built in, many other subtle decisions about relevance must be made upon installation, and if you don't make those calls, then someone will (or worse, won't). Quality search is dependant on your willingness to face complicated decisions. Don't run away!

Moreover, search is not a one-time setup. Maintaining good relevance is highly dependent on your continued, ongoing investment in tuning the engine and the algorithms. In the beginning, you can use subject matter experts (SME) to rank your results in terms of relevance. For example, you could find a person who knows a lot about food and then have her tell you which result set from several different algorythms produced better results.

After your search is launched, you can consider compiling the usage as feedback to tune relevance. For example, if users who search for "gazpacho" constantly click on the third result, is it worth moving it up a rank or two?[7]

---

6 Html for "heading one," a semantically-charged tag.

7 We are wildly oversimplifying here, as we are for the entire chapter. Machine Learning Ranking is big magic requiring programmers of the highest order. Ain't it cool, though? More on the downside: http://anand.typepad.com/datawocky/2008/05/are-human-experts-less-prone-to-catastrophic-errors-than-machine-learned-models.html.

Search Should Be Fast, Easy, and Magic

Now that we can build a search, let's discuss how to build a good (or even great) one! Beyond the inner workings for search, there is a lot to be done in what is known as the "presentation layer" after recall and precision have hopefully been sorted out. The end goal is to be three things: fast, easy, and magic (that word again!). We'll take you through each one of these concepts as they apply to search.

Search Must Be Fast

This seems like an obvious statement, but let's take the time to ask ourselves what *fast* really means, when talking about search.

- People take only a second to search.

- People want to take only a second to search.

1. Results must be retrieved quickly.

We've all seen that little bit of text, "Results 1–10 of about 62,700,000. (0.09 seconds)." The major search engines make sure they have enough computing power to work through their index and get results swiftly. They are also smart enough to brag about it—.09 seconds seems somehow even faster when you see they found 62,700,00 results!

Of course, if you wrote .09 seconds, and it was actually 4 seconds, you'd lose credibility. In search, like many areas of life, you have to walk the talk. While you don't have to load a results set in under a second on an intranet, people are so used to fast search engines that if it doesn't load in one-Mississippi, two-Mississippi, three, your users may think it's broken and complain or worse, give up. You don't have to brag about how fast you are by posting computations, but you do have to be fast. On a consumer Web site, this is truer than on an intranet, and on Web search, it's law.

2. Results must load quickly.

You may have retrieved those results in .09 seconds, but if your presentation layer has images, tables, graphic ads, and other mischief, it certainly won't seem like .09 seconds to your visitors, no matter how accurate that number may be on the back end. Many search engines used to present results in a big table, so when you ran a query, you'd be faced with a big white page for several seconds until it loaded. Very few make this mistake anymore (as we're sure you won't).

Fast and ugly is better than slow and pretty.[8]

8　To get to fast and pretty, check out "High Performance Web Sites: Essential Knowledge for Front-End Engineers" by Steve Souders: http://oreilly.com/catalog/9780596529307/.

3. Results must be scannable.

If fast and ugly is better, do we need design? Absolutely. An aspect of how fast the search feels is how quickly you can make sense of the results. If you have to struggle to figure out what's useful and what's not, then the search is slow. Fast is not achieved via code alone.

These three images (see **Figure 5.2**) are from eye tracking studies done on the three major search engines in 2006 by Enquiro.[9] As you can see, they all follow the "Golden Triangle" pattern typical of search results. However, Google's is the smallest and tightest—this is because users were able to quickly select a result worth clicking without having to scan more of the page. The Google triangle is the most desirable shape for a search results page.

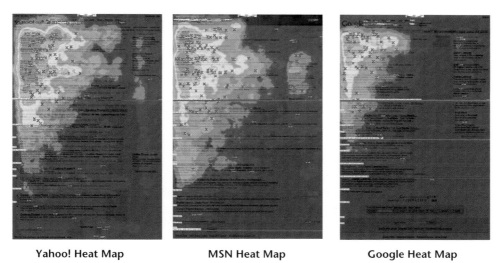

| Yahoo! Heat Map | MSN Heat Map | Google Heat Map |

FIGURE 5.2 Scan time is as important as load time.

Moreover, in the Enquiro report in **Figure 5.3**, Google was the winner in user satisfaction, *measured by speed at finding something the user felt confident clicking.* The speed with which a user can acquire a link to click on is certainly partially dependent on relevance, since the better the first result is, the more likely it will get clicked on. But for users to judge what the best link is, the link has to *look* relevant also.

---

9 To check out all their research, or to dig in deeper into the search studies (350 pages of it!), check out their white papers at http://www.enquiroresearch.com/.

Engine	Success Rates	% of times a listing was clicked after query	Number of results scanned	Average Seconds before click
Google	58.3%	84%	4	8.55
MSN	43.4%	77.8%	5.02	9.53
Yahoo	46.3%	70.9%	5.26	12.18

FIGURE 5.3 This chart reflects the ease with which Google users were able to select an appropriate link, validating the pattern in Figure 5.2.

In **Figure 5.4,** Enquiro has highlighted the areas that get "fixations," for example, people looking at the page for more than a moment. As you can see, searchers scan for the words in the search query. This concept is called *Information Scent*, and it was first coined by the Palo Alto Research Center in the mid-nineties. It means some links just smell like they hold the right information, while some links just stink. If you are researching a digital camera purchase, does the HP store smell like it will get you to browse cameras? Or does it smell like printers and having to dig around to find cameras, which would certainly stink. In less than a second—faster than the user can even comprehend—that link has to be seen with peripheral vision and discarded.

FIGURE 5.4 Where do people look? Anywhere their query is mentioned.

You can speed the scan by using traditional blue links (which "smell" like they can be clicked), by bolding the query term, and by making sure that the query term is always in the result body. This is one reason that snippets can out-perform descriptions (see **Figure 5.5**). A snippet is a quote from the page of the site the result is linking to. A description is written about the page, often derived from either a directory like Dmoz or the metadata in the page. Since the snippet is often taken from the part of the page in which the word is located, it has a strong "scent."

Vanity Fair with Reese Witherspoon, Jonathan Rhys-Meyers & Gabriel Byrne
Official site of the film based on the classic novel by William Makepeace Thackeray, starring Reese Witherspoon.
www.**vanityfairmovie.com** - Cached

Vanity Fair (magazine) - Wikipedia, the free encyclopedia
Vanity Fair is an American magazine of culture, fashion, and politics published ... Starting in 1925
Vanity Fair competed with The New Yorker as the American ...
en.wikipedia.org/wiki/**Vanity_Fair**_(magazine) - Cached

FIGURE 5.5 When you use the part of the page with the search term in it, the user will consider that result more relevant. A description might make more sense, but it is less scannable.

Search Must Be EASY for People to Use

Despite the simple appearance of the single entry box, searching can be really hard for most people. That's because it's difficult to know how to ask for what you want to find. Ever have writer's block? That's what people go through when they see a search box. Unlike browsing where you have a list of words to choose from, you have to think of your own navigation terms when you see a search box.

Is it any wonder that an ordinary guy trying to find the lyrics to "that one song that was used on that sitcom in the seventies" can't figure out what to type in the box?

Articulation problems

These statistics come from a wonderful study by Amanda Spink on the search logs of Excite.[10] Remarkably, private research shows very little change from this behavior since 2001.

- An average search on a commercial Web site is 2.3 words. In 2008, Google announced for the first time their average query length had gone up to four words from the long time average of three. Even if that's the trend going forward, it's still not very big.

- A third of searches are one-word searches.

- Another third are two-word searches—but often single concepts, such as "New York."

So you get queries like "New York pitcher," "San Francisco restaurant," and "1970's sitcom theme song." This puts the search engine in the position of mind reader. Unless, of course, a little more information can be had.

---

10 The most digestible of her findings is "From e-sex to e-commerce: Web search changes." *IEEE Computer*, 35(3), 133-135.

There are three simple steps to making search "easy":

1. Help overcome "query block" with articulation tools such as query suggesters.

2. Use disambiguation tools, such as vertical search and best bets.

3 And finally layer in the magic by giving answers, not just links to pages that might have answers on them.

Query helpers are tools to help get "one more word" out of your users and get the context you need to give a good result. It's all about disambiguation.

- Query suggester
- Vertical search
- Best bets

Query Suggester

Call it type-ahead, call it Google suggest, call it autofill, just don't call it Shirley. Large search engines do a lot of magical things with their data. We can learn from these wizards. If your Web site gets a lot of traffic and repeated queries, query suggestions may also be feasible for you. Basically, as the user types, the search engine begins searching for similar queries (**Figure 5.6**) and populates the query box with them as if it were a drop-down menu, typically ordering them by popularity and similarity, in some secret mix.

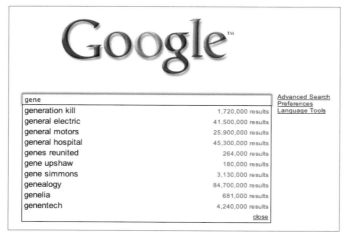

FIGURE 5.6 Google suggest finishes your sentence for you.

A more low-tech approach is just showing the most popular searches right next to the query box. People may choose to click rather than type.

Quintura (**Figure 5.7**) is a search engine whose claim to eventual fame is the query suggestion tool that hangs out on the side of the page, ever ready to help you find that perfect "one more word" to improve your results. There are dozens more experimental search engines working on this problem with the hope that if they solve it, they'll be the next Google! Check out Clusty, Grokker, Mahalo, and Powerset (assuming they are still around by the time this book hits the printer).

FIGURE 5.7 Quintura makes more popular search choices larger, offers images so the user can scan for familiar brands.

The reigning query helper champion is Yahoo! Search Assist[11] (**Figure 5.8**). What makes it so powerful is that it not only finishes your queries for you, but it also gives you ideas for related concepts to explore. It's also very elegantly implemented. Danny Sullivan,[12] search analyst, noted:

> "Search Assist is selective. Ever had one of those moments when you start to type in a query, enter a word, and then pause because you're not quite sure what other words to add to it? Search Assist senses this. It notes that you've paused, takes that as a sign you need help, and magically makes suggestions appear below the search box. Cool!"

---

11 Disclosure: Christina worked on Yahoo! Search for a couple years around the turn of the century, but that was quite a bit before Search Assist came out. Even though Christina is easily impressed, Search Assist is still pretty nifty.

12 July 25, 2007 "Search Suggestions On Steroids: Yahoo Search Assist" by Danny Sullivan
http://searchengineland.com/070725-233903.php.

FIGURE 5.8 Yahoo! Search Assist is happy to correct your spelling, finish your sentences, and even come up with related topics. Such an overprotective mother!

Vertical Search

Vertical search is used by a search engine that explicitly only searches within a particular subset of the vast world of documents. People search, shopping search, music search, and image search are examples of vertical searches.

How does vertical search help make search easy? Vertical search provides one more word for the query by adding context. For example, as you can see in **Figure 5.9**, Chicago has a different meaning in Web search than in music search or in an airline booking search engine.

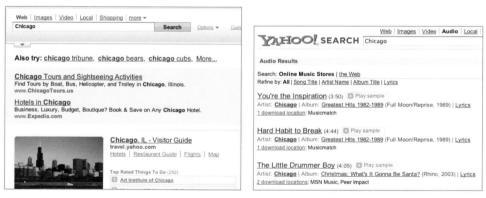

FIGURE 5.9 Two results for Chicago: one for a town, one for a way to rock the town.

Vertical search has a second set of useful disambiguation tools—topical filters, which can be seen by anyone who's been on a shopping or travel site. Because the results set is more or less understood, the site can offer relevant ways to further narrow down results, as you can see in **Figure 5.10**. Shopping often lets you filter by category, price, and other pertinent facets, depending on the item being researched, for example: megapixels for cameras or size for clothing. This sounds obvious, unless you think how hard it is for a Web search engine which might return for a "new york" query—a city, a state, a Wikipedia article, a tourism site, a magazine, and the stock exchange—none of which really share meaningful facets. Vertical search provides groupings of like items, which then can be sorted on like attributes.

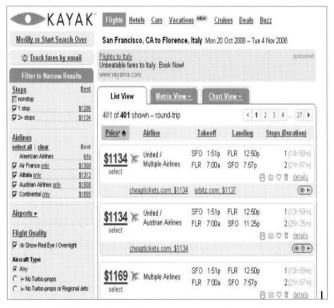

FIGURE 5.10 Because Kayak knows what properties air flights have, they can list useful filters, such as stops, airline, and even aircraft type.

Human Disambiguation

While Yahoo! and Google live by technology and they have the advantage of hundreds of engineers, that's not really what makes their search so good. They have millions of queries, meaning they have the data to create miracles. For example, do you know how their spelling correction works? It's not that they have the best dictionary ever. They monitor when a query with no resulting clickthrough on any results is closely followed by another query with click through on a result in that second query. Example: We type fuschia, but we don't see anything on the page, so we don't click anything and so we type fuchsia and then click on a result. As one data point, the search engine can't be certain the user is correcting their query term. But if thousands of users do it, they can see a pattern and bake that into the algorithm creating features from spellcheck to query suggest or even changing the relevancy of results.

While you might not have enough traffic to begin to make these miracles occur[13] (and honestly, how often does someone type Artie Shaw these days, much less arti chaw?—as shown in **Figure 5.11**) you too can make small miracles, using the brains of people in your organization.

FIGURE 5.11 Google seems to understand us at our least coherent, and corrects spelling errors both rare and unusual.

Best bets

Best bets are when human beings go in and muck with the search results, adding in new results by hand.

Here on HP, we see it in action (**Figure 5.12**).

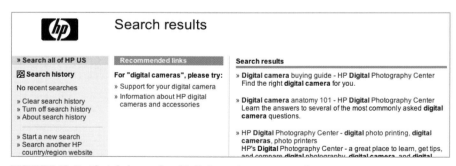

FIGURE 5.12 Best bets help people with their most common queries

---

13 While this was being written, Yahoo! released Yahoo! Search BOSS, so you can now make use of its powerful spelling technology. http://developer.yahoo.com/search/boss/boss_guide/Spelling_Suggest.html. Hopefully, Google will be close behind in sharing their powerful technology, too.

"Digital cameras," despite being a popular query, is not a very clear query. Is the searcher shopping, researching, or looking for help? The smart humans behind the HP search engine figured out that people searching on "digital cameras" were most likely in the market to buy one, or to get some support for one, and added the appropriate links.

Smarter still are the folks at REI, who use best bets not only as disambiguation, but also as promotion (**Figure 5.13**). You're looking for a GPS? We've got them on sale! This is perfectly cricket, as long as you respect the God of Relevance and never show extraneous stuff. That's the quickest path to invisibility. When people are searching, they only see things that match their understanding of their search query (check out those eyetracking results!). Irrelevant=Invisible.

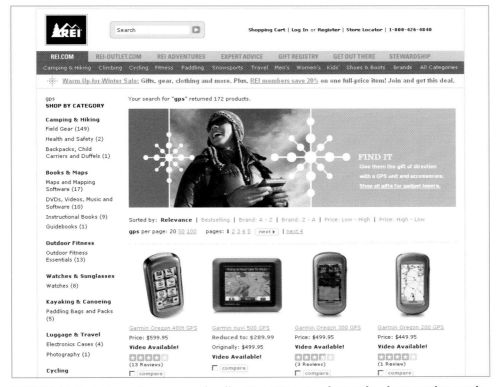

FIGURE 5.13 Best bets can also move merchandise. Here REI creates a banner that shows up when people search for "GPS" in order to promote gadget shopping for the holidays. The idea is good, but the execution is lacking. This best bet looks like a banner ad and is likely to be overlooked.

How do we come up with best bets?

Introducing: The Zipf curve

Thanks to Chris Anderson's popular book, *The Long Tail,* more people are familiar with Zipf curves,[14] and what they mean. Search always seems to be one of the most extreme of the Zipf curves— the head is very tall and the tail very long and low (see **Figure 5.14**). In his book, he's interested in that tail (thus the title), but for creating best bets, the head is the place to be.

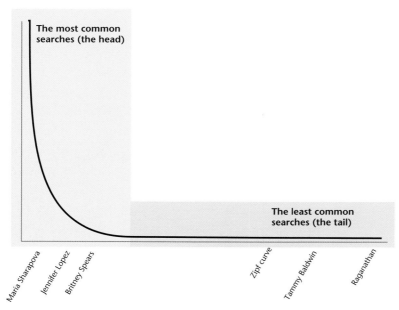

FIGURE 5.14 Imagining a Zipf curve made of queries of the general public. Sure everyone likes cute tennis players, but who cares about the inventor of faceted classification?

Analyze the head

1. Collect your most popular searches.

2. Sort them into query types.

3. Design best bets for them.

---

14 A synonym ring for this concept: Pareto principal, law of the vital few, power law, Zipf curve, 80-20 rule. All more or less discussing the same phenomenon.

For example, let's say you are a local PBS television station, and these were your most popular queries[15] (along with queries that are similar or variations):

- Car Talk

- Cooking shows

- Sesame Street

- Mystery

- News

- PBS Channel

In **Figure 5.15**, we see the current results for the presidential debate the day after the first 2008 presidential debate.

In **Figure 5.16** we see the same results, now with a "best bet" of exclusive PBS content. What's more compelling? More useful?

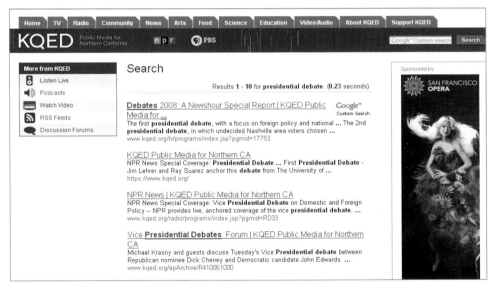

FIGURE 5.15 The typical KQED search results, provided by our friends at Google. They are okay.

---

15 You find these in your search logs. Learn more about Search Engine Analysis: http://www.rosenfeldmedia.com/books/searchanalytics/.

FIGURE 5.16 Search results with a little best bet goodness thrown in for improved visibility and navigation.

As you can see, the new KQED search results are a mix of semi-dynamic templated material and hard-coded. For information architects, designing the rules for what to display in a dynamic system is absolutely as important (if not more so) than designing the organization system.

Google and Yahoo! both handle best bets from within their portfolio of sites in their own way, but one thing to note: there are no borders or backgrounds separating them from "real" results (see **Figure 5.17**). Instead, Yahoo! formats the sports data into a chart while Google decorates the video result with a screenshot.

A line is a wall the eye can't cross. A background color is code word for "advertisement." Resist the urge to put different things in different boxes if you want your user base to actually notice them. There are other ways to designate that these are a different kind of result without "ghettoizing" them to the point where they aren't useful anymore.

FIGURE 5.17 Google and Yahoo! both have a vast amount of information that they own and understand, and thus can be presented in a useful and compelling manner.

The other thing to pay attention to is the fact that both Google and Yahoo! highlight the query term by bolding it in their best bet. Highlighting the query term is critical to having your visitors notice the best bet. Relevance is everything, and one way searchers determine relevance is if they see their query term in the result, especially in the title of the result. And that leads us to our last trick on the road to being magical.

Search Must Be MAGIC

Search, the doctor of the mystical; Search, the prognosticator; Search the MIND READER! For search to be great, it must all be true. Search must be magic. That means having all the answers, not just links to Web sites that might.

Search is a question whose answer is not always a Web site (or an article). When the best result is not a link, you have a chance to create a truly magical experience for your users and deliver beyond their wildest dreams.

Yahoo! and Google approach this concept slightly differently, but it's clear they are both working on providing real answers beyond links.

In **Figure 5.18**, we see Google's answer to the question, "What should I wear today?" and Yahoo!'s answer to the question, "Where can I get pizza?" each in the form of a query. While Google and Yahoo! aren't reading minds yet, they are working hard to make magic happen.

FIGURE 5.18 Google and Yahoo! providing answers, not just links.

In the Google example, they have wisely realized that you want to know what the weather is, not which Web site has the weather, so they provided an elegant shortcut. These shortcuts are hard to measure, because unlike links, no one clicks. The user behavior looks much like failure—a query is made, and no link is clicked.

In the Yahoo! example, they are getting "one more word" from somewhere other than the query box—they know where you are. If you have one of their many services such as Yahoo! Mail or Calendar, you registered with Yahoo! and shared your address. In **Figure 5.19**, Yahoo! gives you local showtimes. You can easily override those showtimes with an edit link, but they get you closer to what you want because they know you. How often do you ask your users to put in personal data, such as location?

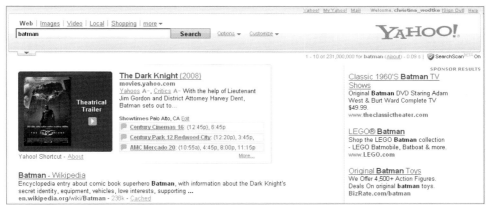

FIGURE 5.19 Yahoo! is able to give you showtimes in theaters within driving distance if you have registered your address with them. The user can be viewed as an anonymous data entry machine, or the user can be a provider of a rich set of metadata used to disambiguate. Oh, and make their searches... and their life... quite a bit nicer.

Personalized search

There are really only a few places that the search engine can look to help define intent without depending on further information from the user:

- They can look at your past history and learn more about you by what you have already done.

- They can look at the context of the task you're currently engaged in, hoping that it will give some clues as to what you're looking for (vertical search or previous queries).

- If they know something about you and your social, geographic, and demographic context, the engine can hope that there is a similarity of thinking within that context, at least when it comes to common interests and intent.

In some ways this approach shares a lot with the other black art, recommendations. Recommendations are built (to oversimplify) by determining which users are most alike, and recommending things you don't already have in common with those users. Let's say on Netflix you and Christina, never having met, agreed that *Princess Bride*, *Casablanca*, and *LA Confidential* were awesome, and *AI* and *Hulk* stunk. You've rated *Spiderman* highly but Christina hasn't indicated that she's seen it, so they'll recommend that to her. Christina has rated *Elizabeth* highly but Christina hasn't indicated that she's seen it, so they'll recommend that to you. This is another bit of magic that works much, much better the more data you have to work with.

In personalized search, we can predict that people who live in Palo Alto and search for "pizza" usually want Round Table Pizza's phone number. It's not hard to see the difficulties in this scenario (not everyone wants a giant chain over a local pizzeria after all), but in search the stakes are high, and the data is hard to get so any opportunity to get more relevant results will be explored. Imagine two users doing similar searches for "Chinese food," "Russian food," and, "French food," and they clicked on the same result. One day, one of them does a search for pizza for the very first time. Is it worth it to show him—highly ranked—the result the other user had clicked on? Or is this the day that user was looking for a recipe and not a restaurant or a band named *Pizza*? Personalization is more likely to work in homogenous situations and with homogeneous user bases. For example, if this same series of searches happened on Yahoo! local, where the context is narrowed to local businesses and the users are all registered, Pizza My Heart might be the better result. And on a site for foodies, Patxi's Pizza (authentic Chicago!) might be a better result still.

One More Thing

It's very tempting to copy Google (or Ask, or Yahoo!) or even just plug their search into your site. After all, they have more engineers, designers, and researchers working on search than you can ever possibly afford. And honestly, it's a strategy that won't get you into trouble. Folks like PBS and CNN have handed their search over entirely to Google, and it produces competent results. Search is hard enough that it is worth handing over to the experts if you can't afford to do it right yourself.

That said, Google and Yahoo! are never going to know your business the way you know your business. They don't have your log files, your user testing results, your internal metadata, and your good old-fashioned know-how. Plus, with the rise of open source search tools such as Lucene, ht://dig, SWISH-E, Solr, Ferret, and many many more, as well as customizable search services such as Yahoo! BOSS,[16] the basic search problem is

---

16 http://developer.yahoo.com/search/boss/

much easier to get right with fewer resources. If you can avoid it, don't blindly hand over the keys to the kingdom to the big guys. Spend the time to apply that array of insights that only you possess to making the search on your site magic.

Mind-reading Is Expected...

...and increasingly delivered.

Do you feel lucky, punk?

Well, do you?

I'm Feeling Lucky

"With the invention of
keyboard and mouse, we're
all back in the story."

6

From A to C
by Way of B

*In which we design a nice path
for the user to get from one
place to another, surviving
such perils as shopping carts
and pop-up windows.*

We humans have loved stories since the beginning of time, and much of our history has involved finding ways to tell better stories to more people.

Before we wrote anything down, there were professional storytellers who wandered from village to village, giving people a rest from their daily struggle to survive by sharing tales of others with them. Each technology that was invented was swiftly put to work as a story delivery machine: the printing press, the radio, and the television. When you sat with a storyteller, you could ask questions. You could even suggest alternative endings: "That's too sad! He should tell her he loves her!" But the technology we invented, while better at getting our stories out to more people, was resistant to participation. It doesn't matter how loud you yell, "Don't go in the house!" at the television set, those silly teenagers always go in and are promptly killed by the monsters.

For the last 1000+ years, we've been designing one-way interfaces. And then one day, someone built something a bit different. A machine that had an output device *and* an input device. Thus, with the invention of keyboard and mouse, we were all back in the story. This made consumers' lives

much more fun, but the storyteller's job 500 times more difficult. How can you tell a story with as many endings (and beginnings and middles) as there are listeners?

Interactive design is the art of making systems that tell stories collaboratively. Sometimes, that story is as banal as, "I'm making a PowerPoint presentation for my boss." Sometimes, the story is as thrilling as, "I'm changing lives with microloans." But all these stories are exciting because no one knows the ending.

If I Only Had a Brain: Smarter Storytelling with Interaction Design

Imagine how much more interesting it is when you are part of the story…

> "There was once upon a time a king who had twelve daughters, each one more beautiful than the other. They all slept together in one chamber, in which their beds stood side by side, and every night when they were in them, the king locked the door and bolted it. But in the morning when he unlocked the door, he saw that their shoes were worn out with dancing, and no one could find out how that had come to pass. Then the king caused it to be proclaimed that whosoever could discover where they danced at night, should choose one of them for his wife and be king after his death, but that whosoever came forward and had not discovered it within three days and nights, should have forfeited his life."[1]

---

1 "The Shoes That Were Danced to Pieces"
   From Jacob and Wilhelm Grimm, *Household Tales*, trans. http://www.candlelightstories.com/Grimms/TheShoes.htm.

Do you:

- Sit outside the princesses' door to discover what they are doing?

- Hide under one of their beds?

- Say, "forget about it" and marry the miller's daughter?

This form is probably familiar to most folks. It is an example of a "choose your own adventure" story. Of course, the limitations quickly become apparent. What happens if you prefer to kidnap one of the princesses and run away to America? You only get to choose from the list the computer (or storybook) offers you. Still, it's a pretty good time.

If you were going to program it, you might lay out the logic in a table. It's easier to keep track of what occurs this way.

ID	If	You do this	then	this happens	with this result
1.1	If	You sit outside the princesses' door to discover what they're doing…	then	You are provided a lovely bed in the antechamber outside the princesses' door. Right before bedtime, the eldest daughter comes to you and offers a glass of wine. "It's a cold night—this will help keep you warm," she says.	Go to wine challenge, 2.1
1.2	If	You hide under a princess's bed…	then	You are a bit uncomfortable under the bed, but it's worth it if you can become king. You wiggle a little, trying to get more comfortable. The youngest daughter says, "I hear a mouse!" She looks under the bed and screams. The guards rush in and kill you.	You're dead.
1.3	If	You say, "Forget about it!" and marry the miller's daughter.	then	You live happily ever after until you die at 52 of a flour-inhalation related disease.	You're dead.
2.1	If	You accept the wine, but toss it in the sink after she leaves.	then	You pretend to fall asleep, and…	
2.2	If	You drink the wine and thank her.	then	You fall asleep. In the morning, you do not know why the princesses' shoes are worn out, and the king has you executed.	You're dead.
2.3	If	You refuse the wine politely.	then	The princess throws a hissy fit for refusing her hospitality, and the guards remove you by force.	You're executed for failing.

You can also map out interactions using flow diagrams. Here's the information from the previous table illustrated as a diagram.

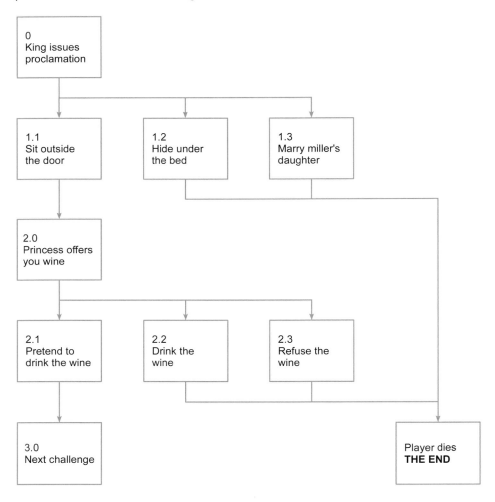

This "choose your own adventure story" is an extremely simple decision diagram. Offering several options adds a level of richness to the story and engages the reader, but try to picture this story now as a video game. You'd have far more choices than simply drink the wine/don't drink the wine. You could hang outside the window, kill the guards, torture the princesses, look for trapdoors, or...whatever. Just picture the number of choices available in any software program. In PhotoShop there is no narrative: there are endless numbers of undo, dozens and dozens of tools each with its own rules... how can you still ensure a level of pleasure with such a crazy level of complexity? The answer lies in understanding your users.

Personas, or Playing Barbies for Designers

Personas are a tool that Alan Cooper[2] developed based on an old market research technique. To be better able to sell to people, advertisers would take their demographics and try to invent an archetypal human from it.

Let's say that the audience for a floor wax was 63 percent female, 43 percent in the 25–35 year-old age range with 1.3 children, and 56 percent were homemakers; advertisers invented a customer named Sally who was a 27-year-old homemaker with two children. And then they did their best to create a commercial to sell floor wax to Sally. By focusing on this one customer who represented their audience, they could create more effective commercials. After all, how do you make a non-specific 25–35 year-old interested in your floor wax? It's too general.

Alan Cooper figured if you could sell floor wax better with personas, maybe you can design more humane software that way also.

So why did we call this section "Playing Barbies for Designers" rather than "The Alan Cooper Method?" The secret of good persona use is pretending *to be* the user, the way little children do when they play with Barbies. You have to relinquish how you think about the Web and become your user. You have to be, *act, and do* as your user would. Let us show you what we mean.

Sam I am

Let's play a game. Your name is Sam. You're a 52-year-old typesetter. You're smart, college educated, and a bit artsy. After all, you are keeping this great old art of handmade books alive! Your daughter, Lucy, just bought you a computer for Christmas. She set it up, ran the wires, and even ordered Internet access. She showed you how to open Firefox, made Yahoo! your start page, and told you there are great pages showing old books online.

---

2 As well as being "The Father of Visual Basic," Alan Cooper is president of a software and application design company, Cooper Interactive, and author of two excellent books, *The Inmates Are Running the Asylum* and *About Face*. Check out his site at http://www.cooper.com for many wonderful insights into making technology for humans.

Sam is not sure if this Web business is worth the hassle.

So, Sam, here you are. You've been looking at your new computer all week, and it's been looking at you. You fire it up, click the Firefox icon, and the screen shown in **Figure 6.1** comes up.

FIGURE 6.1 The Yahoo! homepage.

Um, that's not quite useful. You're looking for old books, so you type "antiquarian books" (that's what you call them) into the search box and see the search results shown in **Figure 6.2**. Suddenly, there are a lot of hopeful looking links to people who sell antiquarian books, art books, and so on.

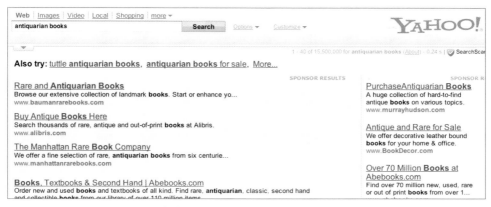

FIGURE 6.2 Yahoo! search results for "antiquarian books."

You decide to try the first result, Bauman Rare Books (**Figure 6.3**). When you arrive, can you tell what the site does? Are you there by mistake? What would you click to look at rare, old, and handmade books? Where could you go to order? Would it be possible for someone to steal your credit card if you ordered online? What happens if your order never comes?

FIGURE 6.3 You're Sam, and you visit Bauman Rare Books. What do you think?

Now pretend Sam is one of your users. Visit *your* Web site and ask yourself the same questions.

You've just seen the power of personas. They let you stop being you for a minute, and have real empathy for your user. As you experience the Web through Sam's eyes, you feel the pain and see opportunities to make your design simpler, clearer, and more valuable.

The archetypal user

Personas are archetypal users that exist mainly to be design targets. Remember the rolling suitcase in Chapter 2, Balancing Acts? In that case, the design target was a flight attendant.

Personas help you understand whom to design for and how to make that user ecstatically happy. Humanizing the audience is the huge benefit of personas. The generic "user" becomes the specific human being "Sam." Each time a team member thinks of a feature and says, "Well, users might like it," you can point to the persona and ask, "Would Sam use it?" Instead of a vague design target of "users" (who are capable of anything), you have a specific, targeted person with things he needs and wants, as well as things he doesn't want and can't use. Suddenly, prioritizing features becomes an easier job.

Suppose you are designing a bill-pay feature—a tool that online banks offer that allows users to have their bills automatically paid each month. You're trying to decide if the steps for that process should be on one page or over several pages. If you are still designing for Sam, you can ask yourself what would Sam think if he saw a huge page with dozens of questions to answer. You might decide to break the process into three pages, each clearly labeled with a step number so Sam would know where he was and have a feeling of accomplishment as he progressed through the setup. Each and every decision can be informed by the designer's ability to channel the persona.

You can design interaction without personas, of course. Plenty of designers do. But the capability to target a specific person makes your design more effective, and being able to prioritize features makes design faster. Why give that up?

How to Create Personas

So where do personas come from? Despite some folks thinking persona creation is nothing but advanced Barbies, creating your personas is a fairly calculated process. The better your personas, the better your interaction design will be. The best way to create personas is to start with user research. As seductive as it is to say, "Hey I know enough, my aunt Helen is just like our user base," don't do it. Go out and talk to people who use your product, who use your competitor's product, or are the people you'd like to have use your product. Find out what their goals are. Interview them, using the methods from Chapter 2, and get the raw materials you need to make personas.

Next, you should hold a workshop to do the initial creation work with the development team and with your stakeholders.[3] Some designers like to do it themselves, but creating personas with both the design team and stakeholders creates a real investment in the user experience. Here's how to do it.

1. Summarize findings. Distribute to stakeholders.

During your research phase, you gathered a ton of information. You probably found audience demographics (or the proposed audience), psychographics, gender, location, maybe even surfing habits, how technically savvy they are, or ways they use competitor products. In your interviews with potential users, you heard stories of their frustration with their current tools, and what works right and makes life easier. You have an insight into what makes the users tick.

Now create a report that includes relevant data about the user base: this is a discovery document.

In Chapter 2, we mentioned research to uncover the user's "goals." Make sure you list these goals in your discovery document. User goals are critical to developing personas. Concentrate on the big goals. People will often give you clues to their goals:

- "I wish there were a keyboard shortcut for 'undo twice.'"

- "I had to wait for five minutes to export a PDF file—it's maddening."

- "I don't know why this program wastes my time—if it were a person it'd be rude."

When you see a pattern emerge in these clues, you can extrapolate goals from them such as, "I would like to focus on my work and not the stupid tools I use!"

Other information in the discovery document depends on the product you are designing. The data might include the following information:

- Technical know-how of the user base

- Age range, gender distribution, and other demographics

- Work flow, if your site helps them with a process

- Usage patterns (both of your product and related products)

- Social patterns—how they relate to family, friends, and so on, in the context of your product

---

3 Stakeholders are people who have a stake in the product. They may include marketing people, business development folks, and customer service representatives.

- Competitors' products of interest to the user base

- Non-competing products of interest to the user base

- Common gripes

- Wish lists

- Psychographics, like morals, values, and cultural background

- And more

Did you extrapolate any specific goals? Find any interesting facts about your users? Any information you've gleaned that's specific, relevant, and universal goes into this document.

- **Specific:** Each piece of information should be as precise as possible. Throw out information like, "Users like it to be easy," and keep information like, "Users need to be able to complete a process in half an hour."

- **Relevant:** Relevant to your product, not to every site on the Web. Don't report, "Users like free stuff," but include, "Many users request free evaluation periods for software to know if paying will be worth it."

- **Universal:** Find things that are true for the entire site, not for a single item on a single page. Weed out things like, "Users couldn't find the Submit button on the checkout page," but leave in, "We have a type of user who knows what he wants already and needs a way to speed through finding and buying."

The discovery document is the springboard for persona creation. Thoughtful creation of this document makes it much easier.

2. Hold a work session with stakeholders and the development team to brainstorm personas.

You need to decide early on if you will design the personas alone or with the larger team. Designing by committee is always a tightrope, and design decisions should be made because they're the right ones, not because they're the political ones. If you choose to do your initial persona creation with a team, keep in mind that politics may play a role. Your work session should concentrate on getting an initial pass at the personas that you can then refine using research data. Refinement should be done alone or with one or two team members.

The big meeting provides involvement and investment; the small team provides precision and depth. Trying to get precision and depth from a meeting of 15 people is like getting 15 cats to do aquatic ballet. But a big meeting is fun and creates a lot of excitement for your project. It also gets everyone on the same page and helps create a unified vision among your team members about who your users are. That alone makes it worth the trouble.

To prepare for your aquatic ballet—er, persona meeting—invite key stakeholders from each department that has contact with, connection with, or investment in the end user to participate in the meeting. Also invite key members of the development team. The final group needs to be small enough to make decisions. For example, a group of 10 to 15 people has worked well for us in the past.

If your company is extremely large, you may have trouble getting the number of people who want to participate down to a manageable number. One technique you can try is choosing stakeholder representatives or holding stakeholder interviews: you or the stakeholder representative can go to each stakeholder and learn what she wants and needs from this project. Although this doesn't provide the same level of involvement, people will still feel they are being listened to and will feel more comfortable about the project.

For your meeting, pick a big room with a couple of dry-erase whiteboards, or bring in giant notepads, or cover the walls with butcher paper. You will want to take notes quickly and loosely, as in a brainstorming session.

Begin the session by explaining that you'll work as a group to put together a clear picture of who your users are. Then start a brainstorm on the characteristics of users. Are they men, women? Age groups? Where do they live? Refer to your discovery document when people seem unsure, or call on quieter folks whom you suspect have the answers. It's important that everyone at the meeting has a stake in the personas. Some people are shy about voicing a thought, and when you ask them for their thoughts, you show their knowledge is valued.[4]

Then move to more subtle questions: Why do users use the product? How do they use it?

After your have filled your board with characteristics, start combining and refining them into personas:

Woman + 25-35 + East Coast, USA = 26-year-old woman from Washington, D.C.

You can even give her a name: Sarah Carlson.

---

4 One peculiar side effect of these persona sessions is it's sometimes the first time different groups talk to each other about the user base in a collaborative fashion. (As opposed to, "Can you get that designed for me by Monday?") Marketing talks to customer service, design to business, etc. These sessions can be amazing team building opportunities and are very effective for promoting communication and building respect for other departments.

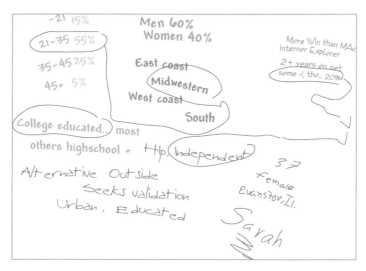

The whiteboard brainstorming session that created Sarah.

Keep going. Create as many personas as the group feels it needs to represent its user base.

Although we've found it useful to involve stakeholders and the project team when creating personas, you may find it simpler to hide in a dark room with your research data, create the personas, and present them to the group afterwards. What you may lose in involvement, you will make up in speed and focus. You also sidestep the potential politics that may water down your personas. It's a trade-off you may want to make.

3. Prioritize and cull personas; develop primary and supporting personas.

At the end of this session, you'll probably have a list of 15 or so personas—too many to design with! Ask the group about each of the personas. Who is the most important user? Who is the most difficult to make happy, or to make the system easy for? Get a rating for all the personas. Take all the data and go off on your own.

Now you need to decide who must be made ecstatic by the product, who can be made happy, and who needs a completely different product altogether. This is done by choosing primary, secondary, and complementary personas.

Primary personas

Your primary persona needs to be a common user type that is both important to the business success of the product *and* is needy from a design point of view. This is usually a beginning user or a technologically challenged one.

Let's imagine that you're designing an online magazine for people who love independent films. When you did your persona exercise, you might have created these three personas:

- **Michael Davies**, an executive from Miramax, who is interested in finding films for general distribution. His goal is to find new breakout films before anyone else does. He does this several ways, including going to festivals, tracking filmmakers with potential, and networking.

- **Sarah Carlson**, a big fan of indie films in general. She wants to support independent filmmaking to keep an alternative to Hollywood going. Her goal is to live a good life, and that includes watching non-Hollywood films.

- **Scott Seamus**, who digs Spike and Mike animations and new film noir. Scott loves to be surprised, shocked, and entertained. He knows film noir will do this, and his goal is to feed that pleasure.

Even though they all read through the magazine, they have different needs. Michael wants "the inside scoop," Sarah likes browsing to find interesting new releases, and Scott's totally focused on, and looking for, "his" content.

Secondary user personas

Your secondary users need to be very different from the primary users. Secondary users may be power users or serious novices who are less valuable from a business standpoint but cost a lot in customer support. (Business is not just about profits; it's also about savings.)

For the magazine on independent film, you might have these three secondary personas:

- **Lois** is an independent film director who is interested in what her peers are doing.

- **Donna** is Michael's personal assistant who needs to book Michael's travel to various film festivals. She's expected to keep up on what is happening where.

- **Melissa** is making plans for her fourth wedding anniversary and wants to pick a good movie for their night out.

Let's look at these users. Is Melissa really so different from Sarah, one of your primary users? Can they be combined? Perhaps Sarah first comes to the site looking for a date movie, and then becomes a regular user of the site.

Complementary personas

There's a third kind of user, the user who has radically different needs for the system, who may even need a specialized design of her own. We call these users "complementary," because they show us a different side of the product, a side we might not have seen otherwise.

- **Linda** is an editor for the magazine, and needs a completely different view of the system. She isn't reading the magazine; she's looking through articles before they go live, editing, and approving. Perhaps she rarely looks at this week's edition; rather, she reads next week's edition to make sure that it is ready to go. Linda has such *completely different needs*, that you may want to build a separate interface for her and others like her. (What about the writers? The production folks? Who else has a different view of the Web site?) Linda, the persona, may well show that you need to design not one Web site, but two: a content Web site for the audience and a Web application to manage the content.

- **Markus** lives in Ireland where he is charged for dial-up. He'd like to download the entire magazine to read offline. Imagine how different a downloadable version of the magazine will be from the Web site version. What happens to links to other sites? Do you want to show big photos that will slow down the download?

Depending on the size of the project, you'll probably want to narrow your entire collection of personas down to three to five personas. The exception is a diverse site with a range of products, like Sony.com. These sites require more personas because their user-base, content, and feature set are very diverse. On a site like Sony.com, each product group may use its own subset of personas to meet the unique design challenges for that section of the Web site. And the company may create a few personas to inform the design of the entire site in order to ensure consistency.

However, our indie film magazine is small and homogenous, so you only need a few personas. Five would be enough. Overall, it's better to have a small collection of well-defined personas than a larger collection of nebulous ones.

4. Make the personas into real people.

Right now, you have personas that look like this:

Sarah Carlson/ 26/ female/ married/ Washington, D.C.

Let's add some personality to these skeletons. The more real your personas are, the more likely you'll be to care about their success or failure and the more likely you'll be to design a good experience for them. Remember, the biggest value of personas is that they help you empathize with your site's users.

Pull as much as possible from your interviews with real people. Create lives for them, backgrounds, and personalities. Create quotes that capture their attitude about the product. We'll use two of our primary personas as examples, Scott and Sarah.

	Scott Seamus 20/male/single/Schaumburg, IL
Quote	"I want something cool and really on the edge. Something you can't get at the multiplex."
Profession	Full-time student
Personal Background	Youngest kid in family of five. Likes to be seen as a little rebellious. Loves movies, and has always gone to as many as possible. He eats Top Ramen so he can spend his money on movies instead. He's a huge film noir fan and spent 12 hours in a noir marathon last year. He is majoring in film studies, but is uncertain if he actually wants to make films.
Goals	Scott wants to know if film is really where he wants to spend the rest of his life. He wants to know not only what new film noir movies are being made and what's good, but also what it takes to make a truly good film. He's always seeking behind-the-scenes stories to understand how film crewmembers work together, how directors fund their films, how to write for the movies, and so on. He's hungry to take apart the magic and figure out how to put it together again.

	Sarah Carlson 22/female/single/ Washington, DC./Originally from the Midwest
Quote	"I like Indieworld because it's just about the films."
Profession	Editor for non-profit organization ($35K/yr)
Personal Background	Liberal arts education at college in the Midwest. Just graduated and moved to DC in hopes of affecting politics. Has a big dog named Chomsky. Likes modernist art and propaganda posters. Went to South By Southwest. Sends out mass emails about causes she cares about or jokes.
Goals	She wants to find well-made genuine films that make a difference. She feels passionately that the world is made up of mass-produced garbage that is contributing to the decline of society, and wants to support any alternative she can find.

Try to make these folks as real as possible without writing a full-length biography. Not only will you believe in them enough to make your design empathic, but their reality also provides insight that leads to product innovation.

For example, maybe a lot of your interviews showed people with young children. If you give your persona a family of young children as well, this will reveal more design issues—children drive large goals, such as "provide for my family," as well as small tasks, such as "keep my kids away from porn." Moreover, in conversation with the team, you can stay grounded by referring to the persona families: "Hey don't remove the parental controls. Maria wants to keep Evan out of the NC-17 chat rooms. Just imagine the trouble he could get into!"

Getting the goal right is one of the toughest parts of persona creation, but it's important. Maybe Donna's goal is, "Spend more time with my family." Now your design can't waste this persona's time: who are you to keep her working late! A goal should be meaningful to the persona's life beyond the product, but still affected by the product. An online calendar can't help a persona with the goal of, "I want to be a rock star." But it can help a persona with the goal of, "I want to manage my time better so I can learn guitar."

The quotes act as mnemonics that keep the team connected to the persona and the persona's goals. It should be something that catches the nature of the persona's personality and her attitude toward the product.

For an online calendar persona: "If I can just keep track of everyone's schedule, there won't be any trouble."

For an online magazine persona: "What makes me good at my job is my ability to stay abreast of the field."

Finally, find a photograph for your persona. It's important that the photo be someone you don't know. Otherwise, it may lead you to warp the persona to be more like the person whose photo it is. For example, you might forget that the persona is less tech-savvy than the photographed person and design something too advanced. Dig through stock photography sites until you find a photo that feels right, the photo that screams "Sarah" or "Sam." A headshot is best. This is the face that will hold you accountable through the design process. Pick a good one.

5. Apply the personas.

There are a lot of ways to keep personas in mind while designing. You can hang posters of them on the walls, or put placemats on people's desks. The important thing is to keep the personas close by to make sure you are constantly considering their needs as you design.

You can distribute these artifacts to the entire company. Customer service reps can look at the persona's image as they talk on the phone, marketing can design ad campaigns for them, business development can think up new products for them, and so on. Personas are a powerful way to get the company to be "customer-centric." The faces of real people, likable, with enough history to make them as real and familiar as a neighbor or a relative, can change the way people do business.

For our purposes, though, the most useful application of the persona is to create scenarios that we'll use to design Web sites.

Scenarios: The Joseph Campbell Method

Here's your chance to put the personas you created into action. Joseph Campbell[5] was a scholar who suggested storytelling was one of the most effective tools humans have for understanding. Humans love stories. We tell them in the morning when we arrive at

---

5 Read Joseph Campbell's most famous book, *The Hero with a Thousand Faces* (Princeton University Press, 1972), and maybe you will become as inspired as George Lucas was. Campbell's concept of the hero's journey was one of the sources for Lucas's *Star Wars* trilogy. Or maybe you'll just have a cool book to read in hip coffee shops.

work. We curl up with stories at night as we watch television. In the past, Aesop's Fables taught us moral behavior, and myths explained how nature worked. Now modern stories told in movies, television, and books provide catharsis, entertainment, and insight into our fellow humans.

Creating scenarios is a way for us to take the pleasure and usefulness of storytelling and apply it to the act of designing interactive systems.

Using scenarios

We typically use scenarios in three ways:

- As a design tool
- As an evaluation tool
- As a communication tool

Scenarios as design tools

To use a scenario as a design tool, start with your primary persona. Create a step-by-step narrative showing the persona using an ideal (for that persona) version of the Web site. Ideally, what would they see on the homepage? How would the site be organized? Where would they click? What features would they love? As you imagine how that persona would use the ideal system, ignore all technical and business constraints. This is the persona's perfect world. If you force yourself to ignore constraints beyond the persona's needs and desires, you can come up with innovative ways to meet those needs and desires.

Next, write a second version of the scenario that reflects the business and technical restraints. The first scenario was the ideal world. This second scenario is more like the *real* world. Walk the persona through this real world scenario. Note where conflicts exist and work with the other team members to bring the second scenario as closely in line with the first as possible. Sometimes a very clever engineer or designer will think of a solution that you hadn't thought possible.

Combining these two scenarios—the persona's *ideal* world and the business and technical *real* world—creates a picture of the Web site and features you should design.

Scenarios as evaluation tools

After you've designed a system, you can also use scenarios to evaluate how well it meets your user needs. Pick a persona and role-play them through the Web site. Try to imagine what their experience will be. (We did this earlier with Sam, the fan of old books.) What works the way they expect? What doesn't? Although this isn't as effective as usability testing, it can reveal flaws in the system while there's still time to change the design.

Scenarios as communication tools

Finally, a scenario can be used as a communication tool. As you saw with the Princesses' shoes, designing interaction can become complex really quickly. A scenario can communicate the way a design will work, how a user will move through and interact with a system, and because it uses a story format, you don't become bogged down in the design details. This enables other members of the product team to understand how the Web site will work. Sales can more easily sell advertisement, business can more easily raise venture capital, and the tech writer can use the context the scenarios provide to make a more usable help manual.[6]

Writing good scenarios

We're going to write a scenario involving Michael, our movie executive and primary persona. Obviously, Michael might want to make more choices than the few we'll offer here. A full scenario might go on for quite a bit longer and cover more ground. The important things to keep in mind are the following:

- **Keep to the ideal experience.** Your boss might insist that users sign in before using the system. It's better to ignore constraints like this in the first version of the scenario. You can always go back and change the scenario to reflect business and technological constraints, but if you don't aim for the ideal user experience, you don't have any chance of achieving it. You can always scale back to reality, but once you're there, it's almost impossible to imagine something ideal.

- **Don't talk about interface decisions.** Save the decisions like how many pages it will be or whether you'll use buttons or links for later. Answer those questions when you're designing. You want to focus on how the persona moves through the system. It's tough. It's so easy to say, "On the next page," or, "He clicks a link," but if you can avoid this, do so. It keeps your mind open to new design possibilities.

- **Don't get caught up in minutiae.** If you get stuck, just keep telling the story. Keep it vague. It's tempting to start answering little questions like, "How do they access movies they viewed in the past?" but just keep moving forward, staying with the intent, of the user in that particular scenario. You can always leave "bookmarks"—little notes to yoruself—to return to side-stories later.

- **Keep with your persona.** Use the persona's name as often as possible (at least once a paragraph). Remember, you're telling the story of how the persona

---

6 Imagine a scenario in which a mom is trying to figure out why the DVD player isn't working. Her daughter is screaming, "I want Thomas," while mom flips through the manual. Now her daughter is strangling her with her scarf while she pages through the FAQ looking for the DVD player's reset button. With this kind of real-world context, the tech writer will understand he needs to create the most efficient FAQ ever.

experiences the site, not how the site handles users. Write what you suspect the persona would say and do, not what your boss would say or what you wish the persona would do.

A scenario in action, designing a new feature: The Festival Planner

IndieWorld.com, our Web site about independent film, has a new feature it wants to launch four months before The Sundance Film Festival. It's called the *Festival Planner*. The Festival Planner allows folks intending to attend a film festival to plan what films to go see. To design this feature, we're going to use one of the personas we created earlier. Michael Davies attends festivals for a living, so he's the right persona for this design job. First, we'll refresh our memory by looking over Michael's profile.

Michael Davies
32, Male, Single, Los Angeles, CA.

Quote	"I don't have time to get lost on someone's site—I'm not playing here."
Profession	Executive for Miramax
Personal Background	Grew up in Oregon, went to San Francisco State University, and majored in film history. Moved to LA to "break into the industry" and ended up working his way up from administrative assistant to his current position, mostly due to his personal charm. Wears nice clothes in grayscale because he's color-blind and can't gamble on trying to match colors. Drives an older model BMW, which he works on during the weekend. Works long hours at his job, and feels guilty when surfing for pleasure at work. Works out every day in the company gym. Worries about health matters. Interested in GQ style fashion information. Single, but doesn't want to be. Has a cat, Rafferty. He wanted a dog originally, but got a cat since he travels so much. Rafferty is good company, though.
Goals	Michael wants to be a producer. He dreams of helping a young director come into his craft. He goes to the film festivals with the dream of spotting the next Chris Nolan or Robert Rodriguez. He reads indieworld.com, hoping they will be ahead of the trades, and he'll get a lead others miss.
Internet profile	T1 at work, DSL at home. Online 15-20 hours/week.
	Technical proficiency: fair. He's a searcher/speed browser.
	Has sites he goes to all the time. If he wants something else, he searches on Google. Will spend an hour a day at atomfilms.com and iFilm.com
	Mostly reads news online.

Favorite sites	Likes CNN.com, ESPN, indiewire.com, indiefilms.com, and variety.com. He listens to a music feed at work and likes to download mp3s.
Technological profile	Has Flash and Windows Media Player, Real Player, and QuickTime.
History with Indieworld.com	Visits indieworld.com's news page to see if there is any interesting news. It's one in a series of sites he surfs as part of a routine, and spends only a few minutes on only the front page before going to the next site. Occasionally, he'll be led deeper into the site by a story, or he'll come to the site to do a bit of research.
Entertainment profile	Goes to movies at least once a week, considers himself a film buff, and watches lots of DVDs (belongs to an online DVD club). His work is also his passion.
Wants and needs	Wants to keep in touch with what's going on while spending as little time and energy as possible. After all, he'd rather be watching a film.

Scenario

To get the scenario jump-started, you can rough out a high-level one: Michael will notice the Festival Planner from the news page and check it out. He will create an itinerary by choosing elements of a film that matter to him and then the system will recommend films he may want to see. He'll choose those he is interested in and save the itinerary.

That's high-level and vague. Let's flesh it out:

> Michael clicks on the "festival planner" link. He then sees a list of names of directors with check boxes. He selects the ones he likes, and clicks the names of a few directors to get a pop-up describing each director's history. When he's done, he clicks the button with the label "next step"....

That's terrible. That scenario is too specific about the interface. It can be tempting when you start to see the design in your mind and dive right in. Resist it. Design will come later. For now, stay with the ideal and abstract.

We'll try it again:

> Michael is doing his morning surf. He's just left indiewire.com and has come to indieworld.com. He reads through the new stories on Sundance and spots the Festival Planner. He's been agonizing over having to wade through the huge number of films and hopes the Planner might make it simpler.

> Michael looks over the Festival Planner intro page. He wants to make sure this is going to save time and not waste time. He sees he can play with it without having to sign up, which is a relief. And he sees he can set up a schedule for any day of the festival. He

sets his watch alarm for five minutes—at that time he'll decide if he wants to continue. Preferably, he'll be done.

Festival Planner asks Michael if he's interested in any particular directors or actors. Michael indicates people he thinks have promise. He notices some names he doesn't know and reads short bios of them. He adds a couple to watch. He notices he can save this information by simply adding his email address and a password. He decides he really ought to because he's put in a bit of effort at this point. He's pleased it didn't ask him for any more personal information; he gets so tired of typing in this and that for registration on every site he comes across.

Festival Planner next asks him if he's interested in any particular genre of film and if he's traveling for business, pleasure, or both. The Planner asks him if he's interested only in films that haven't been signed to a distributor, or if he's interested in all films. He indicates that he's interested only in unsigned films. Finally, Festival Planner asks him if he's willing to see overlapping films, or if he wants the planner to make sure his films dovetail. Michael would rather see complete films, but this is a business trip. He sighs and picks overlap.

Festival Planner now gives him a schedule to review, with three films to pick from and an option to "see all for this time slot." One film for each time slot is indicated as his "best pick." Each shows how well it meets his taste and needs. Or he can choose to "rest" and not select a film for that time period.

Michael goes through the schedule. His wristwatch beeps, and he absent-mindedly shuts it off. He continues to select his films. As he chooses films, he notices an option to get a report on any film when it's available—he's very excited by that. If he can't see them all, at least he can get a sense of what he's missing!

Finally, Michael has a schedule that satisfies him. He notices he can email the schedule to anyone. He sends a copy to his assistant and to himself. After all, he'll have his laptop, but who knows how connectivity will be. Better to have a copy downloaded.

That's our imagining of Michael's ideal experience with the Festival Planner. Even though it's just a story, it provides a clear list of features, as well as a list of design Dos and Don'ts (Don't require an account. Do make bios available.) Next, you'd write a second scenario that takes into account your business and technical requirements. Maybe the business requires registered users. Maybe you don't know which actors are in which films or whether a film has a distributor.

Once you've created your ideal and your real-world stories, it's time to get concrete.

So far, our persona and scenario have provided valuable information. We know Michael is an industry exec, so we need features that help him find movies to distribute. This means asking questions like whether he wants only movies that haven't been signed to a distributor. Second, we know he'd probably want to save and email his festival plan.

But what about Sarah Carlson, another primary persona? She could attend a film festival and want to use the planner. Michael's scenario describes Michael's ideal experience. A movie executive's ideal festival planner isn't necessarily the same as Sarah's. We should write another scenario—one that describes Sarah's ideal interaction with the festival planner—to identify any additional features Sarah might need.

Each scenario will allow you to see how each individual persona interacts with and moves through your site. But you only see each scenario, one at a time. How do you make sure you've identified all the scenarios you'll need for a complete interactive system? Among all personas, what are the most common tasks? What features are used most often? You need to see the entire system at one glance. You need sitepath diagramming.

Sitepath Diagramming

Sitepath diagramming is a sketching system in which you try to determine who the users of the site will be and what sorts of activities they'll try to accomplish. This allows you to decide what you need to design and determine what designs will be most crucial to the success of the Web site.

Sitepath diagramming is especially good for determining site flow, early interaction design, and workflow. By drawing the sitepaths for your different users, you're better able to get your head around complicated problems or see if you've forgotten anything.

They're also really good at showing similar processes you can design for one type of user and reuse for all of them. When you write separate scenarios for different personas, it's easy to imagine designing a different interface for each persona. The sitepath diagram reveals places where your personas can use the same interface. In the end, this means you can design and develop fewer features while retaining the same great experience.

How to do sitepath diagramming

You can create sitepath diagrams by yourself, but they're definitely fun with a group. You'll need a few things:

- Something to draw on, the bigger the better. Whiteboards are great, but you can also use butcher paper or oversize pads of paper.

- Lots of different colored markers.

- The ability to draw some little people. Stick figures are perfect.[7]

- Personas, if you already have them.

Once you have everything ready, it's time to start by drawing your users:

- Begin by drawing a big circle. This is the interactive system. It could be the Web site or a set of interconnected Web sites. That decision can be made later. For now, stick with the big picture and think: "This is the system."

- Put in as many types of people as you think would interact with the system you're designing. We usually put the obvious users of the site in the upper left. These are your usual visitors who come in through a search engine or who type your URL into the address box and enter through the homepage.

- Try to think of alternative ways people might come to the site—a newsletter, for example—and put them in the lower left.

- Finally, try to think of people who would use the site in a very different way and put them on the right. Members of the press, potential investors, and job hunters often fall into this category. These are guidelines only. You can do it any way you please. We do it this way in hopes of having enough space to fit in all the interactions.

The circle is your "system." The little people scattered around the edge are your users.

---

7 Sitepath diagramming is an exercise in visual thinking. If you'd like to master your visual thinking skills, check out *The Back of the Napkin* by Dan Roam. You'll be amazed at the problems you can solve and solutions you can sell with just a few stick figures, some boxes, and some arrows.

Now start thinking about your scenarios. If you've formally documented scenarios, you can return to those. If you haven't, you can make them up as you go along.

Suppose that you are diagramming a small ecommerce site. Let's tell the story of a person who has to buy a gift for a wedding:

- Start at the homepage, find the wedding registry, and search for the name of your friend.

- Then select a gift, purchase it, write a card, and send it off.

For each event that will happen in the system, draw a circle, and draw arrows from circle to circle showing what happens next.

Each circle might be one page, part of a page, or several pages. Don't worry about those details yet. The key is to get the ideas out of your head and onto the page. If you get caught up in details at this stage, you'll get stuck again. Just keep scribbling. Draw out the entire story, and be sure to mark the exit point where your person leaves the system.

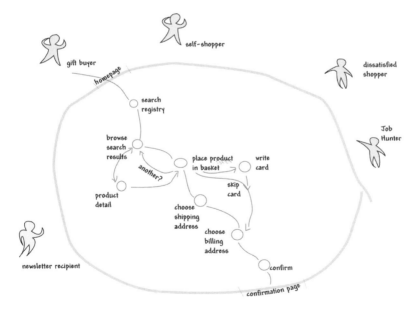

Next, add another path. You may realize you can reuse elements you diagrammed already. Feel free to connect to them. Some people like to retrace the line as well, to show that multiple people may take the same path.

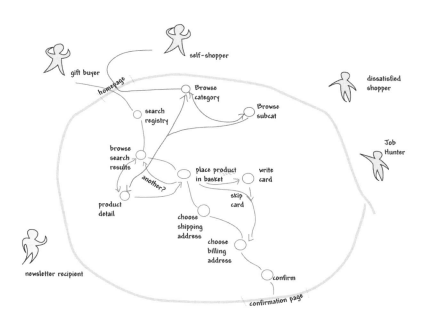

Keep going. You may find areas of the site you think belong together—go ahead and indicate that. You may also find connections that aren't dictated by the scenarios. Note those, too, but you may want to remind yourself that they were gut reactions. A small question mark is a good way to note that. Later, when you move into a more analytical, evaluative mode, you can consider those choices.

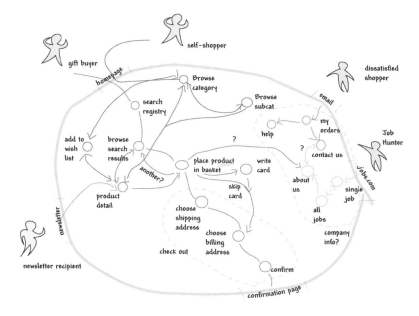

Like your scenarios, the sitepath diagram will reveal features and interactions you might not have thought of. Not only that, but when you're done, you'll have a nice picture of how the system should work.

Task Analysis: Diagramming It All

Task analysis is a discrete, step-by-step analysis of how users do things. It's a careful look at every single action required to complete a task.

Maybe you've got a scenario that provides a general description of what happens, or you finished a sitepath diagramming session and have some fresh whiteboarding to document. You're still not ready to build the html yet. It's time to fill in all the little bits and pieces that make a Web site work. However, it's still not time to pick check boxes or radio buttons. Check boxes or radio buttons is a design question. The task analysis will take our scenario and help us figure out what design questions we need to answer.

First, we start with Michael's task goal:

Michael wants to quickly set up a schedule for Sundance.

Then we go through the scenario and pull out elements from it that relate directly to the task.

1. Understand how it works.
2. Choose films of interest.
3. Select film state of availability (signed, unsigned).
4. Select film scheduling (dovetail or overlap).
5. View recommendation.
6. Select films of choice.
7. Sign up for reports.
8. Save work (available in previous steps).
9. Email schedule.

Here we try to get the basic unique tasks. This sequence isn't necessarily written in stone. For example, in our design, we hope to make "Save work" available at any stage. However, we know that "Save work" is really, really important later in the process. So, for now, we'll leave it in the sequence of the scenario.

Next, we need to get a better level of detail and look for subtasks. If we dive into step two, "Choose films of interest," it might look like this:

2.   Choose films of interest.

   a.   Select directors of interest.

   b.   Select actors of interest.

   c.   Select genres of interest.

We have to do this for all the items. Some may not have subtasks. Finally, we add the system interaction. Table 6.1 shows a full blow out of step two.

Michael's Actions	The System's Actions
1. Michael indicates he is ready to begin.	2. System displays list of **directors**, with option to select as many as Michael wishes, and level of interest (**very interested, somewhat interested**, and default of **not interested**). The system prompts Michael to choose directors of interest.
3. Michael selects as many directors as he is interested in and submits the information.	4. System acknowledges choices. System displays list of **actors**, with option to select as many as user wants, and level of interest (**very interested, somewhat interested**, and default of **not interested**). System prompts Michael to choose actors of interest.
5. Michael selects as many actors as he is interested in and submits the information	6. System acknowledges choices. System displays list of **genres**, with option to select as many as Michael wishes, and level of interest (**very interested, somewhat interested**, and default of **not interested**). System prompts Michael to choose genres of interest.
7. Michael selects as many genres as he is interested in and submits the information	8. System acknowledges choices. System prompts for purpose for trip to festival: **business, pleasure**, or **both**.
9. Michael may choose **business, pleasure**, or **both**.	10. If **business** or **both**, system prompts for interest in availability of film: signed to a distributor or unsigned. If **pleasure**, show results.

TABLE 6.1 Choose Films of Interest

And so on. Task analysis is an extremely effective way to catch each nuance of each step in the interaction. Programmers love these also, because the steps are so clear. Note how the task analysis never specifies what the interface looks like.

Another way to capture this detail is to diagram it.

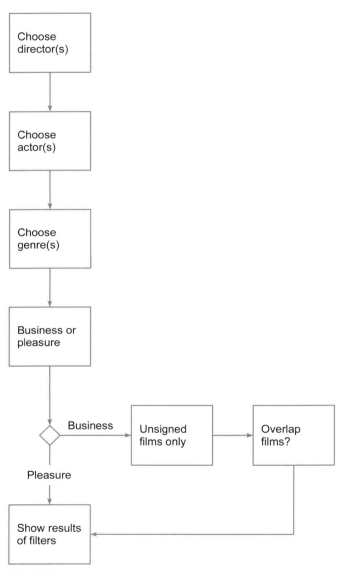

THIS TASK analysis shows how Michael works his way through the Festival Planner.

It really doesn't matter if you use words or boxes and arrows, as long as it helps you to think clearly, and it explains your design decisions to the rest of the team.

Personas, scenarios, sitepath diagrams, and task analysis are all part of the design behind the design. If we were designing a human, this would have been the skeleton phase. Next chapter: muscles!

"The page is the
interface between
the user and the
company, and getting
it right can be the
difference between
that person wanting
to have anything to
do with your company
ever again...or not."

7

From Box
to Page

*In which we transform
abstract thinking into
concrete design.*

Much of information architecture deals with the abstract. You have user and business needs that tell you everyone's goals. Scenario and task analysis tell you what happens and in what order. Personas tell you who uses the site and even why. But so far, none of this provides any nitty-gritty details about how many pages your site has or what lives on each page.

To choose what happens on each page—and how many pages exist on your site—you must balance helping the users accomplish their current task while making certain the tools for what they need to do next are also available. To achieve this balance, a page must do two things:

1. Help the user accomplish one discrete task.

2. Make the next step easy to access.

In this chapter, we'll lead you through the process of mapping user tasks to individual Web pages. We'll explain when to use fewer pages and when to use more. We'll also discuss how to ensure that the user's next step is easy to access. At the end, we'll show how you can document and communicate your page designs using wireframes.

Linking the Chain

User tasks are like links in a chain.

Task 1   Task 2   Task 3   Task 4   Task 5

And each page on a Web site is like a window that shows only so much of the chain.

Task 1   Task 2   Task 3   Task 4   Task 5

In a chain, each individual link is vitally important. Each chain link has the *discrete task* of not breaking. However, it's the relationship between one chain link and its neighbors that creates the chain. The *next step* for each chain link is to connect to its neighbor.

Similarly, when designing your site, helping the user accomplish each task is vitally important; however, it's the relationship between tasks that creates the entire experience. Each page on your site needs to help build this chain.

1. Each page should help the user accomplish one discrete primary task.

2. Each page should provide access to the next link(s) in the task chain.

Balancing between the current task and the next step is important. Focus too much on the current task, and users will find it difficult to get where they're going. Focus too much on the next step, and they won't be able to accomplish their current task.

When you design the page, you are designing a window that shows both a link in the chain, as well as the connected links. You may be saying now, oh that's so Web 1.0— what about Gmail, and Zoho and all the other applications that are on the web? There is still one, primary task on each page. For example, take a look at **Figure 7.1**. When you first come into Gmail, your primary task is to understand what emails you have and quickly act on them. Tasks like chatting, composing mail, and going though your folders are tucked out of the way of the main inbox display. And when you open an email, you are reading it first, responding (or filing, or deleting) second. And while responding to that email appears to happen on the same "page," with a trick of modern web technology, the page is sufficiently transformed to be considered a new page.

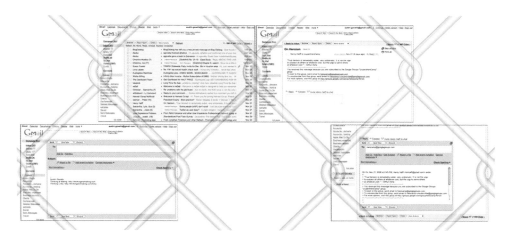

FIGURE 7.1 Gmail and other Web 2.0 applications are less like a chain and more like a chain link fence. First, Gmail's inbox helps you figure out which emails are worth reading. When you select an email, Gmail now helps you read that message. When you choose to reply, Gmail scrolls down to the reply form. It's not technically a new page, yet the screen has transformed completely to keep you focused on your current task.

What's critical is that the browser window is moving along the chain. Even if it's a chainlink fence, and the next task could be one of a hundred, the browser window still focuses on the user's current task. A Web page usually helps users do more than one thing. But design just isn't about allowing access to everything a page can do. It's about identifying the priority for each task, and using those priorities to make good design decisions. First, let's determine priorities for the page.

A note about why we use the word "page."

As a user moves from one task to another, they can move to a different page, or the page can transform itself to support the new task. We use the word "page"—as in our Gmail example—to keep things simple. But when you get into the final design and implementation you may choose to have a page that transforms itself rather than two pages you navigate between. If you choose to have the page transform itself, designers will sometimes refer to "views" of a page—the way Gmail's single email page has a reading view and a reply view. We want to keep things simple for now, so we're going to pretend it's still 1999, and talk about individual pages.

Focus the Page on the User's Primary Task

There are three types of pages on the Web:

1. Navigation pages help users determine where to find what they want, and give them access to it.

2. Consumption pages allow users to consume content.

3. Interaction pages let users enter and manipulate data.

Each type of page is optimized for a different kind of user task. Understanding the type of page you need helps you tailor the interface design. It's also important to understand when users need to move to a new page, versus staying on an existing page.

Navigation pages

Navigation pages exist to send you somewhere else. Homepages, the business section at the *New York Times*, a list of search results, the Gmail inbox, a gallery of thumbnails—all of these pages dedicate their lives to making you go away. If the user's primary task is to navigate to or find something, then you need a navigation page. Design navigation pages so they are easy to leave (**Figure 7.2**).

FIGURE 7.2 A homepage, search results, and a gallery of thumbnails all give you a snippet and then encourage you to go somewhere else to see the rest.

Consumption pages

Consumption pages are the "somewhere else" you usually go to. These are places where articles are read, videos watched, photos viewed, and mp3s played. For example news stories, blog posts, today's weather, YouTube videos, the latest Nick Cave single, recipes, installation instructions, tutorials, wedding photos—things people have spent some energy locating and desperately want. Sometimes, they consume it with a quick glance, e.g. looking at today's weather or watching a funny video clip, and sometimes, it's a commitment, like watching a two-hour movie or reading someone's dissertation. Whatever it is, design the page to make the content as *easy to consume* as possible (**Figure 7.3**).

FIGURE 7.3 Text, videos, and photos—in each of these screenshots, the page is focused on the thing that people want to consume.

Interaction pages

Interaction pages are places where people want to type, drag, slide, push, poke, edit, and delete information. This can be something as simple as Google's homepage with one text input, or something as complex as word processing with Google Docs (**Figure 7.4**). For these kinds of pages, focus on making them *easy to use*.

Easy to use seems pretty straightforward, but easy to use means different things in different situations. Some Web sites need to be easy to use the first time you use them. Others need to be easy to use the 500th time you use them. For example, as most applications move on to the web, you start to see real tools like Excel, Photoshop, and Visio moved online. These tools are often hard to use the first time you sit down with them, but as you use them more and more, you learn and become more effective with them. What you know about the user will guide you in choosing whether you should optimize for easy to use for first-time users, or efficient to use for long-time users.[7]

FIGURE 7.4 Picnik, Google Spreadsheets, and Yahoo! Search all devote almost the entire page to making interaction and manipulation easy. Google Spreadsheets, emulating Excel, has many keyboard shortcuts you learn as you become proficient with the progam, making it grow easier with time.

---

7 And really really complicated apps require more books. Check out Robert Hoekman Jr.'s *Designing the Obvious*, a book on designing web applications. In addition to explaining good design, he explores whether you should optimize for easy or efficient.

Design gumbo (mixing page types)

But, but, but my page is all three?!?!? Maybe. It's possible, especially in this day of Web applications with rich interfaces. But regardless of how much you think your users want to do on the page, there's one thing, just one, primary thing, that's more important than everything else that your visitors want to do, and that task is what the page's design needs to support first and foremost.

We'll stack the deck using Google Maps as an example (see **Figure 7.5**). What takes up more of the page's area? The map for people to look at, or the map for people to drag, zoom, and mark? It seems like Google Maps mixes consumption and interaction, and it does. However, the map is optimized to be looked at; it's optimized for consumption. Google has designed the tools so that they fade into the background (zoom) or has hidden them entirely. You only discover you can move the map if you notice the mouse cursor changing and then experiment with clicking and dragging.

FIGURE 7.5 Although Google Maps offers a map to look at as well as a map to manipulate, Google's designers have optimized the map for viewing.

So, no matter what, every page on your Web site will fall into one of the above three types. Like Google Maps, Web pages will always be primarily one of the three types, supporting the one, primary task, with supplementary tools for supplementary tasks in a subservient role. There can only be one queen; everybody else is a handmaiden.

Match Discrete Tasks to Discrete Pages

When moving from box to page, you should match a user's tasks with the appropriate page type. For example, if the user's task is to choose an article to read, then you need a navigation page. If you've written scenarios or performed a task analysis, you can go down your list of tasks and define them as navigation, consumption, or interaction tasks.[8]

In Chapter 6, From A to C by Way of B, we wrote a scenario and performed a task analysis on a fictional feature that helps film festival attendees choose movies to watch. It was called the Festival Planner. We'll include the task analysis next so we can show you how to match discrete tasks to discrete pages.

When we left our story in progress, our persona, busy film executive Michael Davies, was reading about the Sundance Film Festival, and noticed the new Festival Planner tool. He decided to give it a try. **Table 7.1** shows the task analysis we derived from the Festival Planner. For each task, we've noted the matching page type: navigation, consumption, or interaction.

Discrete Task	Type of Task
Browse new stories on homepage	Navigation
View new story	Consumption
Browse stories in Sundance category	Navigation
View story in Sundance category	Consumption
View Festival Planner start page	Consumption
Choose director(s)	Interaction
Choose actor(s)	Interaction
Choose genre(s)	Interaction
Select business or pleasure	Interaction
If business, limit to unsigned films?	Interaction
If business, overlap film times?	Interaction
View customized film schedule	Consumption
Email copy to self and assistant	Interaction

TABLE 7.1 Task Analysis for the Festival Planner

We could then assign a single page to each and every task in this analysis (**Table 7.2**).

---

8 See! Those three are already popping up on other things. :-)

Step	Discrete Task	Type of Task	Page
1	Browse new stories on homepage	Navigation	
2	View new story	Consumption	
3	Browse stories in Sundance category	Navigation	
4	View story in Sundance category	Consumption	
5	View Festival Planner instructions and explanation	Consumption	
6	Choose director(s)	Interaction	
7	Choose actor(s)	Interaction	
8	Choose genre(s)	Interaction	
9	Select business of pleasure	Interaction	
10	If business, limit to unsigned films?	Interaction	

Step	Discrete Task	Type of Task	Page
11	If business, overlap film times?	Interaction	
12	Save schedule	Interaction	
13	View customized film schedule	Consumption	
14	Email copy to self and assistant	Interaction	

TABLE 7.2 A Page for Every Task in the Festival Planner

This analysis represents the chain of tasks Michael needs to complete in order to customize his film schedule. We've added a page for every discrete task on Michael's list. That's 14 tasks and 14 pages—for now, anyway. Don't worry; we don't plan to torture Michael by making him go through 14 pages: he's a busy film executive! Stick with us and it'll all come together.

For additional clarity, we color-coded each type of page to highlight where Michael switches from one type of task to another. At the top, you'll notice how Michael switches from navigation (in pale yellow) to consumption tasks (light blue) as he browses for and then chooses articles to read. There's also a broad swath of green where Michael sets options to customize his schedule.

Now that we've broken the tasks down like this, it's easier to imagine the interfaces we should build. The navigation pages will have lists of links. The consumption pages will have blocks of text to be read. The interaction pages will have forms. However, that large swath of green signals an important clue about the page flow: there are six interaction tasks in a row. Do we really want Michael to work his way through a six separate pages to complete a form? Although each page should focus on one discrete task, when you have several similar subtasks, you can sometimes group them together on one page.

Group Like Tasks Together

We always have to balance clarity with efficiency in our design. Each page may be devoted to one primary task, but that task may have subtasks or related tasks that make sense to group together closely. Or sometimes, a task may be too small to really deserve an entire page to itself (or may be a subtask disguised as a task!). For example, the six interaction tasks above (choose director, choose actors, choose genres, choose business or pleasure) could each have their own page, but they could also be grouped on one page as a form. Does "choosing a director" deserve a page? Or is Michael's higher task "give preferences in order to get a customized schedule"?

When deciding how many pages to create for a group of tasks, consider these factors:

- The audience's technical sophistication

- The audience's bandwidth

- The amount of information on a page

- The task the audience is trying to accomplish

- How often the audience will complete the task

In interface design, there are three approaches to grouping interaction tasks: Wizards, Control Panels, and Toolbars.

Wizards: Many boxes, many pages

The Festival Planner task analysis shows six discrete interaction steps. If we make each task a page, this would result in a site with a series of pages that looks like **Figure 7.6**.

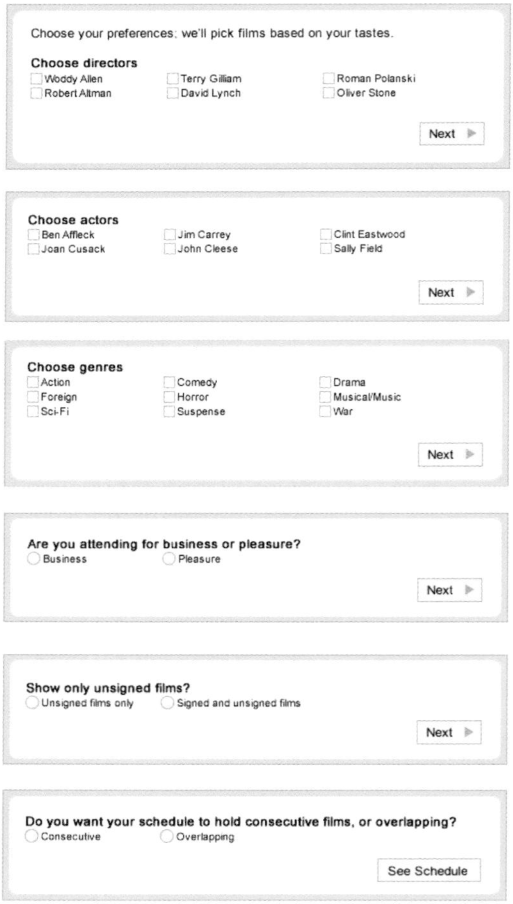

FIGURE 7.6 Each box becomes a page.

In software design, a layout with one-step per page is called a wizard (see **Figure 7.7**). Wizards are used in the following situations:

- When users want to accomplish a goal that has many steps. Wizards are good at making sure you don't miss a step.

- When the steps must be completed in order. Wizards are linear, so it's impossible to complete them any other way.

- When the task is seldom performed. Wizards can seem slow and plodding, so they are best used in tasks you do only once in a while, like setting up a printer.

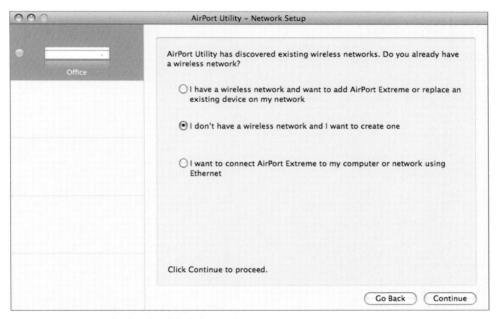

FIGURE 7.7 An example of a wizard in desktop software.

Wizards are a good choice for Web design under all the conditions previously listed, as well as when the following conditions are present:

- The audience is not technically savvy and is likely to be confused by a page with a lot of choices on it. A Web site can have novice users, and a wizard makes complex tasks seem easy.

- Bandwidth is low and downloading a single big page could take forever, or the tasks require several server calls,[9] which would also slow the page's load.

- The task has several steps in it, performed only once a visit, such as checkout.

In applications, wizards are used for one-time situations, such as when a user sets up networking. On your Web site, a wizard is good one-time tasks like registration.

Control panels: Many boxes, one page

A wizard is not the only choice. Just because your task analysis shows several discrete tasks doesn't mean you don't have other choices. You could also combine all the questions in the Festival Planner onto one page, which would make the section look more like **Figure 7.8** and **Table 7.3**.

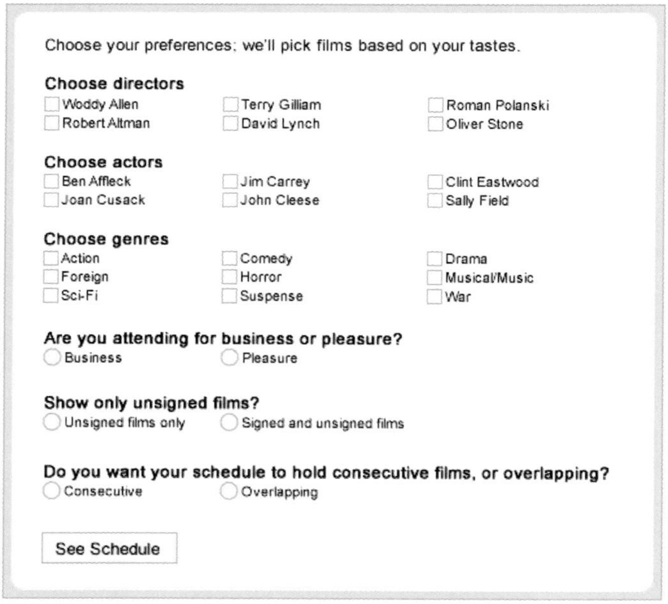

Choose your preferences; we'll pick films based on your tastes.

Choose directors
☐ Woddy Allen   ☐ Terry Gilliam   ☐ Roman Polanski
☐ Robert Altman   ☐ David Lynch   ☐ Oliver Stone

Choose actors
☐ Ben Affleck   ☐ Jim Carrey   ☐ Clint Eastwood
☐ Joan Cusack   ☐ John Cleese   ☐ Sally Field

Choose genres
☐ Action   ☐ Comedy   ☐ Drama
☐ Foreign   ☐ Horror   ☐ Musical/Music
☐ Sci-Fi   ☐ Suspense   ☐ War

Are you attending for business or pleasure?
○ Business   ○ Pleasure

Show only unsigned films?
○ Unsigned films only   ○ Signed and unsigned films

Do you want your schedule to hold consecutive films, or overlapping?
○ Consecutive   ○ Overlapping

[See Schedule]

FIGURE 7.8 All questions are combined on one page.

---

9 This is an example of why getting your engineer on board during design is important. When a user requests a page, the browser requests the page's data from the server hosting the page. This takes a bit of time. Sometimes the browser has to ask for several bits of data, such as HTML and images, and sometimes the browser has to request data from more than one server, which takes even more time. It may prove useful to break up all those requests across several pages so that each page loads quickly. Your engineer can help you determine which design will result in a noticeably speedier page.

Step	Discrete Task	Type of Task	Page
4	View story in Sundance category	Consumption	
5	View Festival Planner instructions and explanation	Consumption	
6	Choose director(s) Choose actor(s) Choose genre(s) Select business or pleasure If business, limit to unsigned films? If business, overlap film times? Save schedule	Interaction	
7	View customized film schedule	Consumption	
8	Email copy to self and assistant	Interaction	

TABLE 7.3 All Interaction Tasks on One Page

A complex layout with many steps on one page is called a control panel. **Figure 7.9** shows its software progenitor. Control panels are good when wizards are not—when the audience is technically savvy and on a fast download. Control panels are also a good choice when the following conditions are met:

- The application is easy to understand, and the choices are straightforward.

- The elements gain context by being placed next to each other.

- The interface is used often enough that the audience will appreciate the convenience of a single page.

Control panels are often used in situations in which occasional tweaking is required, such as configuring a program. If you have several related tasks, you may be able to group them on one page as a control panel. Then the group of tasks becomes one task.

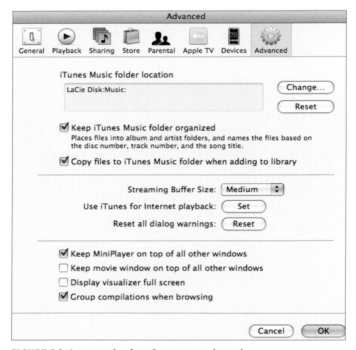

FIGURE 7.9 An example of a software control panel.

Toolbars: When the page isn't enough

There is a third configuration for your interactive elements. Toolbars keep the tools for interaction conveniently close to the workspace they affect. This is useful when frequent tweaking is required, such as when you are writing or drawing. Imagine how painful it would be if you had to go to a different page every time you wanted to go from an eraser to a pencil!

Use toolbars when

- Many steps are in the task, and the steps can be done in any order.

- Steps need to be undone and redone, as well as just plain done.

- The proximity of tools to the workspace is important for the task.

- The user's technology can support the implementation (um, excuse me Ms. Engineer, I have another question for you…).

Although toolbars are common in software, they are not widely used in Web design, mostly because of the technical limitations of older browsers. More and more toolbars are being used, though, as more applications come to the Web and browsers become more sophisticated (see **Figure 7.10**).

If you have a group of tasks that can be accomplished in any order at any time, it may make sense to group them together in a toolbar.

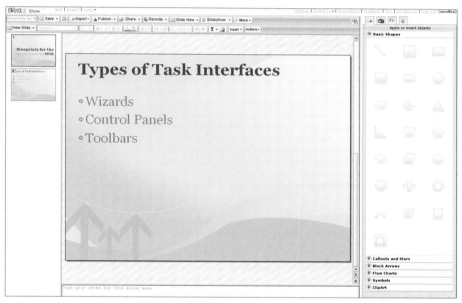

FIGURE 7.10 Zoho's Show, a Web-based presentation creator, uses several toolbars to frame the workspace. You hardly have to interrupt your creative process to change a font or insert an image.

When a box doesn't need a page

You have to make similar choices when you design pages for your content organization. Just because you have a category doesn't mean it should be a page. Some levels of a category only exist to provide an explanation of organizational logic. For example, in faceted classification, you will probably want to label each facet. But should each label be a page?

In our prior task analysis, Michael browses articles related to the Sundance Film Festival. In our example, we created a separate page for the Sundance category, but we didn't have to do so. We could have grouped Sundance articles together on the homepage. It would have been easy for Michael to find them, but we wouldn't need a separate page. This change reduces the number of pages we need from four to three (**Table 7.4**).

Step	Discrete Task	Type of Task	Page
1	Browse new stories on homepage	Navigation	
2	View new story	Consumption	
3 (same page as step 1)	Browse stories in Sundance category on homepage		
4 (same page as step 2)	View story from Sundance category	Consumption	

TABLE 7.4 Grouping Sundance Pages on the Homepage

Epicurious takes this approach with their facets. In **Figure 7.11,** we can see that Epicurious allows customers to browse recipes by choosing facets that include cuisine, meal, and type of dish. These facet labels act as dividers on the browse page, provide context to the list items, and make it easier to scan. However useful they are to navigation, Epicurious has no reason to dedicate a page to each divider. You can select Greek to see recipes for Greek food, but you can't select cuisine to see a list of available cuisines.

The important thing to keep in mind when deciding which pages should exist is that each page should have a purpose. Ask yourself, "What is this page doing?" and if you don't have a good answer, get rid of it. Once you know what pages do and don't exist you definitely have to keep track. You can keep a simple list of all the pages on the site, or you can document both the pages and the site structure in a site map.

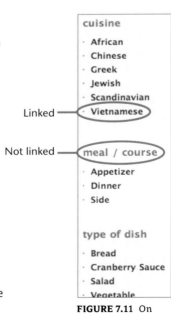

FIGURE 7.11 On Epicurious's browse page, only the actual facets are links. The facet name is only used to give users more context.

Document Site Structure with a Site Map

The site map documents the pages in a Web site.[10] It also includes the relationship of the pages to each other, the interaction between pages, and a number of other facts that change from project to project, potentially including which pages have templates, which pages are dynamic, and which pages are user created. This sounds like a lot to deal with, but you can communicate all of this information with a few boxes and some arrows.

When documenting how information is organized, concentrate on presenting the hierarchy and documenting which pages will exist and where. Show each section of your Web site and any sub-pages inside each section. Also note what other information you want to present, such as the following areas:

- **Access:** Some sites have areas that users must register and/or pay to access as well as areas that are open to the general public.

- **New content vs. archived:** This can be important for magazine sites.

- **Organized by users vs. organized by site owners:** For sites that depend on user-generated content, like YouTube (video), Flickr (photos), or Delicious (bookmarks).

- **Static vs. dynamic:** Some content pages such as articles have content that doesn't change, while other pages change based on user interaction such as "My" homepages (My Yahoo!, My MSN, and so on).

As ever, sketch it on paper first, refine it on the computer second.

Site map layout

Site maps can come in several shapes. The design depends on your project's needs and your personal inclination as a designer. When you evaluate which design to go with, consider whether your map will include the following characteristics:

- **Shallow or deep:** Shallow means that you'll have lots of items at the same level. If everything on your site is only one click from the homepage, you have a shallow organization scheme. Deep means that you'll have levels and sub-levels and sub-sub-levels. If you have items that are eight clicks from the homepage, you might have a deep organization scheme.

---

10 People will throw around the term "site map" quite a bit, often with different meanings. A site map can be the page of links that Google requires you to create on your site to index lots of content. It can also refer to a page on your site that provides access to all pages or all main sections. Here we're talking about a document that illustrates how your site is organized.

- **Large or small:** Few pages on your site (small) means that you can go with simple, very clear layouts, such as the tree layout. If you have many sections and pages (large), that means you'll have to think carefully about how to diagram in order to make the relationships clear.

Some possible site map layout formats include the following:

- **The tree map:** It is great for showing hierarchy; however, it's easy to run out of horizontal space. You can combine it with the comb (see the following item) to avoid this.

- **The comb map:** You'll find this useful in a long work area (most electronic documents are better at going tall rather than wide), with an organization scheme that is deep rather than shallow.

- **The star map:** This is useful when the hierarchy is not strict and when organization is shallower than deep. But it can be difficult to manage if the organization is deep, and it can get a bit messy. It is important to draw the star map out carefully and for each level of item have a unique look (size is most commonly used) to distinguish hierarchy, because it isn't as scannable as a tree.

- **The tab map:** This map is good when items are not so much hierarchical as grouped by similarities. It allows the architect to indicate groupings without feeling the need to create overview pages. The tree map seems to demand that each level of hierarchy has a dedicated page; the tabs group like items without indicating a page.

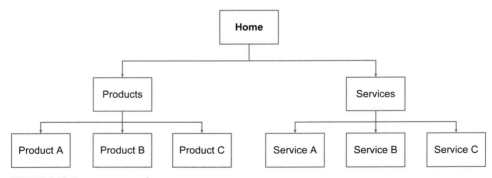

FIGURE 7.12 Tree map example.

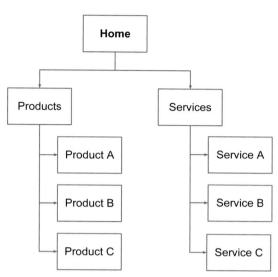

FIGURE 7.13 Comb map example.

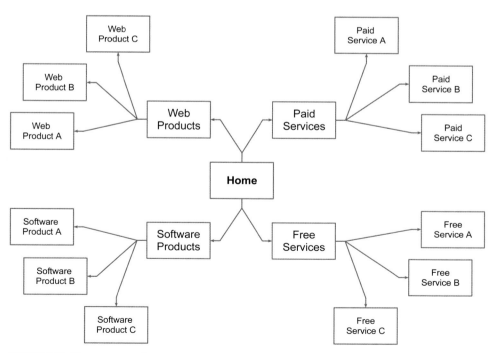

FIGURE 7.14 Star map example.

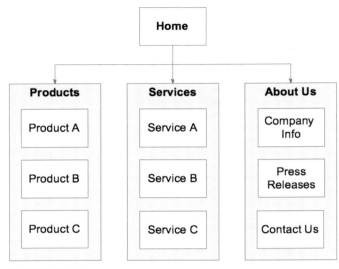

FIGURE 7.15 Tab map example.

Site map vocabulary

In addition to a form for your site map, you'll need a vocabulary for all the objects in it. It should be easy to determine at a glance what is what in your map. For example, you may want to indicate the difference between a Web page, a set of similar pages (such as a section of press releases), or a file that is not a Web page (such as a PowerPoint presentation). You also may want to note decision points, registration areas, and places for user input.

Our number one bit of advice to you on making the site map is this: Don't reinvent the wheel. Buy a book on flowcharting, use an existing set of tools provided with software such as Visio or Inspiration, and take a look at what others in the field have done before you. UML is a very advanced language for modeling interactions. Jesse James Garrett has created a much more accessible one called the "Visual Vocabulary" that is easy to use for whiteboarding as well as formal documentation. It can be found at http://www.jjg.net/ia/visvocab/.

Following is the minimum vocabulary we use in a site map:[11]

- **Page and page stack:** A page is a page. A page stack is a set of pages that are similar enough in formatting to be the same. Imagine, for example, a set of press releases, articles, and book reviews.

---

11 These shapes are used in most flowcharting vocabularies, including the Visual Vocabulary.

- **File and file stack:** As we said, PowerPoint documents are one example of files that you might find online that are not Web pages. Other examples are downloads such as applications, drivers, games, videos and MP3's, or print-friendly documents such as Word documents or PDF manuals.

- **Decision:** This occurs anytime the system has to make a decision. Member or non-member and logged in or not logged in are common decision points for a restricted Web site.

- **Continued:** Keep your site map tidy and readable by diagramming subsections and subprocesses on a second page.

- **Area and conditional area:** Useful for grouping like items (as seen in the tab layout). Conditional is useful for demarcating restricted areas, such as those where login is required.

- **Connectors:** What good is a box without an arrow? Arrows indicate one-way movement through pages. This is usually a step-by-step process, such as when a user is registering or checking out. No arrowhead or double arrowheads (this varies among flowchart languages) indicate bi-directional movement, such as between pages.

- **E-mail:** We find it useful to remind team members that the homepage is not the only way people are arriving at the site. If a site has a newsletter, this icon is well worth using.

Site maps vary from architect to architect and from project to project. As you create your own, ask yourself these questions:

- Do I know what is a page and what isn't?

- Can I understand how a user might move through the Web site?

- Do I understand the organization or interaction being diagrammed?

And always, always ask yourself

- How would I do this better?

Once you've finished your site map, you should have a clear view of all your pages. When you map tasks to pages, you're creating the links for your chain, and when you create a Site Map, you're drawing a picture of the entire chain. You've made sure that each page helps the user do what they came to do. However, if you want to move from useful to indispensable, each page also needs to make the next step accessible. It's time to connect all the links in the chain.

Make the Next Step Accessible

When you look at the task analysis for the Festival Planner, it's easy to spot the next step for every task. For example, when you save and view your customized schedule, the next step is to email yourself a copy. When you design the schedule page, you should do these two things:

1. Focus on displaying the user's customized film schedule.

2. Help users easily email a copy of the schedule to someone.

A sketch of this page shows how you can balance the current task with the next step (see **Figure 7.16**). The film schedule occupies the majority of the page, and a link to Email your schedule is easy to find in the sidebar on the right.

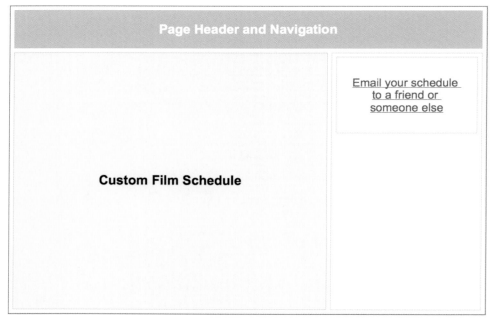

FIGURE 7.16 In this sketch of the View Schedule page, we give users access to the next step by placing it in the sidebar.

In this example, the next step is clear. And, in Michael's scenario, there's only one next step. But what if there's more than one next step? What if Michael wants to—gasp—change what we choose for him?

Manage Multiple Next Steps

Flickr is a Web site where users can post and share photos. Flickr has created a consumption page for each photo that's optimized for viewing. Instead of one next step, Flickr makes several next steps available (**Figure 7.17**):

- A user can view the next photo in the set.
- A user can browse photos that have the same tag or add tags.
- A user can view and edit the photo's metadata.
- A user can read comments or add his own.

And we haven't even looked at the toolbar above each photo that lets users perform numerous other next steps!

Despite the intense complexity of all these tasks, Flickr has emphasized the main task—viewing the photo—and kept the illusion of simplicity.

FIGURE 7.17 Flickr optimizes this page for viewing the photo, but it makes several next steps available.

Most pages on the Web accommodate multiple next steps. There are many different users with many different goals, so pages attempt to make an appropriate next step available to every user. However, you can't design a page to please everyone. You must prioritize your next steps based on three criteria:

1. How many users will it help?

2. How often will it happen?

3. How important—to users or the business—is this next step?

Using Flickr's photo page, we might determine that we have several possible next steps (**Table 7.5**):

Next Step	How many users?	How often?	How important?
View next photo	Many	Frequently	Very important
Browse photos with same tag	Few	Occasionally	Less important
View photo metadata	Few	Rarely	Less important
Read or add comments	Some	Frequently	Very important

TABLE 7.5 Possible Next Steps

By evaluating how many people are affected, how often, and how important each task is, we can prioritize our four next steps:

1. View next photo.

2. Read or add comments.

3. Browse photos with same tag.

4. View photo metadata.

By prioritizing the next steps, the page has a greater chance of giving your users the next step they need or expect. You can then determine a page layout that facilitates the user's tasks.

Zone Your Page for Interaction

In a city, you zone part of the town for business, part for residential. On a Web page, you zone part of the page for navigation, part for advertisement, part for content. In an application, you may zone an area for a toolbar; on a video player, you may zone an area for the controls.

This is so typical that now users will look only in a given zone for a desired control and look no further. In a recent study by Michael Bernard & Ashwin Sheshadri,[12] it was found that the "back to homepage" link was expected to be in the upper-left corner almost exclusively, and shopping carts to be in the upper-right corner. The opposite effect is prevalent as well—users expect advertisement to be in the right-hand column, so useful links on the right-hand side of the page run the danger of being ignored entirely. As you begin your page layout, you may find it useful to create templates for your page types, with the zones marked clearly as a reference as you place your interface objects in them.

In **Figure 7.18**, we've outlined the clear zones for each user need:

- The global navigation at top and bottom, which includes home links, account access, and the core navigation bar itself.

- The user navigation area, where you can flip through your content by the main chronological organization, via "sets" you have created, or by the tags you've assigned to the photo.

- The photo itself, with its associated tools, description, and content.

- The metadata, set off in a corner where it is accessible, but not intrusive.

Each zone holds everything related to the zone's core purpose, and the related tools are easily accessed.

Breaking down the modules

Once you've identified your zones, you can figure out which links, text, and functionality needs to be there. You can also determine the relationships between the different elements. When you find several links are very closely associated in purpose, you can form them into a module.

On Flickr, there are quite a few modules. One obvious one you may have already picked out is the photo toolbar.

This module allows you to manipulate your photo, annotating, sharing, printing, or even altering it. These tools are all links that kick off an interaction with the photo, so they were assembled into one module.

---

12 http://psychology.wichita.edu/surl/usabilitynews/62/web_object_international.asp

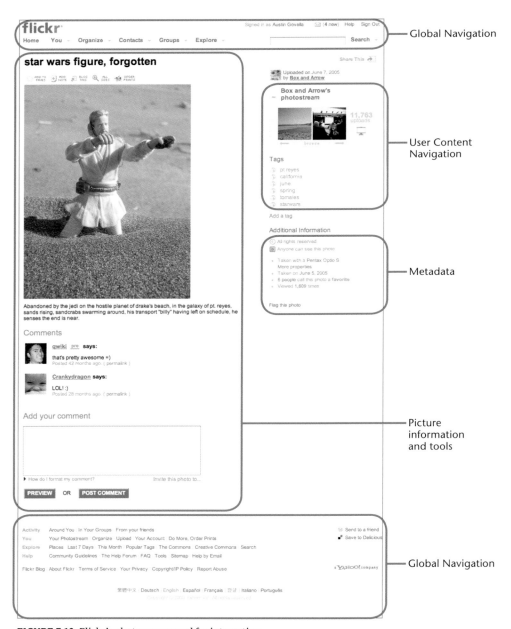

FIGURE 7.18 Flickr's photo page zoned for interaction.

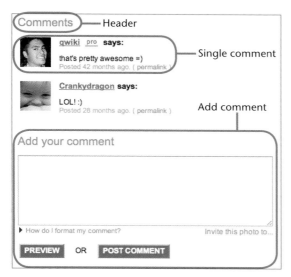

A less obvious module is the commenting module (**Figure 7.19**). Here we see the commenting functionality is supported by a module that groups related functionality, including the header for the module, which sets expectations about which related elements can be found here—comments and the ability to add your own comment.

FIGURE 7.19 The Flickr comment module, composed of the header "Comments," assorted commentary, and of course, the ability for you to dive into the fray.

Interestingly, there is a module within the comments module: the single comment module (**Figure 7.20**).

The single comment module is also built of related functionality, the related elements that make up the display and functionality of a single user comment:

- the user name and avatar that provide attribution
- the content of the comment
- the time stamp
- the related tools—a permalink to a specific comment and the ability for the photo-owner to remove a single bad comment.

By grouping these items tightly in the module, the designer has created a system that can be used everywhere on the site. Take a look at this discussion module in **Figure 7.21**; it closely resembles the comment module. We see the same basic elements: the post owner's name and avatar, the content, the timestamp, and the management tools.

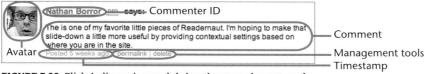

FIGURE 7.20 Flickr's discussion module has the same elements and design as Flickr's single comment module.

FIGURE 7.21 Flickr's discussion module reuses the same basic structure of the comment module, including avatar, commentar ID, content, timestamp and management tools.

So why do we care if a module is reusable? Because it saves money while making everyone's life easier. It's easier for the designer to extend an existing system than it is to create a system from scratch. It's also easier for an engineer to reuse code, and it's easier for the users when everything is where they expect it to be.

The page holds the content, the zones hold related content, and modules hold even more closely related content. Like magnets, everything is closer and closer to its like items. The properly zoned page provides key information about tasks and how they're related to one another, and you will rely on this information when designing the interface.

Document Your Page with Wireframes

After you've chosen your pages and arranged everything on them, you can communicate the design with a wireframe. A wireframe (or page schematic, as it is sometimes called) is a basic outline of an individual page, drawn to indicate the elements of a page, their relationships, and their relative importance. It's much like the wireframe a sculptor will make before adding clay, as it gives shape and provides support.

Wireframes serve two functions when designing a Web site. First, they make an abstract mental picture of a page more concrete. Everyone on a team has a picture in his head of what the Web site will look like, but oddly enough, no two people have the same picture. The wireframe starts the team down the path to a shared vision; it opens up conversation around how the navigation scheme will play out, which tools are really needed for the user's tasks and what the most critical elements of the page are. Imagine having that conversation after your graphic designer had spent three days working on the design? A wireframe gets you to concrete discussions quickly, and since it's simple enough to do on a whiteboard, it's a conversation piece.

Later, wireframes work as documentation devices. In some places, the information architecture is completed separately from design or development. In these situations, a wireframe has to capture all of the decisions you've made with the team for the design and information architecture. And it has to capture them in a way that everyone else downstream will understand. For example, a designer might need only a rough layout, but developers need functionality and error conditions. And poor QA. They need you to document every minute detail since typically they come in so late in the process they have no idea what your site is supposed to do.

How to make a wireframe in 30 seconds

1. Start with a box in the middle of your sheet of paper.

2. Add global elements. (You can handle this with a template in many programs.)

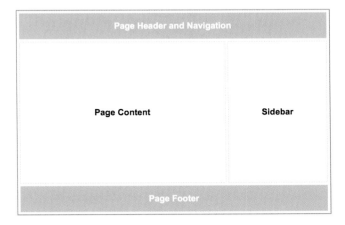

3. Add unique elements to that page. Indicate the following:

    ● Order of importance

    ● Which are dynamic (if any)

    ● Text and GUI type

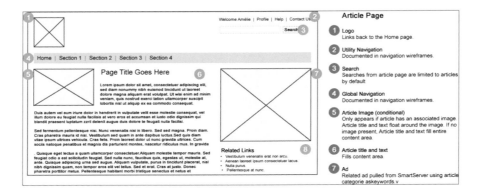

4. Finally—notate, notate, notate. Pretend that the document will have to live without your looking over the viewer's shoulder. Pretend 10 minutes later that you will have no idea why you made the decisions you made. Obvious decisions become obscure over time.

These days, many sites are dynamic, but you can't ever be sure which content will be available on which page. For each element in your wireframe, it's important to consider several questions:

- **Where does the content come from?** If you have a list of related articles, specify how they're related. Are they the most viewed? Most viewed from that section?

- **What is the nature of the content?** Does it vary greatly in length, size, language, and type?

- **Is the element required or optional?** What happens if the element doesn't appear on that page? Does the layout change?

- **Is the element conditional?** Does it vary based on other factors? For example, do administrators see additional links? What happens if an article doesn't have an associated image? What if it does?

- **What's the default or expected state?** Ideally, what's supposed to happen on the page.

- **What are the alternate or error states?** How does the design change when things don't go right?

If you are using your wireframes as an archival documentation tool, you may want to go back and update them so that they reflect the final decisions—so that you can remember why certain decisions were made—and then update them. Alternatively, you can create a style guide that documents both design decisions and architecture decisions and explains how to apply them going forward.

In **Figure 7.22**, we see late-stage wireframes that can be used in conjunction with the final design and a functional spec by the technology team to direct their build of the Web site. These are sometimes called high-fidelity wireframes. Their clearly delineated layout, position, and visual design make communication very clear. They also take longer to produce.

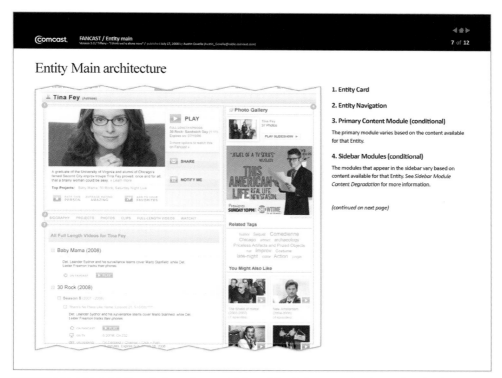

FIGURE 7.22 A high-fidelity wireframe is one with lots of detail that more closely matches the visual design of a site.

In contrast, low-fidelity wireframes are very fast to make. **Figure 7.23** shows a low-fidelity version of the previous high-fidelity wireframe. This wireframe was used during a meeting to facilitate discussion with a product manager, designer, and developer. You can see the different levels of detail between the two. The high-fidelity wireframe was used to document; the low-fidelity wireframe was used to help the team communicate.

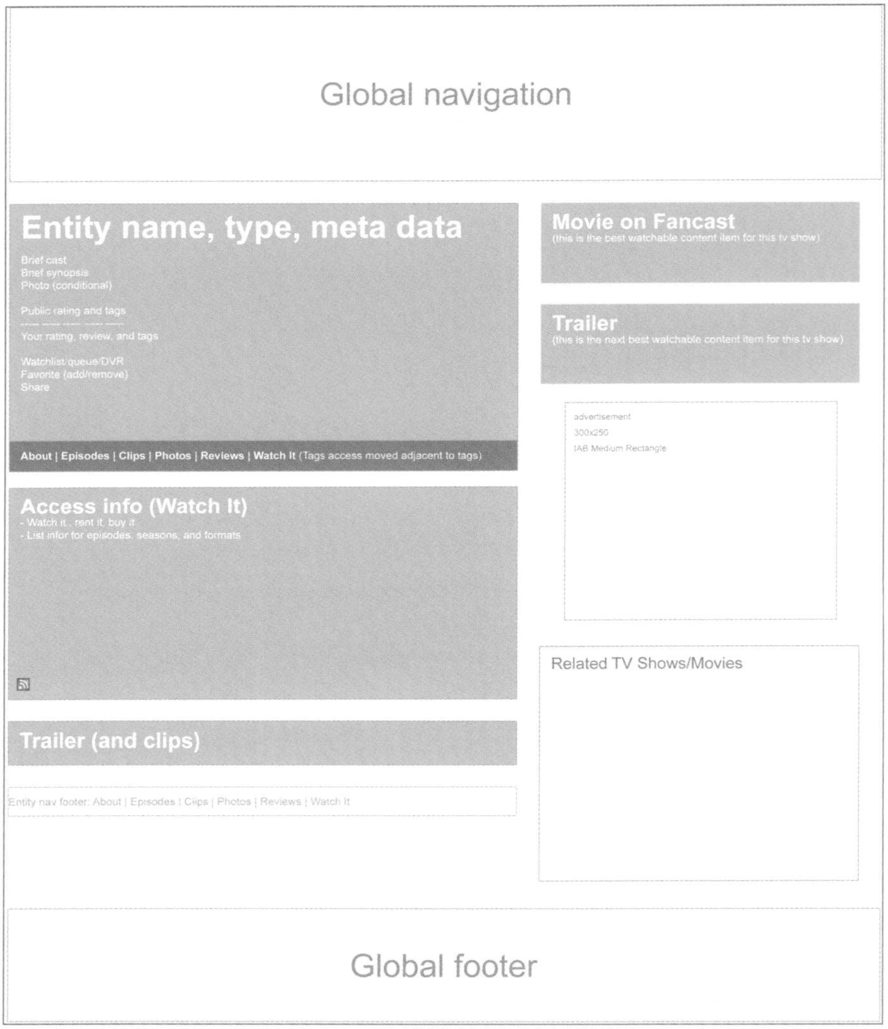

FIGURE 7.23 A low-fidelity wireframe has less detail, but it is faster and easier to produce.

The Trouble with Wireframes

The wireframe is probably the most controversial of the IA deliverables. This is because it is the bridge between design and architecture and between planning and executing. It's where thinking becomes tangible.

The Trouble with Wireframes *(continued)*

When the information architect and the visual designer is the same person playing two roles, there is rarely any conflict (except in those rare cases of split personality). However, when there are two separate people playing these roles, this deliverable can bring the two to blows.

When the information architect and the designer are two people as well as two roles, it's best to make the wireframe a collaborative effort.

Have the visual designer create the wireframe. When the site map and flows are completed, the information architect and designer can brainstorm over a whiteboard on how the pages should work.

Have the information architect walk through the wireframe with the designer after it is created, but before it is finalized. Sometimes thinking through the site map just isn't possible without also considering how the pages will work. In this case, make sure that you indicated in the documentation why you did what you did. Then walk through your wireframes with the designer and ask for ideas on alternative ways to solve those same problems. Note the ideas on the wireframe documentation.

Create a wireframe that doesn't dictate layout. Often called page-description diagrams,[7] this can be a text list of potential pages and page elements, or you can use a design similar to a site map, indicating page elements and their relationship rather than pages.

Work collaboratively and respectfully, and conflicts should remain in the creative realm and not degrade into turf wars.

------

7 Invented by the brilliant Dan Brown. Check out his book, *Communicating Design,* for deep dives into creating excellent deliverables.

The Page Is Important

On the Web, the "page" is a fundamental organizing principle. When designing your site, every page must serve its purpose, as well as supporting all the related goals. Zone the page to give space to the main goal and keep the related activities available yet manageable. Use reusable modules in order to simplify both creation and understanding of the interface. And document everything so that all your crazy ideas can be vetted by your entire team. The page is the interface between the user and the company, and getting it right can be the difference between that person wanting to have anything to do with your company ever again...or not. Take your time, and put your best (inter)face forward.

> "The rules of naviga-
> tion never navigated
> a ship. The rules of
> architecture never
> built a house."
> —Thomas Reid

8

The Tao of
Navigation

*In which we figure out
how to get people to all
that nice content.*

Navigation appears to be one of the easiest and most obvious things about the Web. It's all those links that take you to other pages. Yet how many times do you click a link and get a bad surprise? Perhaps you arrive somewhere you didn't expect, or that new page demands you register…or even installs software and reboots your computer! Navigation seems simple, but it's the most subtle and complex part of the interface. The job of navigation is to clearly state where a user will travel in the information architecture. You may start off simply naming a link, but as you design your navigation you end up representing everything you've done so far in two inches of screen space.

And if users can't navigate to where they need to go, then your Web site will fail.

So, we're going to start with the most obvious bits, and then we'll try to sort out some of the trickier stuff. Lucky for us, the obvious bits also happen to be the most important: structural navigation— the global and local navigation that lets your users traverse your carefully crafted IA. However, before we jump into global and local navigation, we must remember we're helping users find things.

Four Ways Users Seek Information

Users come to your site looking for information. When they see your navigation system, your visitors will use it to help them find content to consume or a task to complete. Knowing what drives them, you can design a navigation system that helps your visitors find what they're looking for. Donna Spencer identified four ways users look for information.[1]

---

1 "Four Modes of Seeking Information and How to Design for Them" by Donna Spencer on 2006/03/14 http://www.boxesandarrows.com/view/ four_modes_of_seeking_information_and_how_to_design_for_the

Known-item search

Often, when people know exactly what they are looking for and what it's called, they'll use search. But not always: sometimes sites don't have search, sometimes the search is badly implemented and sometimes people would just rather browse. Your navigation has to work with search to get people where they know they want to go.

Exploratory seeking

This happens when users may have a need, but aren't certain what will fulfill it. For example, "I'm looking for a new digital camera," or, "I need to know more about typography." People will recognize an answer to their question, but won't know if they've actually found the right answer. For example, if you're looking for a digital camera, you may find one that does what you want, but you'll never know whether or not there's a camera out there that's exactly what you're looking for.

Don't know what I need to know

Sometimes people don't know what they need to know. This happens in a few scenarios. For example, a fellow looking for a new digital camera will discover that before he buys one, he has to figure out megapixels, flash memory, and optical zoom. Or a woman wanting to buy a new house may discover she needs to better understand what regulations exist in her city and state. They're looking for one thing, but discover they really need to know about something else.

Re-finding

People may want to go back to things they discovered in the past. We often forget this in our design practices, figuring the browser's bookmark/favorite functionality will cover it. But why leave things to chance?[2]

Each information-seeking behavior relies on specific navigational tools to succeed. There are three of them.

Three Types of Navigation

There are three types of navigation, each defined by where it takes the user (see **Figure 8.1**). Structural navigation helps users navigate the organizational structure of the Web site. Associative navigation allows users to jump to related information, and utility navigation catches anything important the user needs access to that structural and associative miss.

---

2 Refinding is best supported by account tools like bookmarks, history, and share this (people like to email things to themselves). So we aren't covering refinding much here, except to remind you to change the color of visited links.

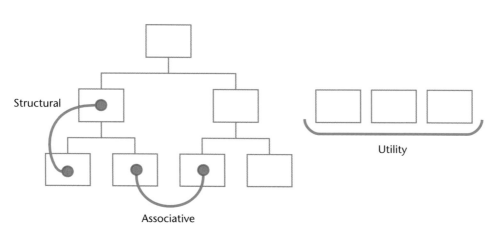

FIGURE 8.1 The three primary types of navigation, adapted from Fiorito and Dalton's model, after James Kalbach.[3]

Structural navigation

Structural navigation represents your content hierarchy and tends to take the form of global and local navigation. Global navigation allows easy access to the most important content hubs—typically, your Web site's top level of categories. Local navigation takes you to the levels of the hierarchy that are near to where you currently are in the site. This is an interface representation of your information architecture. It's particularly useful for known-item and exploratory seeking, and sometimes can help shape users who "don't know what they need to know."

Associative navigation

Associative navigation connects a page with other pages that hold similar content. This answers the user's questions about "What next?" "How do I?" and, "What else have you got?" Associative navigation is particularly good for exploratory seeking and helps users uncover what they "don't know" but should.

Utility navigation

Utility navigation connects pages and features that help visitors use the site itself. This includes features like sign-in and access to user information (profiles or credit card information). This is all the stuff that lies outside the main content organization, yet is critical to the site's functioning.

---

3 See the presentation from David Fiorito and Richard Dalton from the 2004 IA Summit (a conference you should sign up for today. At this writing, it is the single best conference on IA in the world). http://iasummit.org/2004/finalpapers/FioritoDalton_Handout_or__final__paper.ppt

Table 8.1 shows how the three types of navigation support the four information-seeking behaviors.

	Known item	Exploatory seeking	Don't know	Re-finding
Structural navigation	X	X	X	
Associative navigation		X	X	
Utility navigation				X

TABLE 8.1 Three Types of Navigation Supporting Information-Seeking Behaviors

Now we'll explore each type of navigation in depth. When people think about navigation, they usually think about the structural—the global and local navigation—so we'll start there.

Global Navigation

You're probably already familiar with how global navigation works and what it looks like. On a lot of sites, it's the navigation bar or set of links that you see at the top of a Web page. We'll use the Charles Schwab homepage as an example (**Figure 8.2**). It has six links that appear at the top of every page:

- Welcome to Schwab

- Investment Products

- Research & Strategies

- Advice & Retirement

- Active Trading

- Banking & Lending

FIGURE 8.2 The Charles Schwab homepage includes a global navigation bar at the top.

When you categorized your content and chose organization systems, you probably had some items that were more valuable to the users and the business. If you created a hierarchical organization system (like with your site map), you also have some top-level categories. These top-level categories are your global navigation. At Schwab, you can see its top-level categories in global navigation (**Figure 8.3**).

FIGURE 8.3 Schwab's top-level categories

Let's say you find yourself exploring the intricacies of your city government in the "Local" section of your newspaper and the politicians are getting you down. It's simple to fling that section away and pick up the "Lifestyle" section to read the comics. On the Web, a business wants to allow you the same opportunity to scratch whatever random itch you come up with without resorting to Google and possibly using someone else's Web site. So global navigation needs to appear on every page of a Web site. Every page. (Well, almost every page. We'll go over exceptions a little later.) Global navigation gives users access to anywhere else on the site, no matter where they currently are.

Global navigation has a second, less obvious but perhaps more important, function: it tells you what the site is all about and what you should use it for. Take a look at the global navigation for two very different sites, The New Yorker and Sports Illustrated.

The New Yorker	Reporting & Essays, Arts & Culture, Humor, Fiction & Poetry, The Talk of the Town, Online Only, Subscribe, About Us, Archive, Store
Sports Illustrated	Extra Mustard, On Campus, Fannnation, SI Vault, Fantasy, Dan Patrick, Swimsuit, SI Photos, SI Kids, Video, Takkle
	NFL, College Football, MLB, NBA, College Basketball, Golf, NHL, Racing, MNA & Boxing, Soccer, high School, Tennis, More Sports, Sportsman

It doesn't matter if it's The New Yorker or Sports Illustrated, each global navigation bar tells you what the site thinks you might want, what the site is all about, and it does it in the language of the company's brand.[4] Formal, informal, comprehensive, focused,

---

4 You may recall we said you are not supposed to get cute in your navigation labels. Sports Illustrated has chosen to use the language of the insider: tons of jokes and slang. Someone who has never read Sports Illustrated could never figure out where to get baseball scores. But only Sports Illustrated's IA's themselves can tell us if that is a bad choice—perhaps magazine subscribers are all that matter. That said, your humble authors would recommend emulating the New Yorker in naming choices.

biased, unbiased…the items you choose for your global navigation, and how you represent them, tell the users what to expect. They may never use the global navigation, preferring to use inline links, yet the global navigation will always be how they think of you.

Where does it live?

Often, designers place the global navigation at the top of the page because that allows them to focus the entire rest of the page on the content. Charles Schwab does this. Of course, horizontal navigation has its drawbacks. Vertical space on a Web page can increase forever, but there's a limited amount of horizontal space. Comcast.net shows what can happen when you fill your horizontal space (**Figure 8.4**). The designers added a drop-down menu under More+ to give visitors access to the rest of their content.

FIGURE 8.4 Comcast.net has more options than it can fit in its navigation bar, so the designers added a drop-down menu under More+ to give visitors access to everything else.

To counter the limited horizontal space, sometimes the global navigation will live somewhere else. At E*Trade's Web site, they've placed the global navigation on the left (**Figure 8.5**). Even though it's on the left, it's still global navigation because those nine links appear on every page of the site.

FIGURE 8.5 The E*Trade homepage shows global navigation on the left side of the page.

Designers use vertical global navigation less often because it limits the available space for both local navigation and page content. But it's a dance. We'll talk about how much local navigation you need in a little bit.

Overall, it doesn't matter exactly where your global navigation lives.[5] The essential point is that it appears on every page of your site.

Local Navigation

Back at the Charles Schwab Web site, if you click the link for Research & Strategies, you'll jump to the Research & Strategies section of the Web site, and when you do, Charles Schwab adds another navigation bar in addition to the global navigation (**Figure 8.6**). Those seven additional links—Markets, Stocks, Mutual Funds, ETFs, Bonds & Fixed Income, Market Insight, and Portfolio Management—those are local navigation. They're relevant only to the Research & Strategies section and they appear on every page in *that section of the site*. In that way, local navigation is kind of like global navigation, but just for certain sections.

FIGURE 8.6 Charles Schwab's local navigation.

This local navigation helps users in two important ways. First, it aids users involved in exploratory seeking tasks. That is, they know they need something, but they're not sure what. After choosing a global navigation link, local navigation helps users browse to more specific topics until they find what they need. For users who don't know what they need to know, local navigation provides a list of related topics that might be important. For example, let's say you're looking at Schwab's page on mutual funds. Perhaps you're really looking for information on how to manage your portfolio. In Schwab's Research & Strategies section, Portfolio Management is right there in the local navigation.

---

5 Do you remember the Audi Web site from Chapter 1, First Principles, where they put the global navigation on the right? Some crazy kids even put the global navigation on the bottom! http://www.webword.com/reports/sitemap.html

Local navigation is also referred to as section navigation because it provides a set of links that help users find content in a specific section. If you were looking at a site map (**Figure 8.7**), you'd diagram the sub-categories underneath the Research & Strategies page.

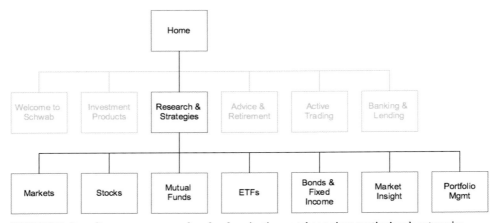

FIGURE 8.7 On a site map, you can see how local navigation matches a given section's sub-categories.

Throughout the book, we've seen several examples where the global and local navigation live in a horizontal bar at the top of the page. Sometimes, local navigation will leave the top of the page to live somewhere else. In **Figure 8.8**, we're looking at the Sapient Interactive Web site. We're in the Services section, where the local navigation is in the middle of the page. At the Web site for the Acumen Fund, the local navigation appears on the right (**Figure 8.9**).

With local navigation, you only need to provide links to other pages in that same section. Local navigation is a way to move within subsections of a Web site. In a complex categorization, users will want to move from category to subcategory and back again. A local navigation system is designed to allow users to navigate easily through categories.

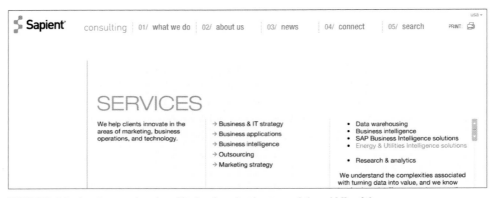

FIGURE 8.8 Sapient Interactive placed its local navigation toward the middle of the page.

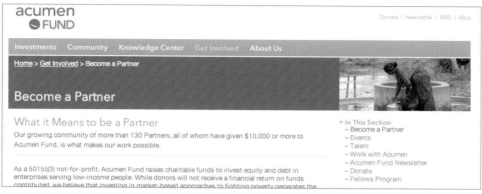

FIGURE 8.9 The Acumen Fund placed their local navigation on the right side.

For example, back on the Charles Schwab site, when a user selects Research & Strategies, the local navigation displays several related links (**Figure 8.10**).

- Markets
- Stocks
- Mutual Funds
- ETFs, et al.

Those are all sub-categories of the main category, Research & Strategies.

FIGURE 8.10 Charles Schwab's local navigation.

Where does it live?

Local navigation often appears "below" the global navigation. This reinforces how your content is organized: conceptually, a category has sub-categories below it. This also places the most relevant links closest to where the user needs them. When a user visits a page on your site, he spends his time staring at the content of the page, almost totally ignoring your navigation. If the page he's looking at does not have what he's looking for, the local navigation is usually laid out in closer proximity to the page content than the global navigation. When the user looks for somewhere else to go, the local navigation is the navigation he looks for first.

Let's say you wanted to know when you could register for online classes at the University of Houston. You might navigate to the When can I register? page on the Distance Education Web site (**Figure 8.11**). After glancing over the page, you decide you're really looking for details about what's involved with the process. The local navigation on the left collects several links related to registration. Maybe Before you register is what you're looking for? It's definitely closer to the content you're looking at than the links to Admissions, Degrees, or Courses in the global navigation.

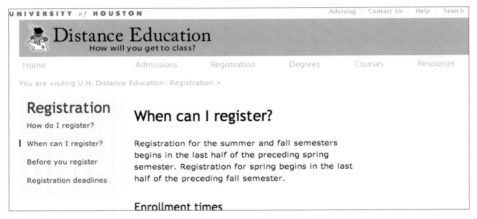

FIGURE 8.11 The local navigation for the U.H. Distance Education Web site lists several pages all related to the same topic, Registration. And, the local navigation is closer to the page content than the global navigation.

How much is too much?

The trickiest part about local navigation is figuring out how much you need. At the Charles Schwab site, the links beneath Research & Strategies work pretty well. But what happens when you select Mutual Funds? Turns out you get an entirely new chunk of navigation on the left side of the page (**Figure 8.12**).

Local navigation is sometimes called sub-navigation because it's the links that live below (sub) a given category. Here on the Schwab site, though, we see what happens when your sub-navigation (Mutual Funds) has sub-navigation. All of a sudden, our page is a lot more complicated. Now we have two local navigation schemes.

FIGURE 8.12 The Charles Schwab site has a third level of navigation, sub-sub-navigation.

Navigation can also be identified by "level." Your global navigation is navigation level one. Level two is the first level of your local navigation. Level three is one level of navigation down. Can you have a navigation level four? Can your sub-sub-navigation have sub-navigation? In **Figure 8.13**, we see how a fourth level of navigation appears below Find Funds. On a site map, it's easier to see how the navigation goes four levels down (**Figure 8.14**).

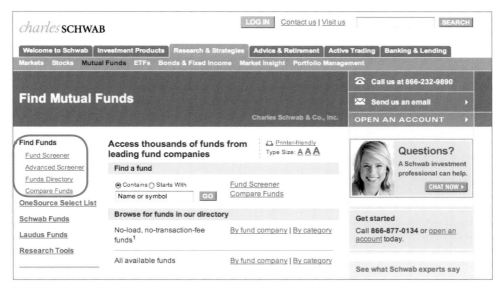

FIGURE 8.13 They're still going. Charles Schwab has a fourth level of navigation.

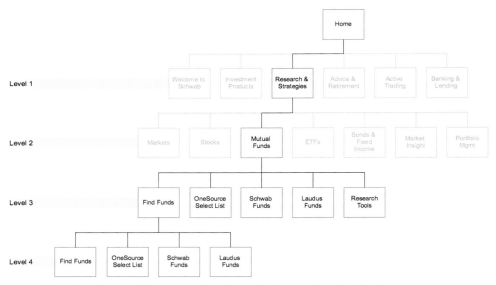

FIGURE 8.14 On a sitemap, it's easy to see how the navigation goes down four levels.

So, how many levels of local navigation do you create? As many as you need without making the user have a nervous breakdown. Schwab feels each level of navigation helps users zero in on their goals. With a lot of new sites, you may only have enough content for two levels of navigation—the global navigation and one level of local navigation. Even though that's all you have right now, it's wise to plan your navigation design to expand to a third level. If you never need a third level of navigation, fine, no harm done. However, sites grow over time. It won't be long before your nice two-level navigation system starts needing sub pages. If you haven't at least planned for a third level, you risk needing to redesign your site very early on.

Working with the global navigation—models for navigation access

Your navigation will necessarily shape how users find content. The two basic patterns of access to content via navigation are called *pogosticking* and *crabwalking*.[6] Each one has advantages and disadvantages, and you'll choose the right navigation behavior based on the nature of your site and users.

---

6 Obviously, this is not a complete list of every type of local navigation, but because we're not writing the encyclopedia of web navigation, we'll just look at a couple of common examples. Consider starting your own collection of navigation forms to refer to when you're designing. Here's a great one on Flickr http://www.flickr.com/photos/factoryjoe/collections/72157600001823120/, and another http://www.flickr.com/photos/morville/collections/72157603789246885/.

Pogosticking

In pogosticking, users go to a subcategory, and then must go back to the parent category to choose a different subcategory. This type of navigation is typically used when users are browsing very large, heterogeneous collections of content. The bookmarking site Delicious, photo site Flickr, and the iTunes music store all designed their navigation for pogosticking by using breadcrumbs (**Figure 8.15**). In each experience, the only way to access previous navigation options is to move back up the breadcrumb trail.

FIGURE 8.15 Delicious, Flickr, and the iTunes Store all use breadcrumbs to facilitate moving within subsections.

This navigation scheme is also used for large Web portals where a large number of sub-sites are collected under one brand. Yahoo! and Comcast.net both collect large, diverse groups of sub-sites under one banner. Whenever you dive in to one site—in this case, News—the rest of Yahoo! and Comcast.net falls away, and you only see navigation related to finding News (**Figure 8.16**).

FIGURE 8.16 Web portals Yahoo! and Comcast.net focus navigation solely on the section of the site you're in.

In every case, pogosticking works for two reasons. First, if you have too many top-level categories, then hiding them as users move through the site makes it easier to use. In iTunes, if you're in Music, you're probably not worried about TV Shows or Movies. Along those same lines, pogosticking can be easier to design. For sites with lots of content, it's not possible to squeeze in all top-level categories alongside all of your local navigation. Consider the alternative: you'd have hundreds of links on a page. Pogosticking is a viable solution when there are many categories holding a lot of content.

Crabwalking

In crabwalking, users can move in a sideways fashion through categories, like the locomotion of a crab. Users choose a category and can choose links to sibling categories provided on the page. Business Week designed its local navigation to support crabwalk-ing (**Figure 8.17**). You might be in Innovation, but Technology and Investing are just a click away.

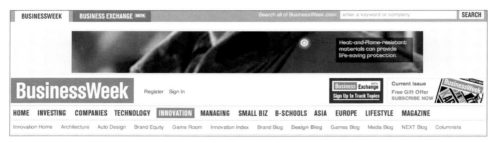

FIGURE 8.17 Business Week lets users navigate by choosing sibling categories.

If you've designed the global and local navigation well, then users will be able to browse your Web site. Good structural navigation will support all of your customers' informa-tion-seeking behaviors: users looking for known items, those exploring, those who don't know what they need to know, and those re-finding something they saw in the past.

If you've done a really awesome job, your users will never click a single one of those links. If you've really honed your design ninja skills, your users will rely solely on associative navigation.

Associative Navigation:
What's Next and Safety Nets

When you assign your boxes and arrows to pages, your site starts coming into focus. Even if you haven't even thought about the final colors and fonts, everyone has a picture in his or her head of what a homepage looks like, or an article page, or a gallery of thumbnails. More importantly, you've used page types in the previous chapter to help you optimize each page for a given activity—navigation, consumption, or interaction. So the user visits a page on your site. What then? Did you think you were done?

Let's say you read an article over at *The Huffington Post*. You get to the end of the article and see two links to More In Politics… (**Figure 8.18**). These links take users to content that is related to the article they just read. These links are called associative navigation because they *associate* additional content with the article on this page.[7] They can easily

7 We touched on associative navigation in Chapter 3, Sock Drawers and CD Racks. Associative navigation answers two important questions: "Do they have anything better?" and "What do I do now?"

be forgotten because they act as shortcuts cutting across the hierarchy of your IA, but they are actually the single most powerful driver of usage on your site. If you have 10 hours to spend on navigation, spend nine on associative.

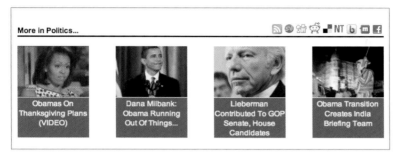

FIGURE 8.18 The Huffington Post uses links at the bottom of every article to associate additional content that users may find interesting.

Associative navigation addresses two important situations for every page on your site:

1. What happens once the user has successfully interacted with the page? What next?

2. What happens if this page isn't what the user wants? What's the safety net that catches him before he leaves your site?

What's next?

Imagine success. Your user has navigated your site, found what he wanted to do, and done it. Now, he sits there, staring at the screen. Pretty soon he types Google in the address bar, and he is gone. Is that really what you want? Of course not. If you sell things, you want him to see more things to buy; if you sell advertising, you want more page views. But most of all, you want him so happy and engaged that his five-minute visit turns into 15, and the next day he comes back wondering what else you've got!

Ask yourself, what do our visitors *want* to do with what they've found? What's the next step? If they read an article, give them links to more articles to read. If they watched a video, give them more links to videos to watch. Keep them happy and engaged; your business depends on it.

What happens after you've read a news article? In **Figure 8.19**, we see the bottom of an article from Comcast News. They offer options to email, discuss, print, Digg, or use Delicious to bookmark the story. Or, chances are, you're in the mood to read another article. Comcast has placed links to the Most Viewed, Recommended, and Emailed stories. Hopefully, what's next is that you'll check one of those out. YouTube offers similar next steps after you've watched a video (**Figure 8.20**)—share, replay, or similar videos to watch—all show how YouTube handles what happens after you watch a video.

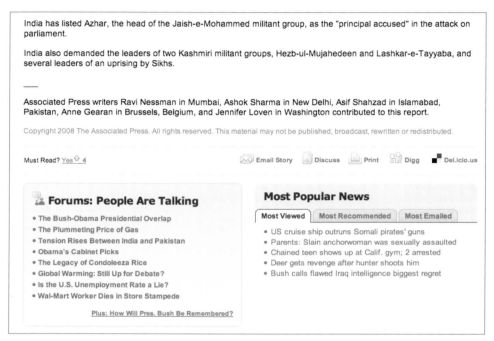

FIGURE 8.19 Comcast News offers tools that give visitors obvious "next steps" for when they're done reading an article. They also offer more articles.

FIGURE 8.20 YouTube's clear next steps keep you in their video-watching world.

If a user finds a product on an online store, an obvious next step is to buy it. That's why Add to Cart buttons are always so prominent (or should be). But what if the item's not available? No page should be a dead-end. In **Figure 8.21**, we've found a toy we want to buy online from Toys "R" Us. Unfortunately, it's out of stock. We can't buy the toy, so what's next? Toys "R" Us offers to let us know when it's available again. Contrast this to what happens when we try locating the same toy in nearby stores (**Figure 8.22**). Toys "R" Us doesn't know whether or not any of the stores have the toy in stock. So what's next? Toys "R" Us leaves us hanging. If Toys "R" Us moved the store's phone number into the right column and prompted us to call, we still wouldn't know if it was in stock, but at least we'd have a next step—call the store.

FIGURE 8.21
Toys "R" Us's product page offers to let you know when something comes back in stock.

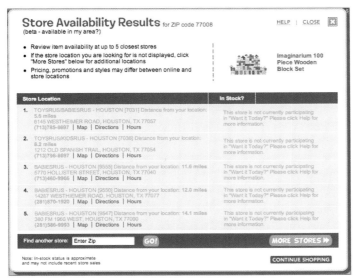

FIGURE 8.22
Unlike the product page, Toys "R" Us leaves us hanging when their locator tool doesn't know anything. What do we do now?

Next steps aren't just for online stores and browsing articles. They're critical for online applications. **Figure 8.23** shows the story composition page for PublicSquare, a content management system. At the bottom of the screen, after you've typed in or edited your story, PublicSquare provides the obvious next step: Save. (In fact, they give you three separate options for saving.)

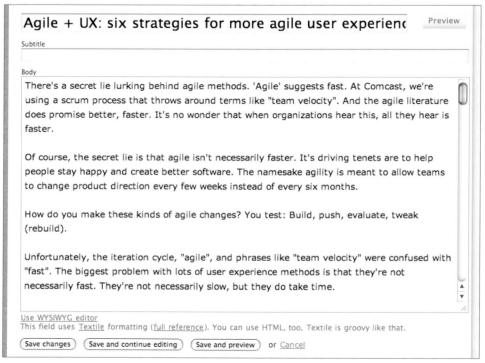

FIGURE 8.23 PublicSquare offers three, clear next steps for users who have finished writing or editing a story.

Always provide a next step. There's always one more thing your users want to do.

Safety nets

Now imagine failure. Your user has navigated your site and found something he didn't want. Now, he sits there staring at the screen. Do you really want to force him back to try again? Do you want to take the risk that he'll decide it's a waste of time and go somewhere else? If your visitors arrive at a page and decide it's not what they wanted, give them another page to go to with something new to look at. Link to something on a related topic, or link to the same content in a different format. CNN does this. If an article has a related video, it's linked at the very top of the page. If you'd rather watch than read, they've got you covered (**Figure 8.24**).

FIGURE 8.24 At CNN, if you'd rather watch a video than read an article, CNN has you covered.

If the user doesn't like what he sees on a page, he might fall through the cracks and leave your site. The New York Times is fabulous at creating safety nets to catch wandering users. **Figure 8.25** shows their article page, packed with safety nets. If you'd rather not read, they offer video, photos, and even audio. And at the bottom you get links to past coverage and related searches.

Safety nets are useful everywhere. At Ask.com, a set of related searches at the right of the page helps you refine your query. If your first search doesn't work, what's to stop you from going over to Google or Yahoo! or MSN or anyone? Safety nets imagine what might go wrong and then create a mechanism for helping the user out of that problem (see **Figure 8.26**).

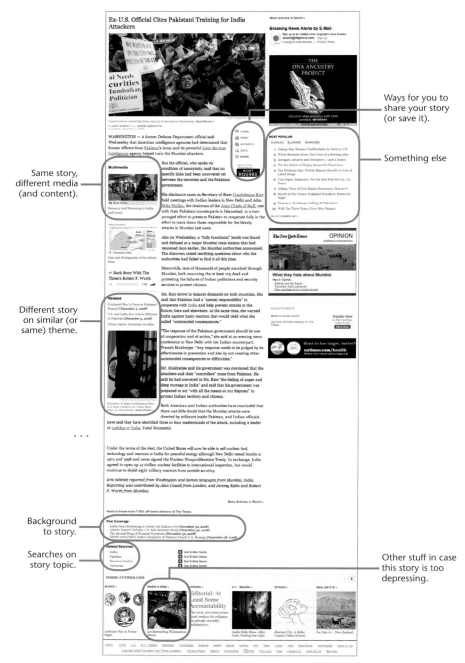

Ways for you to share your story (or save it).

Something else

Same story, different media (and content).

Different story on similar (or same) theme.

Background to story.

Searches on story topic.

Other stuff in case this story is too depressing.

FIGURE 8.25 The New York Times offers a wide range of safety nets to keep readers on their site.

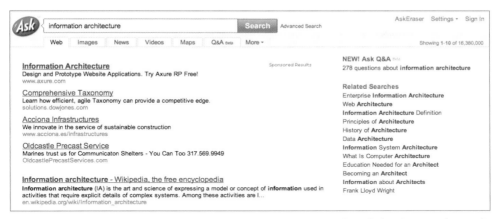

FIGURE 8.26 Ask.com's related searches help users who are having trouble formulating the query they need.

Driving associative navigation with metadata

Associative navigation is all about associating more content with whatever content the user is currently looking at. You can make all kinds of associations:

- **By time:** Items that occur, were published, or were saved around the same time. On blogs, these might be the next and previous entries. On a news site, they could be earlier and later articles on the same news event.

- **By type:** More articles, videos, or photos, based on what the user is looking at. On YouTube, more videos are always just a click away.

- **By topic or subject:** More items in the same category. Previously we saw how The Huffington Post offered links to more articles in the same section of its Web site.

- **By interest:** Most popular items. Comcast.net offers links to the most viewed, the most emailed, and the most recommended items.

- **By owner or group:** More items by the same author or from the same group.

- **By community:** More items based on what people like you are checking out. Last.fm links to artists that users with similar tastes also enjoy.

All of these associations can be created auto-magically using metadata. For large sites, you almost have to rely solely on metadata. For a site like Yahoo! News that aggregates news from numerous sources all over the world, there's just no way for individual editors to add related articles to every story by hand.

Before you sit down to design your associative navigation, grab one of the programmers or product managers and ask him what kind of information you have about each piece of content. Use this information to have the site automatically generate the associative navigation. Your users will love you because that next step is always close at hand, and the business will love you because you're driving traffic where they want it to go.

That may seem like a lot of navigation. So far, pages include global navigation, one or more levels of local navigation, what nexts, and a safety net. Believe it or not, there are still a few things we've left out, and that's what utility navigation is for.

Utility Navigation, the Red-headed Step-child

James Kalbach defines utility navigation best: "Utility navigation connects tools and features that assist visitors in using the site."[8] On the Charles Schwab site, the utility navigation consists of Log In, Contact Us, Visit Us, and Search. At Amazon, the utility navigation includes Your Account and Help.

A convention has emerged where the utility navigation lives at the top right of the page (**Figure 8.27**). Usually, it lives there because the rest of the navigation system occupies the top and left of the page. So, the top right of the page is somewhere both out of the way, yet still accessible.

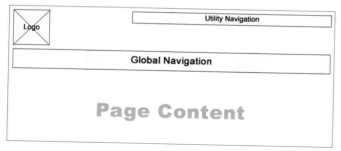

FIGURE 8.27 In this diagram you can see how utility navigation usually lives at the top right, out of the way, but is still easily accessible.

Ask yourself—what common or important tasks are ignored by your global navigation? What links will your visitors want or need if browsing your taxonomy isn't what they want to do? Common items that appear as utility navigation include sign-in and sign-out, access to a user's account or profile, help, contact info, links to physical locations (branches for banks, stores, offices), and search. Even though these links are important and necessary, they're usually the last to be considered. This is unfortunate since many of them, like help and contact information, serve as lifeboats for visitors who arrive at your site and find themselves adrift in a sea of information.

Often utility navigation is placed adjacent to the global navigation, because it also needs to be accessible everywhere on the site. However, when designing utility navigation,

---

8 From James Kalbach's excellent book, *Designing Web Navigation*, (2007, O'Reilly, p 98).

it's important that you separate it from the global navigation with both visual cues and physical location on the page. Users have learned to focus on the global navigation to understand what a site is about, and they know to look elsewhere when they need something other than content. E*Trade does this really well (**Figure 8.28**). They've moved their global navigation to the left side of the page. The entire top of the page is reserved for utility navigation. E*Trade includes useful user account links (Log On, and Open an Account). They also include lifeboats like Customer Service and Search. E*Trade also adds a couple of quick shortcuts to content. The Quote field saves users from browsing through Investing & Trading. Similarly, Employee Stock Plans and International Sites both provide quick access to specific content for specific groups of users.

FIGURE 8.28 E*Trade locates global navigation along the left of the page and distributes utility navigation across the top.

Utility navigation can also hold oddball stuff like jobs, blogs, and press releases. And it can hold bookmarks, favorites, and history. This can help users who are trying to re-find something they've already seen before.

Together, global and local navigation help users narrow in on your content. Associative navigation connects users with related content, provides next steps, and offers safety nets. Utility navigation provides a place for any other important links not handled well by the other three types of navigation. Nail these three pieces of the navigation puzzle and you'll have a usable Web site. However, navigation has its own inscrutable black art—a set of nuances you should consider—that really make it outstanding.

Designing Navigation—
Three Questions to Ask Yourself

When you design your navigation system, it can be tempting to fill the global, local, associative, and utility navigation with links. Just so you have them. You don't need to *find* links for the various types of navigation. Start with the content you have and see what navigation you need. But what kinds of links should appear in the global naviga-tion? What goes in the local navigation? When designing your navigation system, there are three questions you need to answer:

1. How is your content organized?

2. What do your users want to do?

3. What do you want your users to do?

The answers to these three questions will ensure your navigation includes the links it needs, while leaving out what it doesn't.

How is your content organized?

Back in Chapter 3, Sock Drawers and CD Racks, we looked at ways to organize your content. If you'd been working for Charles Schwab, you might have discovered that your content fell into nice categories like Research & Strategies and Investment Prod-ucts. Charles Schwab organizes its content according to a category-based organization system.

Sometimes, users will already have an expectation of how your content and features will be organized. Employee directories are often organized alphabetically. Events are organized by date. Other times, metadata may offer an alternative way to organize your content. Letting users navigate content by the way it's organized is a good way to make sure they can find what they're looking for. Sometimes, though, you don't want to rely on users to browse around. Sometimes, you want to make sure users can do what they came to do.

What do your users want to do?

Figure 8.29 shows the global navigation for Hulu, an online video site. Like Charles Schwab, Hulu also organizes its content by category: TV or Movie. However, they've tried to imagine other ways someone might want to find online videos. They have Most Popular videos, Recently Added videos, HD Gallery, and more. Hulu uses administrative metadata to determine recently added videos, and it uses intrinsic metadata to find the most popular videos.

FIGURE 8.29 Hulu assumes users want to navigate less by topic (TV or Movies) and more by newness and popularity.

Hulu has decided that what users want—Most Popular and Recently Added—is more important than organizing videos by genre, date, or something else. In Hulu's case, they have two answers for "What do the users want to do?"

1. Users want to catch up on missed TV, so they want links to the newest videos for a show they missed.

2. Users want to entertain themselves, so they want links to the most popular videos.

This *want* question is pretty important. You may have a wonderful organization system, but users may prefer to navigate another way. Your organization system and your navigation system are not necessarily the same thing. They can be. That's how Charles Schwab's navigation works. However, if there's something users come to your site to do, your navigation needs to help them do it, even if that's different from how your content is organized. If there's a mismatch, you'll have a lot of frustrated users. Even worse, they'll have trouble finding what they need, buy less, register less, download less, and see fewer ads. Hulu understands this. TV and Movies are organized by genre, year, actors, and directors, but users come to the Hulu site looking to watch videos, so Hulu optimizes its navigation to help.

Helping users do what they want to do will please your users, and that can be a path to success, but what about your organization? Your organization has a business model that needs users to complete some task.

What do you want your users to do?

All Web sites have a reason for existing. For commercial Web sites, this *raison d'être* usually follows from the current business model. Helping users to do what they want to do makes the site work for users, but that doesn't mean you'll actually make any money. However, you can't focus solely on making money because then your users won't come back (if they ever come at all). For example, let's say your organization makes money off every ad viewed by a user. If you were totally focused on your business model, then you wouldn't even bother with navigation. You'd just have one page covered with nothing but ads. Of course, no one would visit, so no one would see any ads, and you'd be looking for a new job. In contrast, users want to view content. If they had their way, they could find their content and consume it in a nice ad-free environment. If you built a site to please these users, you wouldn't make any money because there wouldn't be any ads.

A successful Web site emerges from a balance between what the user wants and what the business needs. Navigation should help your users do what they want, but it also needs to help them do what *you* want them to do. Navigation facilitates your business model. Good navigation makes your business money.

Fancast is a Hulu competitor. In **Figure 8.30**, you can see Fancast approaches the navigation question a different way. Rather than browsing by newness and popularity—like Hulu—or by category—like Charles Schwab—Fancast wants you to navigate by type of video (Full Episodes, Movies, Trailers, and Clips). The difference between Fancast and Hulu and Charles Schwab reveals the answer to our last question: What do you want users to do?

FIGURE 8.30 Fancast's navigation helps users do what Fancast wants them to do.

When it first launched, Fancast was a lot like IMDb, the Internet Movie Database. It listed every TV show, movie, and person involved in TV shows and movies going back several decades. Just like IMDb, users could search for a favorite movie or TV show, find a synopsis, a rating, and a list of people involved. At that time, Fancast's content navigation followed its primary organization scheme. The global navigation had links to TV, Movies, and People. The navigation matched how the content was organized. Fancast earned money for every ad viewed on a page, so a pretty Web site and quality content were how they drew people to the site and encouraged them to come back.

Fancast also knew where and how you could watch anything; kind of like IMDb meets TV Guide. Looking for an old movie? Fancast knew if it was on in the next couple of weeks, if it was in theaters, On Demand, or on DVD. Fancast also had a growing collection of online videos, so if you were looking for a show, it could tell you if it was available on Fancast and then you could watch it—right there—without leaving the Web site.

It turns out not only do ads in a video pay more than ads on a page, but Fancast was signing deals to host more and more full-length TV episodes and movies on the site. It wasn't much of a leap to shift the focus from content about TV shows and movies to watching the actual shows and movies, themselves. Fancast no longer wanted you to look for info on TV, Movies, and People. Fancast now wants you to choose a type of video to watch: Full Episodes, Movies, Trailers, or Clips.

The navigation changed to support a shift in business model from page views to video views. The design hasn't changed. The underlying organization schemes haven't changed. The functionality hasn't changed. But now, the Web site makes more money because the navigation takes you to videos (and ads) to watch, which is, of course, why they're in business.

This doesn't mean that what *you* want users to do needs to displace what *the users* want to do. In **Figure 8.31**, Target does a great job of helping users and helping themselves. The Target Web site functions as an online store. In that role, Target helps you to browse or search for something to buy online. This is what the Target online store would like you to do. However, they also support users who want to use and participate in registries and gift giving with a navigation bar for GiftCards, GiftGiving, and GiftRegistries. This is what their users want to do—give and receive gifts from their friends and loved ones. The gift-giving navigation is more likely to drive you into a physical Target store. The Target online store won't make money there, but users will come back to the Web site next time (and maybe they'll buy online).

FIGURE 8.31 Target's global navigation balances what Target wants users to do with what users actually want to do.

Pagination—Navigating Multiple Pages

Pagination is a special form of navigation. It's a simple tool that lets people flip through multiple pages. Breaking a large group of items into bite-sized pieces is a common wisdom. It allows a faster download and prevents information overload. It's useful for categories that hold a large number of products, or for extremely long documents, such as e-books or in-depth articles. And, of course, it provides more pages for advertising spots.

Amazon has a nice design for pagination « Previous | **Page: 1** 2 3 | Next » . It tells you what page you're on, offers links to the previous and next page, as well as links to specific pages.

If moving through page after page is too tedious for impatient users (like us), Fancast provides links Results Per Page 10 | 30 | 50 to show more results per page... or fewer!

Printing is a common task for long articles; offering pagination for online reading is nice, but removing it in a printer-friendly version is even nicer (the pagination is handled pretty well by the printer). Business Week does this. Articles are broken into multiple pages (to make them easier to read and to generate more ad revenue), but when you select the print view, you're presented with the entire article on one page.

View All is similar to a print view. At Office Max, a user can choose to browse through page after page of products, or they can choose to View All and view all products on one page [Page 1 of 4] 1 2 3 4 Next | View all . By offering the View All, users get to choose how many items their bandwidth can handle, rather than having the designer dictate to them.

This works best for collections that only have a few pages. If there are too many items in the list, View All threatens to take too long to load (the browser will eventually give up) and be too long to scroll through.

Pagination can have its own downside. When Boxes and Arrows split its articles across several pages, they noticed each additional page had 50 percent fewer readers. That is, every time users were presented with a link to go to the next page in an article, only half of them clicked. When we did usability testing with our users on a one-page article, we saw they might get bored in the middle, and scroll down to the end to determine if they should continue. This was far more satisfying for the end-user, so Boxes and Arrows put everything on one *ginormous* page.

Search results have this same problem. On Google or Yahoo!, if your site isn't on the first page of search results (in the first 10 results for a given query), it may as well not exist. Searchers rarely look past the first page of search results. A long page is better than several short ones; users will scroll before they'll click.

Paginating forms and processes

The preceeding examples show what happens when you paginate a list of links (a navigation page) or a piece of content (a consumption page). You can also stretch a form across several pages (a series of interaction pages).[9] Whereas you paginate pages of content and links to offer visitors more, when you paginate a form, you don't want page two to be optional. An e-commerce checkout is a good example. You need users to confirm their order, enter payment information, and tell you where it's to be shipped. Amazon puts each task on a separate page. The next step for each task isn't optional. It's required if you're going to buy that book.

In this case, Amazon removes all of the global and local navigation on the page. The only navigation available to the user is the button that takes her to the next step (**Figure 8.32**). With the global and local navigation removed, Amazon hopes the user will click all the way through and buy the book.

FIGURE 8.32 During the checkout process, Amazon removes the global and local navigation, leaving only a logo. The only links users can click moves them closer to finishing the purchase.

---

9 We talk about the three types of pages—navigation, consumption, and interaction—in Chapter 7, From Box to Page.

This is different from the Amazon search results page (**Figure 8.33**). If a user is on page two and doesn't see the book she wants, then Amazon actually would rather she choose an item from the global navigation if that means she might be able to find something to buy. Similarly, Business Week splits its articles across several pages. If the user would rather browse to another article than click to page two, that's ok. Business Week keeps the user on its site (viewing another ad).

FIGURE 8.33 Amazon has left the global and local navigation on its search results. They don't mind if the user would rather skip the next page of search results and navigate somewhere else on the site.

When deciding to paginate a form or process, you should decide how important it is that users complete the form. If it's ok for users to abandon the form and go somewhere else on your site, then leave the global and local navigation visible. If, however, it's critical that they finish the form, then remove the global and local navigation. The user will have fewer distractions and be able to focus on completing the process.

What Does It All Mean?

Because navigation is everywhere and because everyone touches it daily, everyone thinks they know which navigation works best. Often, you can get into some brutal arguments with someone who's been burned by a bad navigation scheme. But by keeping the business goals in mind, and talking with users regularly, you can figure out what navigation system makes the most sense. And this is critical to a Web site's success.

If users can't navigate the way they need to, or the navigation isn't helping the business realize its goals, your site will fail. Up until now, all of our design decisions have been about optimizing for one audience or another. Personas focus on who your users are. Scenarios focus on the user's experience. Your organization scheme focuses on your content. Navigation is where you take all these pieces and fit them together to support your business's goals and your user's needs.

"Because we're going to be serving steak, we're going to be using steak knives. And since we have steak knives, people might be stabbing each other. And therefore we need to put fences around all the tables."

9

Architecting Social Spaces

In which we map the unknown territories of profiles, forums, and user-generated content, encountering trolls and flamers along the way.

In 1977, a new book on architecture was published. It was filled with the collective wisdom of the cultures of the world from centuries of building human housing had a resounding effect not only on architecture and urban planning, but also on software design. It was called *A Pattern Language: Towns, Buildings, Construction* and in it, Christopher Alexander and his co-authors listed 253 patterns of the best design solutions architecture had created. Here is an excerpt from the introduction: "Each pattern describes a problem which occurs over and over again in our environment, and then describes the core of the solution to that problem, in such a way that you can use this solution a million times over, without ever doing it the same way twice." This pattern approach had not been seen before, and it proved to be an effective way to describe best practices in architecture.

For example:

203. Child Caves

Conflict
Children love to be in tiny, cave-like places.

Resolution
Wherever children play, around the house, in the neighborhood, in schools, make small "caves" for them. Tuck these caves away in natural leftover spaces, under stairs, under kitchen counters. Keep the ceiling heights low—2 feet 6 inches to 4 feet—and the entrance tiny.

What resonates as you read Alexander's book is how the patterns are all about the design of space to meet human needs and promote happiness. It doesn't take a great leap of imagination to bring these principles from architecture to information architecture, and out of the real world and into the digital. Information architecture is social architecture, as long as it is designed for human use. But when many humans use it, when the use is primarily for human interaction, even greater care must be taken. In this chapter, we add five more principles to those laid out in Chapter 1, First Principles, and then describe patterns of architecture in social spaces that have worked well in solving human needs.

Principles for Social Architecture

Humans are funny animals, and they behave in surprising ways. In an information space, a human's needs are simple and his behavior straightforward. Find. Read. Save. But once you get a bunch of humans together, communicating and collaborating, you can see the madness of crowds or the wisdom of crowds. Digg, an online news service in which the top stories are selected by the readership's votes, is as likely to select an insightful political commentary as it is an illegal crack[1] for a piece of software as their top story. This makes architecture in social spaces the most challenging work an IA can take on.

---

1 Cracking software means removing the protection built into the software that prevents things like copying and allows you to rid yourself of adware and nag screens.

While your designs can never control people, they certainly can encourage good behavior and discourage bad. The psychologist Kurt Lewin came up with a formula to understand why people do the crazy things they do: $B=f(P,E)$, or **B**ehavior is a **f**unction of a **P**erson and his **E**nvironment. You can't do too much about a person's nature, but you can design the environment he moves around in. Here are a few principles to guide you in this challenge.

Trust and monitor

We spend an inordinate amount of time worrying about what will happen when barbarians overrun our site when what we should worry about is if anyone will show up at all. Jimmy Wales, founder of Wikipedia, tells a marvelous story about the creation of the world's biggest collaboratively created encyclopedia[2] in which he asks what would happen if we designed restaurants the way that we design Web sites.

> *"Imagine if you're designing a restaurant. And in this restaurant we're going to be serving steak. And because we're going to be serving steak, we're going to be using steak knives. And since we have steak knives, people might be stabbing each other. And therefore we need to put fences around all the tables. We need to have cages so that people are protected from each other, because who knows what godawful thing they might do, sitting there with knives.*
>
> *That isn't a good idea. It isn't a good way to design a restaurant; it isn't a good way for us to live our lives in society."*

Worrying about the worst-case scenario is exhausting and often pointless. There is a point-of-view emerging among folks who do social software design that both avoids excessive design for every edge case and also embodies the belief that most people are mostly good: *trust and monitor.*

Wikis are a good example of this. No one watches and approves every article's creation, editing, and publication. Instead, the system records changes, and if a complaint is made, it's easy to go back and see who did what and revert the changes back to an earlier version. Some software automatically sets off an alert if potentially troubling activity is detected. For example, if multiple people edit a page more often than the average, a system might alert an administrator to come see if there is a flame war[3] going on. Some folks are even working on algorithms to detect particularly hostile language. Still, when you consider how well Wikipedia has done with just simple software and a lot of humans, you have to think twice about being too clever with automating decisions that humans may be better at.

---

2 http://blog.longnow.org/2006/04/19/jimmy-wales/

3 Geekspeak for fight. Back in 1959, Xerox Parc (inventors of the computer) had an email program that marked emails containing potentially emotional content with yellow or red text. The color was reminiscent of "flames" and that became the term for mean-spirited email exchanges.

Rely on emergent discoveries, rather than on curatorship

In previous chapters, we discussed a lot of approaches to organization that are dependent on the modern equivalent of indexers—designated employees who go through and add metadata and categories by hand. But in social sites, often the volume and dynamic nature of user-generated content precludes this approach; you'd have to have as many information architects as you have users! The role of information architecture in a socially-generated information space is very different—it's all about rules and tools. First, you must create classification tools the end users can use to become information architects of their own personal information. Second, you need to create rules for the system to recognize when common behavior is significant, in order to do things like create an emergent disambiguation system (as seen in **Figure 9.1**), or trainable recommendation systems that correlate people and content patterns.

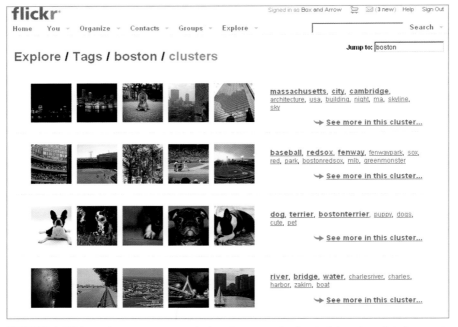

FIGURE 9.1 Flickr analyzes common proximity of tags to each other to determine related concepts; in this case, that Boston can be a place, a baseball team, a dog, or a river.

Default to public

If you ask your users if they'd like their photographs automatically to be public or private, even today they'd say "private." Yet Flickr is the single largest photo site today, despite having the opposite behavior. When Facebook first launched News Feed, a service that aggregated all the activity of your friends into one place where you could easily see what was going on with your social circle, the users flipped out. There was a massive backlash against what they felt was an invasion of their privacy. Over time, the users became accustomed to the News Feed. After all, all it did was put the information they were already sharing in one place. And coincidentally, they started logging in just to find out what was new with their friends. Now Facebook is the fifth most trafficked site on the Web because of the compelling nature of the News Feed. Similarly once upon a time, all Internet wisdom said that you needed to prevent people from putting content you provided on their own sites because you needed to drive them to your site to get more page views. Then YouTube made it dead simple for anyone to embed any video on his own site. Openly allowing anyone to share publicly any of a site's content is now a pattern on video sites everywhere, and it drives more traffic than ever to the parent site.

You always want to protect your user's privacy (and your site's intellectual property!), but in social sites over and over it appears that defaulting to public is the right approach. If people don't share their lives, there is no opportunity for community and activity. Privacy is important, but when we are overprotective we can miss a chance to be the matchmaker who connects people. You do still have to give your users the opportunity to opt out of living their lives in public, but that initial default setup can make or break a site.

Architecture must be adaptive

Successful social architecture supports both individual and collective human needs. In Pattern 251, Alexander notes, "People are different sizes; they sit in different ways. And yet there is a tendency in modern times to make all chairs alike."

A profile on a social Web site must allow users to be identifiable, yet give them the capability to reveal what they want about themselves. Users should be able to edit at will as their lives change, including replacing photos and even changing their birthdays as they become more comfortable (and hopefully honest). The degree of customization of the profile appearance varies from site to site. MySpace made a name for itself by breaking an unwritten rule and allowing its users to completely customize their pages, down to changing the html.

Moreover, a social Web site should learn about you and your preferences and become more personalized over time. Facebook encourages you to refine the presentation of your News Feed by letting them know what and whom you really care about (see **Figure 9.2**). As you get hundreds of friends who produce hundreds of news items, this input informs an algorithm that makes sure you don't miss what's important to you. Over time, the social site becomes as comfy as an old chair.

FIGURE 9.2 Facebook encourages users to adjust the News Feed so it fits their lives better.

Size matters

We would all like to think there is a universal, perfect design that we could find and then never change. However, differently-sized people require more than differently-sized clothes; they require clothes that make them look leaner, taller, more powerful, or less imposing. And differently-sized Web sites with their differently-sized audiences demand different design approaches. This is true of both information spaces and social spaces.

Wikipedia is only interesting as a result of the huge numbers of people who use it. Experts on every topic on earth join in writing, editing, and contributing citations, collectively creating the most complete entries you can find on any topic. Because Wikipedia has so much traffic, and because most people are nice, if the occasional idiot defaces a page, it is repaired in less than five minutes. And so goes the marketing spiel, and many of the entries do indeed realize this promise. But some entries on each end of the spectrum of usage show the problems that result from both too large an audience and too small an audience (see **Figure 9.3** and **Figure 9.4**).

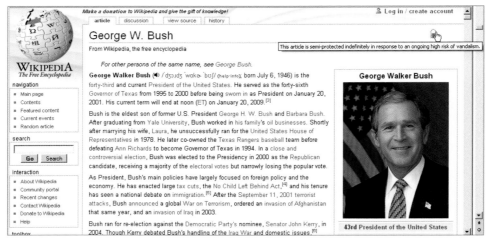

FIGURE 9.3 The extremely popular entries or extremely controversial entries (often the same) can't be left open to be edited by everyone, no matter what the Wikipedia philosophy is, because the number of people vandalizing it is too high to guarantee a useful entry at any given time. Wikipedia is forced to lock these entries against open editing.

FIGURE 9.4 Here we see a typical Wikipedia article, illustrating the power of collaboration. The top image is the article page; below on the 'talk" page we see Ciphergoth, Melcombe, OliAtlanson, Aastrup, and many others discussing how to make the article more accurate and complete.

And here in **Figure 9.5**, we see a page that gets almost no traffic. In fact, it didn't exist until one day Christina started to wonder where the name (and the food) jalapeño poppers came from.

FIGURE 9.5 Wikipedia didn't have an entry about these little bits of tasty goodness until Christina wrote one.

She searched everywhere, including Wikipedia, but all she could find was a Chow discussion board article that thought they might be related to chiles rellenos. Christina posted what little she knew on Wikipedia, and wandered off to ask the question on another discussion board. As we see in **Figure 9.6**, most people don't realize size and authority are correlated. Too many cooks in the kitchen, and you've got a big opinion fight. Too few, and you've got one guy (or gal) spouting off their theories as if they were true.

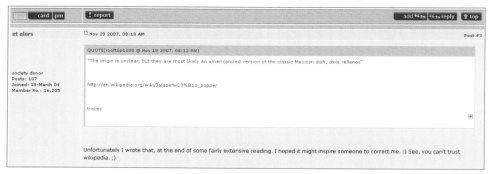

FIGURE 9.6 Christina has found her question being answered by her own words out of someone else's mouth.

People are so used to Wikipedia being extensive, complete, and expert that no one questioned this entry. Meanwhile, while Christina went out to perfect her popper recipe, people started adding bit by bit to her entry, contributing a photo and some suspiciously marketing-esque information about John Neutzling. That has been removed since this screenshot, but in the stubs,[4] updates are slow, and vandalism—especially subtle marketing-driven vandalism—remains up. The truth is arrived at with fewer miracles—if it arrives at all.

The *Los Angeles Times* tried to leverage the power of wikis with its wikitorial. On June 17, 2005, they launched it, and on June 19, 2005, they took it down. Users were posting obscene photos and comments at a pace that no one could manage. The *LA Times* had the large numbers needed to create interesting content, but hadn't learned the lessons of Wikipedia's controversial entries. After all, if Wikipedia, with its vibrant community, couldn't keep George Bush under control, how could a brand-new newspaper site? It still hasn't returned, and maybe it represents a problem that can't be solved.

When you look at examples on the Web to learn from, make sure that you are dealing with similar problems of scale. Do you have enough traffic to create rich collections of content? Do you have too many users to create coherent communities? What will you do when you begin, and what will you do if you make it big?

Elements of Social Architecture

Alexander had the good judgment to write about architecture, which has been refined over thousands of years. The Web is much younger, even if communities are not. In the last five years, there have been a number of models for the architecture of social software and media[5] that have been passed around from blog to blog, collectively evolving. New patterns of excellence are still being identified.[6] Consider these a foundation from which you can build.

---

4 Stubs are the Wikipedia term for funny little "almost" pages where someone began an entry and ran out of steam. They also include pages that aren't really up to the Wikipedia standard. They're often annotated with what needs to be done next...if a serious Wikipidian has found them, that is.

5 Matt Webb http://interconnected.org/home/2004/04/28/on_social_software
Steward Butterfield http://www.sylloge.com/personal/2003_03_01_s.html#91273866
Gene Smith http://nform.ca/publications/social-software-building-block

6 For example, Bryce Glass' excellent Reputation pattern in the Yahoo! Pattern library http://developer.yahoo.com/ypatterns/parent.php?pattern=reputation

Identity

Conflict: Who can you trust online?

Resolution: You must give each user an identity, and then allow him to customize it as he sees fit. The identity acts as a way for the user to express his personality, and is typically accessed and protected via a unique log-in. Participation is rewarded in the identity with a combination of reputation and ability to collect items in the system (bookmarks, history, relationships, and so on).

In the brilliant "A Group Is Its Own Worst Enemy,"[7] Clay Shirky writes, "If you were going to build a piece of social software to support large and long-lived groups, what would you design for? The first thing you would design for is handles[8] the user can invest in." Identity is the bedrock of social architecture; get it right, and your site will stand firm despite the tempests that blow through communities. Identity, over time, will hold a user's reputation, and that is what allows users to relate to each other, trust each other, and ultimately trust your Web site.

Elements of identity

To allow your user to create an identity on your site successfully, you need to provide certain tools. The elements of online identity are:

- Profile
- Avatar
- Presence
- Reputation

Profile

A profile is a collection of information about the user, typically including a short biography and the results of a questionnaire, such as the one in **Figure 9.7**. The questionnaire shapes the view that others will have of the user, and it sets the tone for the site's purpose. For example, Orkut, Google's foray into social networks, collects and displays gender and marital state prominently. The rest of the profile circles around hobbies and interests, including many personal items like politics and vices. This sets the tone for a romantic environment suitable for dating. LinkedIn, a business-networking site, doesn't touch any of these bits of information, focusing instead on job history, skill set, and education. Slideshare, a site devoted to sharing PowerPoint slide shows, collects very

---

7 http://shirky.com/writings/group_enemy.html

8 Truckers were the first to use "handles" or callnames on their CB radios. Online, people got usernames and referred to them as "handles." Hey, it was the '70s. We liked paisley, too....

little explicit information about the user beyond name, work, and homepage. It focuses instead on collecting the user's activity, such as slideshows shared and favorite items.

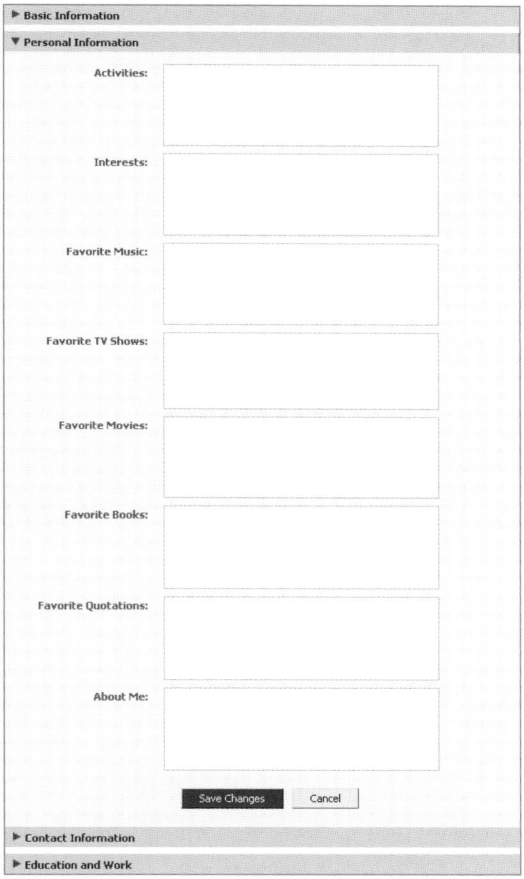

FIGURE 9.7 Facebook asks a series of personal (but not too personal!) questions to get you to write a profile your friends will recognize.

Avatar

An avatar is geek-speak for the little image that follows your name around and represents you on the Web site. It can be a photo or a picture of something you care about. Some systems insist you use only a photo of yourself, while others don't care and don't moderate.

An avatar can set the tone for a system. Yahoo! originally envisioned Yahoo! Answers as a human supplement for search, in which smart people could answer complex problems. Instead, it's become a teen hangout. Could the choice of using avatars from messenger that make everyone into a young hip cartoon character (see **Figure 9.8**) have influenced this perhaps?

FIGURE 9.8 A typical question on Yahoo! Answers. Can you see rocket scientists discussing launch velocity with this avatar?

Because avatars are important to lend personality and humanity to a site, a number of sites have tried to think up ways to get users to use theirs. Vimeo cleverly encourages users to upload an avatar by using a monkey as the default image. No one feels very happy about being portrayed as a monkey. (Or perhaps it's a Cro-Magnon man. Nonetheless, not flattering.)

SocialMedian.com, a social news site, chooses a famous person for your avatar. If a Mac fan gets Bill Gates or a Democrat gets George Bush, he may feel very motivated to change it. Christina? She never looked so good.

Presence

One thing any community needs for it to be inviting and vibrant is a sense of life. Things are happening here. That is manifested in presence, which is defined as footprints freshly left in digital sand. These footprints manifest in a number of ways. Here are some examples:

- **Status:** A brief message to the world about your state of being, as seen in **Figure 9.9**. It started as a message of availability on IM, and it has turned into a place for commentary. "Out for lunch" or "BRB" has become "looking for my misplaced optimism" or "bellybutton gazing." Twitter concatenated statuses into a smooth flow that reads like the world's biggest chatroom.

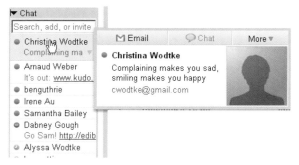

FIGURE 9.9 Status on Gmail gives your friends a conversation starter, as well as letting folks know if you are around to chat.

- **History:** Similar to status but usually auto-generated by the system; for example, "Last log-in 3 hrs ago," or "Edited by Christina at 4.15 10/22/02," or "Submitted 44 mins ago" (**Figure 9.10**).

FIGURE 9.10 History on Basecamp lets you know the last time a coworker checked in

- **Statistics:** A way of communicating how many people are on the site, to create a feeling of life; for example, "457 users" or "2 members and 5 guests in this forum" (**Figure 9.11**).

FIGURE 9.11 Statistics on the food forum eGullet.org make you feel like you are in a crowded restaurant

- **Signs of Life:** These are more varied types of proof that humans are actually on the Web site and doing things; for example, "Latest uploaded" or "New comment," and timestamps such as "posted 1 minute ago." (**Figure 9.12**).

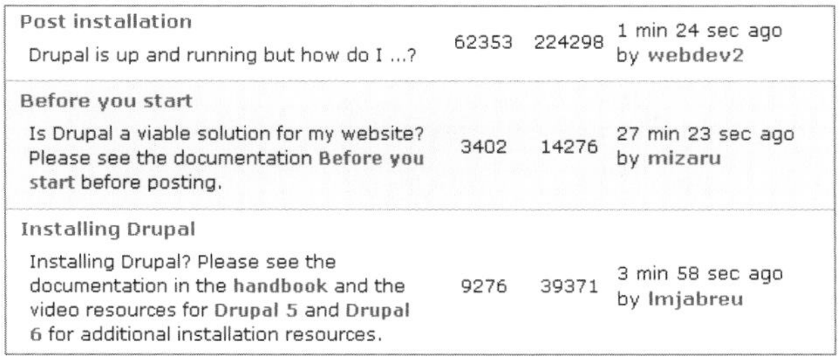

FIGURE 9.12 Signs of life on the forums for Drupal: new posts every minute!

- **Keeping company:** This means giving you a way to keep company with other users. Typically, it's a list of who is present in the system, adopted from chat room conventions. MyBlogLog shows what other users have recently visited, although it won't show if the other users are there at the same moment as you (**Figure 9.13**).

FIGURE 9.13 MyBloglog makes the invisible readers of a blog visible to keep you company while you read.

- **Location:** With the pervasiveness of geotagging and cell phones with GPS, there are more and more tools that place you, digitally, in the real world. This can turn strangers into neighbors, offer cultural context, and make face-to-face meetings more likely (**Figure 9.14**).

FIGURE 9.14 Location is Dopplr's reason for existence. It takes Web presence and turns it into real-world presence.

IM is the master of presence. It not only broadcasts presence and absence, but also avoids false-positives by displaying messages such as "idle." Also it can redirect messages to mobile devices and other communication channels keeping present while away from your computer and can embrace group and asynchronous[9] communication.

Working communities have a very pragmatic use for presence. If you are collaborating with a coworker, then knowing when he is available and how much he's working is invaluable. Basecamp and PublicSquare take a cue from presence indicators to let you know who's working and who's slacking.

Reputation

Your reputation on a site is equal to the sum of all your past actions on the site, good or bad, with good/bad being defined by the community. Since human memory is fallible, and, of course, new members to a site (or visitors to a site) don't know the history, reputation systems are built into the Web software to track behavior and the community's judgment of it. See **Figure 9.15** for an example of a user's reputation.

FIGURE 9.15 Anatomy of a reputation. The badges include a ranking: the fact that she's using her real name and that she participated in a prestigious event.

Reputation is something all communities manage in their own way. Small closed communities such as mailing lists rarely need formal mechanisms for reputation, because the name is enough for everyone to get to know each other, and ranking people is sometimes even considered offensive. ("I don't care if George has 20 points or 2,000—I know he's a good guy!") Conversely, in public communities where there are a large number of drive-by visitors, dilettante participants, or too many people to keep track informally, reputation mechanisms are useful. In the medium-sized communities, it gets tricky. Ben Brown, founder of dating site Consumating, writes about how their point system backfired:

> *"We built a point system into Consumating because we thought giving direct feedback to people about their conduct on the site would encourage them to be nice to one*

---

9 Email is asynchronous, which means any amount of time can go by between responses; the telephone is instant. IM lives in a funny, but very useful space, between the two.

another—you get a thumbs up when you are nice (treat!), and a thumbs down when you are a douche (electric shock!). Anyone who joined the site immediately opened themselves to cavalcades of negative feedback from existing members whose goal was to protect their own ranking. Our brilliant design where every post could be individually ranked meant that the more you participated, the more you could be punished by other members. Members could gang up and "thumb bomb" other members, giving a thumb down on every single post, causing points to disappear and rankings to drop."[10]

Digg was able to use a leaderboard showing its most active users to encourage participation; later on, it caused more trouble than it was worth. In the words of founder Kevin Rose:

"Which leads me to a disappointing trend that we've noticed over the past several months. Some of our top users—the people that have spent hundreds if not thousands of hours finding and digging the best stuff—are being blamed by some outlets as leading efforts to manipulate Digg. These users have been listed on the "Top Diggers" area of the site that was created in the early days of Digg when there was a strong focus on encouraging people to submit content. The list served a great purpose of recognizing those who were working hard to make Digg a great site, as well as a way for new users to discover new content. So what does this all mean? After considerable internal debate and discussion with many of those who make up the Top Digger list, we've decided to remove the list..."[11]

What had started as a useful feature to get people motivated to participate turned into a feature that mostly drove gaming and damaged the overall quality of the site's content. This doesn't mean it wasn't useful in the early days, it just means that, as we noted earlier, community size affects design choices. What works for a thousand people may not work for a million, and you have to be ready for the backlash that comes with removing features if it makes the community as a whole better.

On big sites, though, the choice of if and how to manage reputation is often a bit more clear. For example, Amazon needs a solid reputation system because the community is too big for people to know each other, and advice is being given to strangers ready to spend their hard-earned cash.

Amazon addresses reputation a couple of ways. "Top 500 reviewer" reflects the reviewers who write the most reviews marked by readers as useful—a task for which a computer can easily keep an accurate and honest tally. "Real name" also helps promote people to own their ideas and take responsibility for their words, which in turn makes those reading the reviews trust the writing. You are less likely to be lazy or snarky when

---

10 Read the entire painfully insightful post at http://benbrown.com/says/2007/10/29/i-love-my-chicken-wire-mommy/.

11 A Couple Updates… by Kevin Rose Feb 1st, 2007 http://blog.digg.com/?p=60.

your actual name is attached to a post. And Amazon can verify the name's authenticity because they have the user's credit cards, making the review even more authentic.

Amazon wisely rewards users who are real, rather than preventing anonymous comments. Since a certain amount of anonymity is useful to get honest feedback, they trust that the large number of voters will flag the morons who leave non-useful posts. In many ways, the size of Amazon's community protects them the way Wikipedia's does.

eBay needs a reputation system because it is also brokering sales between strangers. eBay collects ratings on everything a user does on its site from buying to selling, from paying on time to answering questions, which aggregates into a reputation (**Figure 9.16**).

FIGURE 9.16 eBay puts the combined reputation of a seller next to every item he sells in order to increase confidence in a purchase.

Many forums (such as the example shown in **Figure 9.17**) have named their reputation levels to reflect seniority, participation, and financial contribution. While it's often hard to know what these titles mean, it's clear they bequest a certain weight to that individual's posts. In the case of egullet.org, they are accompanied by statistics that often tell a richer tale than the official titles. For example, who's going to argue with Fat Guy, member #1?

FIGURE 9.17 Manager, participating member, society donor... who's the most important member? They all are, and are proud to earn each badge.

It's worth noting that Wikipedia still works well without any formal reputation monitoring or management. There, they just trust that passionate readers who care will check on articles they care about and correct untruths. And Wikipedia's gotten remarkably accurate[12] overall with this approach. On the other hand, unlike eBay, Wikipedia can roll back[13] an untruth, while eBay can't roll back a shipped iPod. Before implementing a

---

12 A 2005 study by Nature magazine found that Wikipedia's science articles were roughly as accurate as Encyclopedia Britannica, with an average of 2.92 mistakes per article for Britannica and 3.86 for Wikipedia.

13 Wikipedia's approach for protecting of their valuable content is to save every single version of every article ever created, and if some mischievous devil comes by wreaking havoc, any concerned Wikipedia reader can "roll back" the article to a previous, better version.

reputation system that is rife with unintended consequences, it's worth thinking about your best and worst case scenarios.

Relationships

Conflict: On a Web site of thousands or millions of people, how do you make sure you can keep track of the people whom you care about?

Resolution: Create ways that people can identify, connect, and organize the people they care about, as well as the information those people produce. The complexity of the classification of relationships depends on how your customers will use your Web site.

Relationships are always present in communities; it's up to the host software to manifest and categorize those relationships according to the community's needs. A lighter touch creates less overhead, such as Twitter's flat following mode seen in **Figure 9.18**. Twitter is based on the concept that people are broadcasting to each other and subscribing to each other's broadcasts as they would to a magazine. The Twitter system design doesn't recognize that mutual following might be a proxy for friendship. The entirety of the relationship is, "I'm interested."

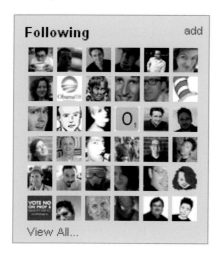

FIGURE 9.18 Twitter lists everyone you are following, whether they follow you back or not.

If you offer more choices for defining the nature of relationships, you can allow for greater levels of control by the user, but it also introduces complexity. Flickr offers the categories of Friends, Family, and Contacts, but leaves one with the question of which friends are really family and which family are really friends? When your contacts can grow to 100, Friends becomes a useful shortcut for people you simply want to watch a little closer, because they are at the top of the page (see **Figure 9.19**). Because you set viewing permissions based on these distinctions, a college student might show his most intimate photos only to a list of close friends labeled *family*, and put his actual family in the friends or even contacts list. Each label has a built-in set of assumptions that may or may not be applicable to the user's needs.

FIGURE 9.19 Flickr shows photos from friends and family before they show you the masses.

Elements of relationships

Relationships on your site are just as important as your users' relationships in real life, at least you hope they will be. The elements of relationships are:

- Contacts
- Groups
- Norms

Contacts

Relationships, or *interpersonal ties* as they are called in sociology, are defined as information-carrying connections between people, and they come in three varieties: *strong*, *weak*, or *absent*. *Strong* ties are defined as people you see once a week, *weak* are less than every two weeks but more than once a year, and after that they are considered *absent*.[14] On a traditional Web site, all ties are absent, so you don't know which members know which other members. In order to organize your site's world via the people in it, you need to give your users a way to create a classification system of humans. It can be as

---

14 Granovetter, M.S. (1970). "Changing Jobs: Channels of Mobility Information in a Suburban Community." Doctoral dissertation, Harvard University.

simple as just saying, "I know him," or, "I don't know him," or as complex as saying, "We were college roommates, but we haven't spoken in 10 years."

LinkedIn.com focuses on *weak* ties, creating a flat hierarchy of contacts. You know someone, or you don't know someone. It's up to you to remember if a contact is someone you never met but whom you email with regularly, or someone you met once two years ago at a conference, or the guy in the cubicle next to you.

Orkut allows you to express how close you are to a person with terms like "acquaintances," "friends," "good friends," "best friends"—but this is a lot of mental overhead. How much does Christina like Austin anyhow? In **Figure 9.20**, we have to figure out if he's an acquaintance, a friend, a good friend, or a best friend. That's a lot of subtlety for a checkbox to carry.

FIGURE 9.20 Orkut wants to know how much Christina likes Austin.

Facebook does its best to pull out information about the nature of your relationships (see **Figure 9.21**). For a while, the powers that be at Facebook tried forcing their users to add details upon adding a contact. Now they merely encourage users to add a few details once they have confirmed the relationship's existence. The intercept approach probably was annoying enough to lower the number of connections made, and a social network survives by the completeness of the social graph.[15] It's what allows you to receive information; the more connections you have, the more news articles, applications, photos, and gossip you get. The more accurate the connections (i.e., they are actually friends rather than random strangers you collected to make yourself look cool), the better the stuff you get. The more "better stuff" you get, the more you come back, and the more the Web site thrives via page views and advertising impressions.

---

15 Hot buzzword of 2008 and term most likely to make this book look dated, the social graph is the uncharted map of everyone's relationship to everyone else. Facebook's stated goal is mapping the social graph.

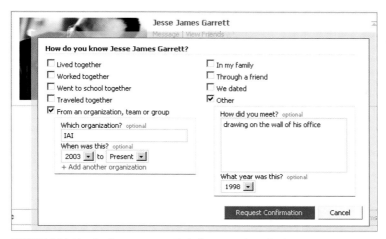

FIGURE 9.21 Facebook encourages Christina to say how she knows Jesse James Garrett.

Groups

Groups are another relationship structure, based on shared interests or experiences rather than personal affection. They include alumni groups, work groups, and professional organizations. We usually think of groups as something users explicitly join, such as a mailing list or a discussion group. But groups can be formed by shared activities or even tags. For example, 43 Things is a site that helps you meet life goals. If you state you are interested in, say, learning French, you'll land on a page that collects all the other people who have said they are interested in the same thing. This group is loosely connected, and people come or go as often as their need for support grows or wanes, but for a little while you can find support and advice from your peers. It's a little like a drop-in alcoholics anonymous support group, where the shared life experience is enough to tie these people together.

Explicitly choosing to join a group will create greater commitment to participate and nurture that group. Barriers to participation, such as the pay-to-participate model seen on The Well, can keep the level of conversation very high, or it can kill it when there are many free alternatives. The Well is one of the oldest and possibly the most prestigious of virtual communities, started in 1985 by Stewart Brand and Larry Brilliant. Yep, that's not a typo: 1985. Before the Web. You have always had to have a subscription, originally because the cost of the technology was high, but eventually because it was good for the quality of the community's dialogue.

Groups are usually formed around a subject of interest, and the Internet allows for aggregation of passionate people into a viable group that might not normally be possible in the physical world. You may be the only person in a hundred miles who cares about carrying your baby in a sling, but on the Yahoo! group "babywearing," you've got 3,221 friends. Even in the "real" world, virtual communities can connect people who might not otherwise find each other, acting as an idea matchmaker. Meetup is the most well known in this category, and was launched into the spotlight when it enabled passionate supporters of presidential hopeful Howard Dean to meet up and plan. But now it allows pug owners, knitters, and ghost hunters to gather and discuss their divergent passions. If it weren't for Meetup, Christina might never have guessed she was driving distance from fellow origamists.[16]

Groups, formal and informal, online and off, are marked by similar characteristics:

Norms

A group will decide what it considers good and bad, and will eject those who don't share those norms (unless one of the norms is embracing diversity, of course). Groups are usually formed for one of two reasons:

1. **Vilification:** Some groups are formed just because they all hate something.

2. **Veneration:** Others are formed out of love.

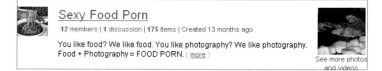

While walking into a biker bar wearing a Yamaha T-shirt might get you killed, wandering into a Star Wars forum and saying, "George Lucas ripped off Joseph Campbell, and he didn't even do it well!" will just generate 500 posts an hour. On the Internet, we call these people who violate norms "trolls," and it's best to be prepared for them by creating and posting clear rules for behavior as well as designing consequences for violation of the rules, from time-outs[17] to full-out banning.

Banning is often problematic because of the difficulty of identifying people on the Internet. On The Well, they have your credit card so they know your real name, and, if they really

---

16 People who fold paper into shapes and animals for fun. Christina thinks it's fun, anyhow, and on Meetup she found a dozen others who agree.

17 It works for kids from 2 to 52!

wanted, could keep you out for dreadful behavior. Another approach to managing bad behavior is encouraging people to build up rich profiles so they are less willing to destroy their hard-crafted identity. A simpler approach is allowing the site community to "flag" inappropriate posts in order to identify misbehavior (as seen in **Figure 9.22**), and then giving the miscreant a time-out in which he/she can't post. This will allow them to acclimate to the group's norms, or if they are truly just seeking a fight, they'll wander off. Some groups don't allow posting until you've been a member for a period of time, to avoid this drive-by nuisance making.[18]

please <u>flag</u> with care:

<u>miscategorized</u>

<u>prohibited</u>

<u>spam/overpost</u>

<u>best of craigslist</u>

FIGURE 9.22
Craig's List has fine-tuned flagging categories.

Activity

Conflict: If there is nothing to do on a site, then it doesn't matter if all your friends are there. The site has no more usefulness than an address book, and it won't get affection or traffic.

Resolution: Find activities to support on your site that are useful to individuals but are much improved by group participation.

The third major pattern in social software is community activities. This is just like being a party planner: you've brought people together, now what? Happily, humans have things they like to do together anyhow, and if you get them in the same spot and give them even rudimentary tools, they'll start talking, sharing, and collaborating.

Elements of activity

The more things your users are able to do on your site, the more time and energy they'll spend there. The elements of activity are:

- Sharing
- Conversations
- Collaborating
- Collective wisdom

Sharing

Gifting is a primitive human behavior—it binds us. When one person gives something to another, there is gratitude, and a desire for reciprocity. In community settings online,

---

18 Since trolls are best handled by ignoring them (they start arguments to gain attention), it's been suggested that software should hide the trolls' posts from everyone else, so the trolls don't realize they've been banned. Thinking they are being ignored, the trolls will wander off. It has yet to be proved that this will work over time.

where the digital nature of files means anything you give to someone you still have a copy of, gifting manifests itself as sharing. Sharing first gathers people of like interests, then it allows for an exchange of digital assets, such as photos, recipes or essays, and, as the community tightens, permits an exchange of dreams and hopes, secrets and fears.

You can share pictures, stories, recipes, drawings, habits, and hopes. If it can be represented digitally, you can share it. **Figure 9.23** shows a page of 43 things on which abmasterflex has shared some very personal revelations about himself in order to help others suffering from anxiety. This intimate revelation is far more binding than sharing a favorite song or photo, although those can tie communities together also.

FIGURE 9.23 People share hints on how to get through life, and they grow emotional connections along the way.

Conversations

Conversations and communication—that's the heart and soul of a community. No matter how much software we build, people build the relationships, and they build them out of words first. If you don't have a place for people to put their words, no community is ever possible, only a viewership. There are fanfiction[19] sites that have

---

19 Fanfiction! The Internet is a marvelous place where, if your favorite show is cancelled, you can join others to write new episodes. Some sites even let the fans film those episodes and upload them. Do a search for any old cult movie classic or cancelled popular TV show, and you'll find a joyous riot of copyright infringement.

outlived their original inspiration. Communities last if the people within them can talk to each other.

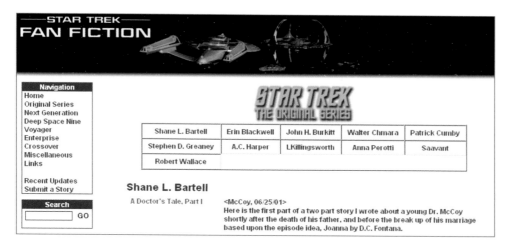

Twitter blends presence with conversation by little tweets of, "I am here, alive! Aware!" If you add an @ to the user's name, you can cobble together a public back-and-forth, rather like chatting at a noisy party. In **Figure 9.24**, you can see our stalwart tech editor Robert Hoekman trying to carry on a debate with Joshua Porter and Christina.[20] It's a testament to the passion people have for conversation that they will cobble it together, even out of clunky, command-line approaches.

Conversely, Amazon has long made it impossible to conduct conversation in reviews because of their usefulness rating, which changes the order of the reviews so a thread's history is disrupted. Unable to guarantee chronological display of their comments, reviewers can only

FIGURE 9.24 Robert, spoiling for a fight, uses the @ sign to indicate whom he's disagreeing with.

broadcast their views. They have recently added "comment" to the reviews, to overcome this problem, yet still allow for "useful" reviews to float to the top (see **Figure 9.25**).

---

20 A note from Christina: "@wodtke is my dad, not me. I'm @cwodtke. If you plan to stalk... er... follow me."

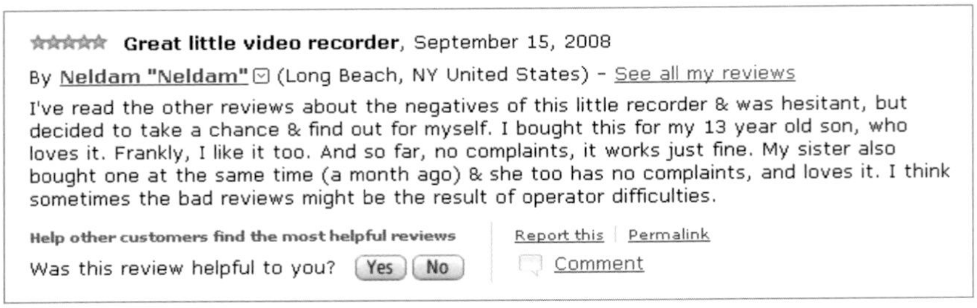

⭐⭐⭐⭐⭐ **Great little video recorder**, September 15, 2008

By <u>Neldam "Neldam"</u> ☑ (Long Beach, NY United States) - <u>See all my reviews</u>

I've read the other reviews about the negatives of this little recorder & was hesitant, but decided to take a chance & find out for myself. I bought this for my 13 year old son, who loves it. Frankly, I like it too. And so far, no complaints, it works just fine. My sister also bought one at the same time (a month ago) & she too has no complaints, and loves it. I think sometimes the bad reviews might be the result of operator difficulties.

Help other customers find the most helpful reviews

Was this review helpful to you?   (Yes)(No)   ☐ <u>Comment</u>   <u>Report this</u> | <u>Permalink</u>

FIGURE 9.25 Although the reviews are ordered by usefulness, rather than chronologically, Amazon has added "comment" to allow for conversation.

LinkedIn similarly kills conversation in their Answers section by allowing only one response to any given question; they have optimized for quality rather than participation. Conversation is not always the most important thing in user-generated content.

Collaborating

Social software was originally envisioned as a tool to allow workgroups to collaborate. While the "social" part may have swept the Web, there are still plenty of tools that focus on letting smaller groups with focus get things done.

One of the best known is Basecamp, and it was our pick when we sat down to try to find a way we could share chapters, files, and debates about how the second edition of this book should be. Unlike Microsoft Project (which it was designed to displace) it is multi-user, conversation-focused, and drop-dead simple (see **Figure 9.26**).

Collective wisdom

As opposed to collaboration, in which the approach is working together toward a known goal, collective wisdom approaches on Web sites leverage people acting individually in self-interest and then aggregate those choices into patterns. This approach can be remarkably effective. The Iowa Electronic Markets and the Hollywood Stock Exchange both reproduce Wall Street, allowing anyone to buy, sell, and trade "stock" in political outcomes or films. The Iowa Electronic Markets has proven to be more accurate in predicting election results than polling. It predicted the vote totals of the past two presidential elections within two-tenths of a percentage point, outperforming national polls. It's theorized that the market is more accurate because people are motivated to buy and sell on what they think is the most likely outcome, rather than what they'd like to see happen.

FIGURE 9.26 Here you see Austin and Alyssa discussing how to write the book. Conversation is how things happen. Basecamp also supports collaboration with wiki-style "Writeboards" where people can edit each other's work, and overviews that show new activity.

Dell's IdeaStorm (**Figure 9.27**) is one of the most successful of the new breed of demand aggregators. Demand aggregators encourage folks to post ideas or requests to a company. The customers then vote the ideas up and down. IdeaStorm led to Dell's very first PC with Ubuntu[21] preinstalled. *Boxes and Arrows*, a user-experience magazine founded by Christina Wodtke, encourages authors to post their story ideas publicly and then encourages the readership to vote for stories they'd like to see written, and

---

21   An open-source operating system competing with Windows and Macs.

comment on the partially-formed concepts. This helps the authors refine their ideas, and it allows the editors to better understand their readership.

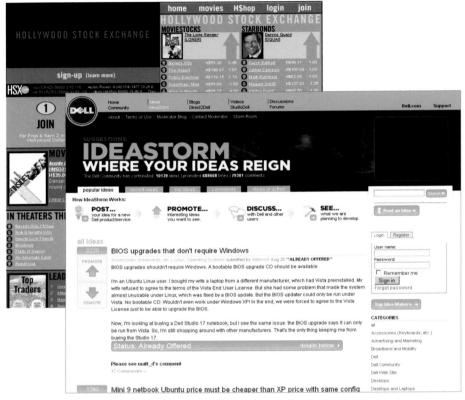

FIGURE 9.27 Hollywood Stock Exchange and Dell's Ideastorm both use collective behavior to decide what "best" means—a new movie, or a new operating system.

Finally, you can combine collaboration and collective wisdom effectively. Cambrian House uses collective wisdom to vet ideas and collaboration tools to build new companies. Anyone with an idea for a business can post it, it gets voted on, and others can join that person to build a business out of the best ideas.

Architecture for Humans

Humans are complex, and the Web is dynamic. It's likely there will be many more new innovations and new patterns of excellence as they are refined. Yet human contact and collaboration is not new.

36. Degrees of Publicness

Conflict

People are different, and the way they want to place their houses in a neighbourhood is one of the most basic kinds of difference.

Resolution

Make a clear distinction between three kinds of homes—those on quiet backwaters, those on busy streets, and those that are more or less in-between. Make sure that those on quiet backwaters are on twisting paths, and that these houses are themselves physically secluded; make sure that the more public houses are on busy streets with many people passing by all day long and that the houses themselves are exposed to the passers-by. The in-between houses may then be located on the paths halfway between the other two. Give every neighbourhood about an equal number of these three kinds of homes.

This pattern was written about the design of a town, but it can be easily applied to the design of a social network. Facebook was initially lambasted over what has become its most popular feature: the News Feed. The News Feed is the equivalent of the town square where you can hear everything that's going on with everybody and chat about it. Some people want to live on the town square, so they don't miss a thing. Others would like to live at the edges of town, away from both prying eyes and overwhelming updates. An ongoing challenge for social architecture will be figuring out intelligent and subtle ways to allow people degrees of publicness (including shelter from other people's publicness.)

If we remember the *social* in social architecture, we can continue to make new products that delight.

"If you give a problem
to an architect,
you'll get a building
for a solution."

10

All Together Now

In Which We Design a Web Site.

Finally, the moment we've all been waiting for. We've gone over all the tools and how to use them. Now it's time to put what we've learned into action by working on a real project. We need a guinea pig. It turns out, both Austin and Christina work with Boxes and Arrows, an independent online magazine, and we know they were having some problems with their current design. Let's go work for them.

Project: Boxes & Arrows, an Online Magazine

Christina founded Boxes & Arrows in 2001. In the last eight years, it has published almost 400 articles. Day-to-day activities are overseen by Chris Baum and Jorge Arango, the chief and managing editors, respectively. Chris and Jorge will be two of our primary contacts. Christina is still the publisher, so she'll also have a serious say in what does and doesn't get approved. For the purposes of this project, Chris, Jorge, and Christina are the stakeholders. In our case study, Austin is the lead architect and will drive the approach, while Christina will add details to the issues and review the work.[1]

Step 1: What Does B&A Need?

To get started, we asked Chris and Jorge to list some of the problems they'd seen with the site:

- Entering B&A via a story or the homepage can be a dead-end; if you don't see a story you like on the homepage, the classification system isn't great for helping you find it. If you

---

1 One thing we know is it can be hard to get distance on your own site, especially when you've been running it for eight years! Christina is happy to let Austin take the reins on this long-neglected problem.

read a story, there is very little associated navigation to help you find more to read. (Chris suggested: "I'd love to have links to other stories/ideas and "guides" based on important topics—for example, "Getting Started on B&A," "Usability," etc.)

- There is no way to promote new material that's not a story (for example, news, podcasts, and editorials).

- There is no way to drive attention to new community activity, such as forum posts.

- The classification system is almost the same as it was when first created in 2001, and new categories have been tossed in. The result is a classification that is both incoherent and doesn't really match the content.

- There is a variety of interesting content that's not articles, but it's not really integrated well with the main magazine (like events). This means readers may not notice it.

- The B&A folks have wanted to add a book reviews section (and maybe software reviews) for years. If we can create a special section with book reviews, we may be able to drive more traffic to it, increasing money we need to fund the site via the Amazon Associates program.

- They have also wanted to add richer member profiles. Users have asked for better profiles (bios) for a long time. With the economic downturn, could Boxes and Arrows help people find jobs?

You'll notice that this is an odd mix of complaints; some seem to be general problems, while others seem to be feature requests. For example, "Entering B&A at a story or on the homepage can be a dead-end"—that's a problem. That means people aren't reading that next article. Some of the other problems aren't really problems; they are the stake-holder's way of pushing to the solution to the problem quickly. It's been said that, *"If you give a problem to an architect, you'll get a building for a solution."*[2] And as is often the case with a Web site, a solution to a problem is framed as a new feature.

Look at how Chris phrased one problem: "Entering B&A via a story or the homepage can be a dead-end." He then followed his problem with a proposed solution: "I'd love to have links to other stories/ideas and 'guides' based on important topics—e.g., Getting Started on B&A, Usability, etc." He breezed past the problem to what he thought could be the solution, and this is normal. But our job is to dig a little deeper. He is the B&A expert, but, on the other hand, an outsider can sometimes shed light where no one else dare tread (or has time to). Analysis to the rescue!

We'll split our initial list of problems into two lists—one of problems and another for new features (**Table 10.1**).

---

2 Herb Caen, the late great newspaper columnist for the San Francisco Chronicle, who also said, "A man begins cutting his wisdom teeth the first time he bites off more than he can chew."

Problems	New Features
There's no connection between Ideas, Stories, and the homepage.	There's no way to promote new material that's not a story (for example, news, podcasts, and editorials).
Entering B&A via a story or the homepage can be a dead-end.	No way to drive attention to community activity like forums.
The classification system is outdated and isn't very flexible.	They've wanted to add a book reviews section (and maybe software reviews).
There's a variety of interesting content, but it's not really integrated well (like events).	They've wanted to add richer bios.
	There's isn't any way to add tags or keywords.

TABLE 10.1 We've split our initial list of complaints into two lists—one for problems and another for new features.

If you can delineate the problems from features, you gain two pieces of knowledge. First, it's often easier to fix a problem than it is to build a new feature. This isn't always true, but it's worth identifying fixes versus new features. Second, new features are always problems in disguise, and your list of new features tells you where you need to do some more digging.

Step 2: What's the Problem, Really?

When trying to decide what you should work on next, it can be difficult to compare the benefit of a new feature with the benefit of fixing an old problem. The sneaky thing about new features is that they are the solution to a problem someone hasn't specified. A good way to dig an underlying problem out of a new feature is to ask "Why?" five times. Let's try it with one of the new features: a way to add tags or keywords to stories.

1. *Why?* So we can add more categories to stories.

2. *Why do we need more categories?* Because our current classification is outdated. It doesn't match up with what our stories are about.

3. *Why does it need to match up with the stories?* Because users have trouble finding content on the topics they are looking for.

   It only took three "whys" to get to a real problem: users have trouble finding content on specific topics. Let's see where five "whys" take us.

4. *Why do users need to find content on specific topics?* Because we want them to turn to Boxes and Arrows whenever they need insight on how to do their jobs better or help to grow in their careers.

5.   *Why do we want them to turn to B&A?* Because we want them to get amazing information, grow, and feel a sense of gratitude and obligation, so they contribute back to the community, helping the community continue to grow.

Now, that's a problem: Users won't contribute back to the B&A community because the site doesn't engage them on topics they're interested in. That sounds awfully concise and tidy. Could that be the problem we're trying to solve? Talking with Christina, she echoes this idea: "Right now someone comes via Digg, or a blog, or whatever and reads an article, and leaves. We are just another site on the Web. And when they consider where to submit an article they've written, if they aren't thinking of us they could blog it, or put it on another Web site. And maybe we don't deserve it!"

It sounds like several of our problems and new features are oriented toward improving engagement by improving how content is classified. If we can group several similar problems together, we might be able to fix them with one solution.

Step 3: Reframing the Problem

Like any organization, Boxes and Arrows has more things to fix and more new features to add than it can or will ever get done. This isn't a unique problem. All organizations have wish lists that exceed the realm of possibility. That doesn't mean you ignore all but the most important. Instead, you reframe your problems so they change from a long, insurmountable to-do list to a couple of problems that you can solve. This isn't always possible. But if it means we get more done with less, then it's worth some time.

To reframe your problems, it's useful to look for commonalities between them. Often, the common thread running through several problems is also the loose end you can sew up to solve with one stitch. together. To group similar problems together, let's do a card sort. In Chapter 3, Sock Drawers and CD Racks, we performed a card sort to organize Web site content by grouping similar content with similar content. Here we're using a card sort to solve a similar problem: Which problems are similar to each other. To do this, we'll write all of our problems down on note cards. (You can also use sticky notes, scraps of paper, or anything you can move around easily.) Whenever we encounter a problem we think needs to be rephrased, we'll jot down the original problem, and the rephrasing on the same note (see **Figure 10.1**).

Don't worry about the labels being fuzzy. We're not trying to sum complex, intricate problems with singular, clarifying phrases. We just want to remember the gist of what the problems are about. It's also important to note there's no one right way to group items. The way we grouped the problems listed in the table is almost certainly not how you would do it. And that's okay. The point of the exercise isn't universal truth, but to think about how our problems are related to one another. We're thinking.

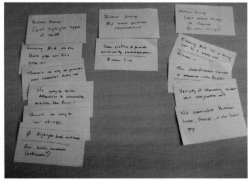

FIGURE 10.1 We wrote each problem on a card and then grouped similar problems with one another.

In **Table 10.2**, we've unpacked our problems using the five whys and collected them into three groups.

Publication has no way to draw attention to featured content	Bios don't promote participation	Difficult to find related content
1. There's no way to "pin" things. 2. No connection between Ideas, Stories, and the homepage. 3. There's no way to promote new material that's not a story (for example, news, podcasts, and editorials). 4. No way to drive attention to community activity like forums. 5. Entering B&A via the homepage can be a dead-end. 6. There's no way to highlight book reviews, which could make money for our infrastructure costs. 7. No place for administrative content like news from the Editorial department.	1. User profiles only have a short biography and a list of the member's stories and comments. 2. Users can't add outside links to things such as their portfolio or stories on other publications. 3. Users can't indicate if they are looking for work or to consult. 4. Users can't "follow" other users to find more interesting content via peer activity. 5. Users can't message each other.	1. Entering B&A via a story can be a dead-end. Few related stories. 2. The classification system doesn't help users find stories. (It's outdated and Frankensteinian.) 3. There's a variety of interesting non-article content, but it's not really integrated well with the articles (like events). 4. The bottom of the page trails off into comments, and leaves the user wondering what comes next. 5. Hard to be sure if you've found everything pertaining to a topic, whether you browse or search.

TABLE 10.2 When we looked at all of the problems, we found they fell into three groups.

In all, we list 17 different problems. However, when we reframe the problems by looking for common threads, we find three main problems:

1. Publication has no way to draw attention to featured content (book reviews, forums, news, podcasts, and so on).

2. Bios don't promote participation.

3. It's difficult to find related content.

If we can solve the first reframed problem—publication has no way to draw attention to featured content—then we have the potential to solve seven separate items on our original list of problems. However, at the back of our heads is this nagging thought: if we can figure out how to relate other content to stories better, it will help us with the first problem of promoting content. Boxes and Arrows needs better tools for sending users to associated content. Boxes and Arrows needs a better way to categorize its stories, podcasts, and news so we can give users access to related content. Since these are classic IA problems, we'll solve them first using the tools from the previous chapters. For now, the profile problem will have to go on hold.

Step 4: Who Are the Affected Users?

When you're working on only part of a site, you don't need to worry about all of your potential users. You can focus only on the users who will be affected. Unfortunately for us, tweaking the way content is organized on B&A is a pretty global change that will affect all users.

If you were building a site from scratch, or redesigning a site from the ground up, you would ask yourself: "Who are my users?" The playing field is almost totally wide open, and you'd want to do user research to figure out who all of your users were. For our project, we're fixing a specific problem with an existing site. The users are already there and have formed opinions about the site's good and bad points. And luckily, the B&A staff ran a comprehensive online survey recently. Austin spent a Saturday sifting through 483 responses to uncover who B&A readers were and what makes them tick. He had enough information to put together a couple of personas.[3]

---

3 You won't always have a large user survey waiting around for you to come by and craft personas. And maybe you can't conduct a survey, or interviews, or anything. But dig around, and you'll find you know something about your users. While more information about your users is better, a little information is better than nothing. We cover sources for information about your users in Chapter 2, Balancing Acts.

Lindsey Mason
26/female/single/St. Louis, MO

Quote	"I'm trying to improve my user experience skills, so I can move my career along."
Profession	(Interactive) graphic designer for MegaCorp
Tech Skill	Low Intermediate
Personal Background	Lindsey has been designing Web sites for two years. She used to focus solely on graphic design, but in the past two years she's shifted toward interactive work. She works for a small corporation where project teams typically have an owner, a dev guy, and her. She visits Boxes and Arrows whenever one of her friends posts a link to an article (about once a month).
Goals	Lindsey is trying to learn more about specific user experience topics so she can improve her work as well as move up the ladder.

Phillip Kuyklander
34/male/married/Philadelphia, PA

Quote	"I'm in a hurry and really need to find that article about how that company did this."
Profession	Information Architect/User Experience
Tech Skill	Intermediate
Personal Background	Phillip has been involved with Web design for almost 10 years, mostly focusing on the user experience. He usually contracts with large organizations on large projects with lots of moving pieces. He's on the B&A mailing list and always checks to see what new articles have been posted, reading several each month. He's been in the business for long enough that he doesn't want to get stale so he needs to keep up with the latest thoughts in design.
Goals	Phillip wants to reference a specific article because it covered something he wants to do on his current project. He hopes finding it will solve a specific problem he's having with a current project.

	Samantha Evans 41/married/Ann Arbor
Quote	"I need to make a name for myself so work finds me."
Profession	Interaction Designer
Tech Skill	Senior
Personal Background	Samantha has been doing Web design for 10 years and interaction design for eight years on the Web. She has recently left employment at a major pharmaceutical company to move into consulting, and she wants to increase her rates. She reads Boxes and Arrows when she sees links on the listserves she follows, but wonders if it's worth writing for them.
Goals	Samantha is looking to prove how knowledgeable she is in order to get more work, and perhaps even score a book contract some day. She hasn't published outside of intra-company reports, and wonders if she should start a blog or something.

Not only was there enough info to generate personas, but Austin also noticed many of the survey respondents mentioned having trouble with the classification system:

- "I don't use it as a source where I 'look for things.' I'm more likely to respond to the latest articles or announcements."

- "Strictly speaking, the navigation on the left is arbitrary and unusable. I can't actually 'find' any damn thing on the site."

- "The organization system and labeling! (Just what are those categories, anyway?)"

- "Do something different with the navigation; it seems to be organized in an odd way."

Our problem set came from the stakeholders, but it's good to know both stakeholders and users are seeing the same problem. Moreover, we created the third persona so we could keep in mind our end goal of eliciting more participation from the B&A members.

Since we're focusing on solving the problem of how content is organized, we're going to design for personas that are trying to find things. That makes Lindsey and Phillip our primary personas. Samantha will have to wait until later in the project.

Step 5: What Do the Users Want to Do?

Now that we know who our users are, we need to figure out what they're doing. We want the final product to be ideal for our users, so we'll write a scenario for each user that describes that person's ideal experience.

Lindsey is looking for more information about personas. Phillip is looking for a specific article on negative personas.[4]

Lindsey's Ideal Experience

This afternoon, Lindsey will meet with the project team to kick off the next project. Lindsey wants to grow her UX toolset, and she thinks this project might be a good time to try using personas. Also, she's been feeling frustrated with the team's process. Her product manger pushes her to go from meeting to mock-up—but with 500 layers, it can be a hassle to change. For today's meeting, she wants to see if the team will whiteboard wireframes with her. Hopefully, that means her mock-ups will go through fewer changes. To make that argument, though, she feels that she needs some ammunition from Boxes and Arrows.

Since she has a couple of hours before the kick-off meeting, she decides to do a quick refresher on personas, so she hops online to look for tutorials over at Boxes and Arrows. On the homepage, she notices information about both personas and UX 101. Both sound right up her alley.

She opens UX 101 in a new tab and—along with articles on the various practices that make up user experience—she sees a collection of introductory articles on personas.

Back in the other tab, she dives into all the articles on personas. It has a section of introductory articles, but it gets deep fast. She decides UX 101 is what she wants, but adds the personas page to her favorites, so she can come back later if she needs any more help.

UX 101 also has a section on wireframes, but it looks pretty basic. She knows how to draw gray boxes. She's really looking for help on creating collaborative wireframes, so she explores all the articles on wireframes looking for something more advanced, and there it is: an article on sketching wireframes with a team! It looks a little in-depth to read right now, so she prints it out to read it later.

Back at UX 101 on personas, the intro articles are just the right depth and level to go through right away. She alternately skims and reads two articles until it's time for lunch.

She saves the third persona article to her favorites, grabs her purse, and heads to lunch. She'll go through the last article later today after the kick-off meeting.

---

4 If you remember the information seeking behaviors we talked about in the Chapter 8, The Tao of Navigation, this task is an example of "exploratory seeking," and Phillip's is an example of a "known item" search.

In **Table 10.3**, Austin breaks Lindsey's scenario into a step-by-step analysis of each task. In Chapter 7, From Box to Page, we also assigned tasks to pages. Since we're adjusting how people navigate an existing site, many of these tasks are already being completed on existing pages. We'll note this in our analysis and see if it should be adjusted or where we may need new pages. Austin does the same for Phillip's scenario in **Table 10.4**.

Austin added a column to show what page Lindsey is on at any given time. (Those question marks mean we might need to design a brand new page.)

Step	Task	Page
1	Views homepage	Home
2	Views articles related to "personas"	???
2a	Adds persona article to favorites	???
3	Returns to homepage	Home
4	Views articles related to "UX 101"	???
5	Views articles related to "wireframes"	???
6	Opens article on "sketching"	Article page
7	Prints article	n/a
8	Opens articles on personas	Article page
8a	Saves article to favorites	???

TABLE 10.3 An analysis of the tasks Lindsey completes to find an article about personas

Phillip's Ideal Experience

Phillip just got out of a meeting. It looks like the project might be swinging off track—and fast. The project team is losing track of whom they're designing for. Phillip thinks personas will help, but more importantly, he has to educate the team about who *not* to design for. He remembers an article about negative personas he read at B&A a little while back. Those would be perfect.

Back at his desk, Phillip directs his browser to the Boxes and Arrows site. After he searches for "negative personas," he finds the article he wanted on the first page of results. He glances over the article and thinks he might be able to find some more nuggets of useful information in other articles. He takes a look at all persona-related articles, looking for some of the more advanced techniques and some case studies.

Under case studies, he finds an article about personas that seems to match his current situation and reads the intro. It looks like it matches what he's looking for, and he has 15 minutes before his next meeting, so he reads the article. When he's done, he doesn't want to forget it, so he saves it to his favorites to find later.

It's time for his meeting, so he pulls up Outlook to check the room number and heads out.

Step	Task	Page
1	Views homepage and searches for "personas"	Home
2	Views search results	Search results page
3	Opens article on "negative personas"	Article page
4	Views articles related to "personas"	???
5	Opens persona case study	Article page
6	Views articles related to "wireframes"	???

TABLE 10.4 Austin Converts Phillip's Scenario into a Task Analysis

The scenarios and task analyses help us understand how Lindsey and Phillip will navigate the content. We know how our personas would like our solution to function, but we still haven't reorganized our content so the right content and navigation is available to them at the right time. We're ready to find a better way to organize B&A's articles.

Step 6: What Does Our Content Look Like?

The personas give us an idea of who our users are. And we've framed the problem as one of finding a better way to categorize the Boxes and Arrows content, so now we need to figure out what our content looks like.

Currently, the Boxes and Arrows site organizes content in an odd series of buckets:

- Big Ideas
- Business Design
- Case Studies
- Deliverables
- Findability
- Forerunners
- From the Editors
- Interactivity
- Interviews
- Learning from Others
- Methods
- Podcasts
- Professionalism
- Reviews
- User-centric
- Visual and Visible

What's wrong with these labels? Some of these labels are pretty clear. *Findability* is a core focus of information architecture, yet findability is a bit jargon-y. *Business design* was a hot topic a year ago that has since simmered down, and is often called "design thinking." These labels describe the topics discussed, but they rub against labels that identify types of content like podcasts, interviews, and case studies. Methods and deliverables are vague in an entirely different way. For example, just about everything's a *method*, and any method you can squeeze onto paper and hand to someone is a *deliverable*. In these 16 categories, it's clear that Boxes and Arrows has a lot of content, but it's not clear how it is organized. It's not clear to users where they'll find the stories they're looking for from these categories.

One of the problems the editors mentioned was that they were unable to highlight special content like podcasts and news. When Boxes and Arrows began, everything it published was a story, so there was no need to highlight special content. Now, that has changed. They've already added a category for podcasts to help manage the new content format. Since we're reorganizing the content, we're going to split content type from content topic. Type includes things like News, Podcasts, Reviews, and Stories. Topic includes things like Business Design, Findability, and Interactivity.

In **Table 10.5**, Austin looked at the current site and came up with four ways to group the content:[5]

Format	Type	Topic	Audience Level
Stories	Article/tutorial (how to do something)	prototyping	Introductory
News		sketching	Intermediate
Podcasts (audio)	Editorial/opinion	xhtml/css	Advanced
Discussions (comments and forum discussions)	Case Study (how the user did something)	ia summit 2008	
Ideas	Interview	wireframes	
Events	Conference	findability	
Jobs	Book reviews	usability	
	Software reviews	professionalism	
		business design	
		accessibility	
		card sorting	
		interface design	
		forms	
		user registration	
		audio	
		icons	
		search analytics	
		social media	
		personas	

TABLE 10.5 Four ways of Grouping Boxes & Arrows Content

Since we had the request to add book reviews (and maybe software reviews), Austin went ahead and added them. And, because Lindsey specifically looked for introductory content and Chris had requested a way to highlight basic material for new practitioners, Austin added Introductory, Intermediate, and Advanced content groups, as well. (This also helps Phillip, since he most likely will prefer to avoid introductory articles on topics he's familiar with.)

If you read about metadata in Chapter 4, A Bricklayer's View of Information Architecture, then you might remember that there were three kinds of metadata: intrinsic, administrative, and descriptive. When you organize your site, you're identifying the kinds of metadata you will assign to your content, as well as figuring out what metadata will make the best findability system (for both browsing and searching). In this case, Format is intrinsic metadata, Category is administrative, and Topic and Level are both descriptive.

When you organize your content, it's also important to think about how the content will evolve over time. Organizations evolve and change and their content changes with

---

5 Four *main* ways. There are auxiliary ways, like "author" and "chronological," that already exist because of inherent metadata. We're ignoring those for now, but they will always be there, and useful for creating associated content.

them. When you create a content model, it's important for it to be flexible enough to grow alongside the rest of the Web site. For example, the list of Formats will probably grow very slowly, if at all. The editors might add video, for example, but there aren't that many other Formats to add. Similarly, the Types represent reasonably static types of content. However, Topic is a long list that could easily be longer. Some topics are newer, like "social media", and others have been around since the beginning of the Web, like "interface design." Others, like "business design," evolve into newer terms ("design thinking"). Where Format and Type will change slowly, if at all, Topics will change constantly.

We have a first pass on how we'll organize our content. Let's make sure the Content Management System (CMS) can handle it.[6]

Step 7: How Does the Technology Work?

Boxes and Arrows runs on PublicSquare, a hosted CMS designed specifically for independent publications with active, involved audiences. Because we're using an off-the-shelf solution, we won't be able to just apply whatever metadata we want, however we want it. We'll have to work with what the CMS is designed to accommodate. **Figure 10.2** shows PublicSquare's story screen. Each story has fields for a custom list of Categories, and a custom list of Story Types. This feature was created so that publications could apply different layout templates for different types of articles. Right now, Boxes and Arrows is only using Category metadata. This is good news for us, since it means we have one entirely empty bucket to play with, and we can use it for a different purpose than the one for which it was designed; we can create a simple faceted navigation system.

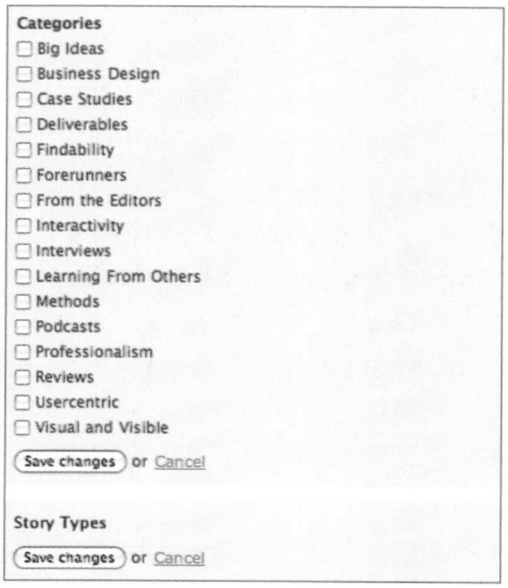

Categories
☐ Big Ideas
☐ Business Design
☐ Case Studies
☐ Deliverables
☐ Findability
☐ Forerunners
☐ From the Editors
☐ Interactivity
☐ Interviews
☐ Learning From Others
☐ Methods
☐ Podcasts
☐ Professionalism
☐ Reviews
☐ Usercentric
☐ Visual and Visible
(Save changes) or Cancel

Story Types
(Save changes) or Cancel

FIGURE 10.2 Boxes and Arrows only uses two metadata fields for each story. That means we can use Story Type to assign additional types of metadata to all of our content.

---

6 One of life's most frustrating lessons: Never assume the CMS can do anything basic, obvious, simple, or standard. Most of them don't.

In **Table 10.6**, we show how we can align our content model to the available fields in PublicSquare.

PublicSquare Metadata	Boxes & Arrows Content Model
Category	Type
Story Type	Format
???	Topic
???	Audience Level

TABLE 10.6 We've lined up PublicSquare's metadata fields with our content model.

Two parts of our content model don't line up with the technology—Topic and Audience Level. We could give up now and go with what we have, or we could ask the developers if we could add more fields. Lucky for us, the engineering team at PublicSquare has been meaning to get around to adding tags and keywords[7] for some time, since it's a popular feature.

When we sat down to talk with the engineers, they mentioned keywording (adding keywords) was trivial to implement, as long as it was just another field in the story's metadata area. Creating a navigation system that leveraged it would be even more work, and tagging would be slightly more difficult. After talking this through with the engineers, we decided to implement the keywording first and add the tagging later.

It's always important to discuss desired functionality with your engineering team early (if you can!). Sometimes things you think are hard aren't, and sometimes things you think are easy are difficult. The reality often lies between the two poles; via conversations with the programmers, you can probably figure out a way to make a complex feature simple enough to be executable.

With engineering on board to add keywords to the CMS, we only have one metadata category without a home, Audience Level. If we squeeze that in with Format, then our new PublicSquare approved Boxes and Arrows content model looks like **Table 10.7**.

---

7 Tags and keywords are similar, but different. The difference is that keywords are added by editors, and tags are keywords that are created and added by users. They frequently look and act the same, but it's best if we keep our terms straight.

Story Type/Classification (Format)	Category (Type)	Tags/Keywords (Topic)
Stories	Article/tutorial (how to do something)	prototyping
News	Editorial/opinion	sketching
Podcasts (audio)	Case Study (how the user did something)	xhtml/css
Discussions (comments and forum discussions)	Interview	ia summit 2008
Ideas	Conference	wireframes
Events	Book reviews	findability
Jobs	Software reviews	usability
	Level	professionalism
	Introductory	business design
	Intermediate	accessibility
	Advanced	card sorting
		interface design
		forms
		user registration
		audio
		icons
		search analytics
		social media
		personas

TABLE 10.7 Final Content Model

So far, everything seems great. Of course it seems great—we haven't had any feedback on the new metadata scheme. No one's been able to disagree with us. It's time we brought the stakeholders in to review. Christina offers some good comments:

> "…no users look for an editorial or an interview per se… they want to learn about search, or prototyping. Our current system is crappy for the same reason, and we compound it with silly names. I recommend a system where we reflect standard topics and use tagging to supplement for esoteric subjects. For example, the editors might set categories to be Design, IA, IxD, Business and Career, and Technology but users and authors might create tags like prototyping, kissing up, sitemaps, managing sideways, omnigraffle tips, etc."

After a little more discussion, Christina reveals an important tidbit:

> "We've also run into problems with how-to, deliverables, and case studies, as they overlap a bit. That [category] list should reflect how we want to express what B&A is about."

Chris Baum echoes Christina's new set of categories:

"I see two facets here:

1. *The communities of practice.*

2. *Other topics (prototyping, sketching, special event coverage, user reg, personas, etc.). These could also be divided into subgroupings, but don't necessarily need to do so.*

I'd like to be able to treat the former differently from the latter."

It's not uncommon to uncover tidbits like these as your initial designs are reviewed. Ideally, you hope your initial conversations with stakeholders and users will reveal everything you need to know. In practice, however, showing someone a proposed solution provides something for her to respond to.[8] It allows that person to clarify issues she might not have communicated earlier in the process.

Fortunately (or unfortunately) for Boxes and Arrows, all of the stakeholders are also IAs, so some of the feedback comes from very experienced and knowledgeable Web folks. In Chapter 8, The Tao of Navigation, we wrote about three questions to answer when designing your navigation system. Austin's taxonomy answered the first two questions: "How is your content organized?" and "What do your users want to do?" When Christina recommends the categories shift from types of content (like How-tos and interviews) to disciplines (like Information Architecture and Interaction Design), she's answering that third question—what do you want your users to do?

It's not rare to have a client recommend a totally different organization or navigation system. However, their recommendations will vary from really good to really bad. That's why it's important to communicate with the client as much as possible to make sure both of you have the same users in mind and are working toward the same business goals. You won't always have such wonderful feedback. But you can always have wonderful communication. In this case, Austin understands why Christina made the recommendation she did, and he understands why it might be better. Design isn't about being perfect. It's about making sure the site works despite its imperfections.

With Christina's comments about using the categories to reflect what B&A is all about, we end up with a new list:

- Information Architecture
- Interaction Design
- Information Design
- Interface Design
- Usability

---

8 "In theory, there is no difference between theory and practice. But, in practice, there is."—Yogi Berra

- Strategy

- Your Career

- Reviews

- Conferences

This new list of categories replaces our previous organization by type that included things like Article, Case Study, and Interview. And they'll also appear on the homepage. However, we still need to accommodate audience level—introductory, intermediate, and advanced. According to our task analysis, these three additional categories only appear on a mythical Tag/Keyword page that collects all articles related to a specific topic. (Lindsey wants to pull up all articles on personas and narrow in on introductory articles.)

Mixing a category like Usability with a level like Intermediate might seem odd. A story's category and a story's audience level are totally different pieces of metadata. That's still true for Boxes and Arrows. However, the technology limits the number of fields we can use. So, inside the CMS, we'll combine our categories with our audience levels. **Figure 10.3** shows what this looks like inside PublicSquare.

Changing our categories calls for a change to the B&A homepage—the category navigation at the top left of the page will change to match these new categories. That's pretty easy, so we'll whip up a quick wireframe and send it off to everyone for comments (**Figure 10.4**). While our stakeholders review it, we'll work on the keywords page.

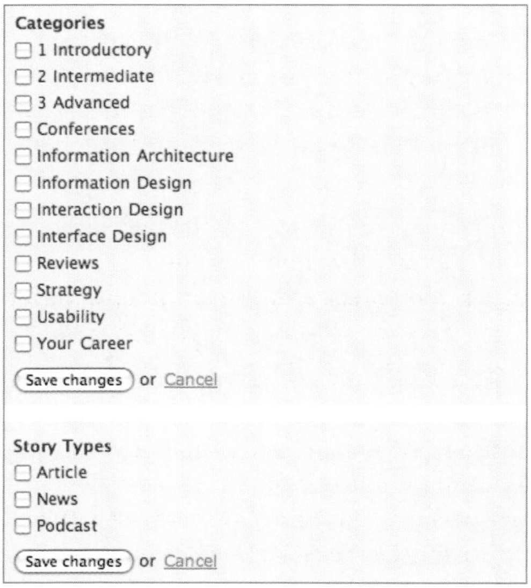

Categories
- [ ] 1 Introductory
- [ ] 2 Intermediate
- [ ] 3 Advanced
- [ ] Conferences
- [ ] Information Architecture
- [ ] Information Design
- [ ] Interaction Design
- [ ] Interface Design
- [ ] Reviews
- [ ] Strategy
- [ ] Usability
- [ ] Your Career

(Save changes) or Cancel

Story Types
- [ ] Article
- [ ] News
- [ ] Podcast

(Save changes) or Cancel

FIGURE 10.3 This is what our metadata looks like inside the CMS. Every story will be assigned at least two categories—at least one for its topic (like IA, Reviews, or Usability), and another for audience level (like Introductory or Advanced).

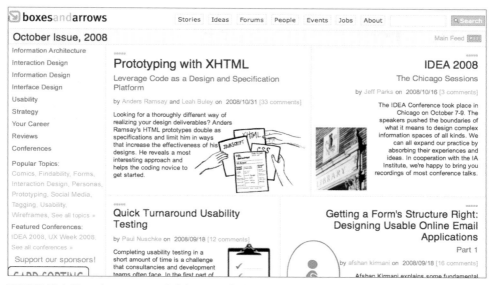

FIGURE 10.4 Since the recommended change to the homepage was minor, Austin took a screenshot of the current page and added the new categories to the top left. He also added keywords as a tag cloud ("Popular Topics") and a special collection of conference-related keywords.

Step 8: Designing the Keywords Page

In our task analysis, we came across mystery pages (represented with question marks). These mystery pages collected all articles related to specific keywords. Essentially, it's just a list of articles. In fact, we'll refer to it as a "list page." Boxes and Arrows already has several pages like this one. There is the search results page, and there are also the category pages. But the Keyword page will be different.

For starters, Lindsey wants to see all the introductory articles and avoid the advanced ones. Phillip wants to avoid the introductory articles and dive right into the more advanced stuff. Right now, the existing list pages don't break articles into groups. Maybe they should? Maybe not. Luckily for us, we don't have to make that decision now. We'll group articles on the Keywords page, and later, someone can figure out whether we should change the other list pages.

There's another way the Keyword pages are different. With both search results and category pages, you're only looking at one slice. You're looking at all articles in the Business Design section. Or, all articles with the phrase "negative personas" in them. One of the neat things about keywords is the way you can combine them. **Figure 10.5** shows how you can combine keywords on the social bookmarking site, Delicious.[9] Since we assume each article will have several tags assigned, it would be neat if we could let people combine them.

---

9 Delicious actually lets you combine tags, not keywords.

FIGURE 10.5 The bookmarking site, Delicious, lets users find links that share multiple tags.

That's kind of hard to visualize, so let's sketch some solutions, but before we start, we'll jot down a quick list of all of the elements we want to appear on each page:

- The keyword

- List of articles

- Breakdown by level (introductory, intermediate, advanced)

- Related tags

This is our shopping list. As we sketch, we need to make sure we're working all of these elements in. **Figure 10.6** shows Austin's first three sketches. In the first, Austin sketched the standard list page, just to get his bearings. In the second sketch, he adds in the breakdown by level, and also realizes he'll need to sort the articles in some way. His first thought is to sort by rating, with highest-rated articles listed first. The third sketch adds in related keywords, and that definitely makes the interface more complex.

Figure 10.7 shows sketches four through six where Austin continues to develop and iterate the Keyword page. Thinking about Lindsey, Austin decides she might need some kind of introduction to some of the more esoteric topics, so he adds a description or definition of the keyword and a friendly image to the top of the page. The Keyword page should also drive a lot of search engine traffic, and an intro will make the page more inviting for visitors arriving from Google or Yahoo! And if you're searching for a specific topic—like wireframes or personas—and you arrive at Boxes and Arrows, then maybe you'll want to keep up with all new articles on that topic. Austin adds an RSS link near the intro.

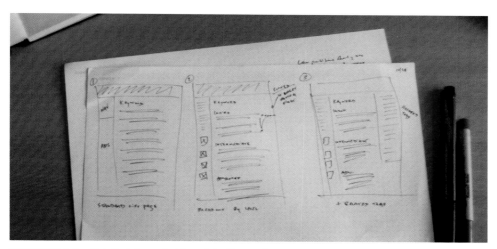

FIGURE 10.6 Austin's first three sketches of the Keywords page.

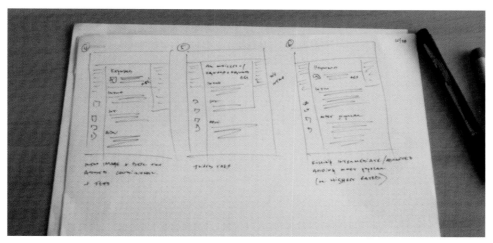

FIGURE 10.7 Austin continued to iterate with three more sketches.

Sketch #4 packs a lot of information in at the top of the page. In sketch #5, Austin sketches what it would look like if you were looking at a list of articles for two joined keywords. The top of the page is too busy, so he removes the intro text and image. Lindsey really digs the collection of introductory articles at the top, but we'd probably annoy Phillip if we made him browse through two separate chunks of intermediate and advanced articles. Phillip is probably more interested in the highest rated or most popular articles. Sketch #6 keeps the collection of introductory articles, but replaces intermediate and advanced with one list of articles that are sorted by what's most popular. But should they be sorted by most popular or by highest rated? Sketches #7 and #8 (**Figure 10.8**) show Austin zooming in to flesh out a little more detail.

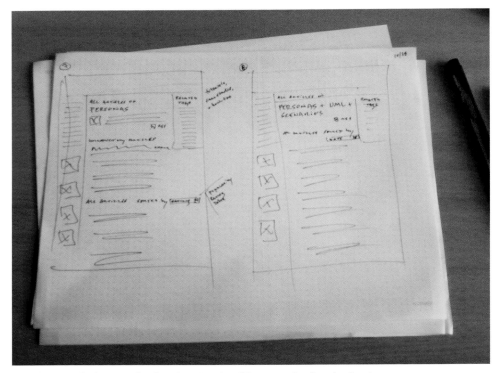

FIGURE 10.8 The last two sketches show Austin adding more detail to the sketches.

The sketches help us work though different ideas very quickly. Once we've worked out our ideas, we can try and crank out a couple of wireframes. **Figures 10.9** and **10.10** show our finished wireframes. We'll annotate these and email them to our stakeholders for comments and changes.

After reviewing the wireframes, we get back some good comments. Adding a description and image for individual keywords receives the most push back (Figure 10.9). Jorge is worried because it isn't scalable. You can't describe every keyword because hopefully, there will be lots of them and editors will be adding more all the time. Christina notes we probably couldn't describe the keywords, but probably could add descriptions for the categories: "It's not manageable to create a description for all of them. Categories will be limited to a manageable number and controlled by the editors, and thus it's possible to describe them."

FIGURE 10.9 Wireframe of the Keyword page. We've included introductory articles for Lindsey, but made the rest easy for Phillip to find.

FIGURE 10.10 This wireframe shows a variation of the Keyword page where the user has combined several keywords. It also demonstrates a couple of design variations. First, we see what the title looks like if there's no image or intro. Second, we see what happens if there are no more than two introductory articles. (There's no link to view more.)

Christina also provides some feedback about the new categories, noting that case studies are one of the most often requested types of stories. We add Case Studies. Our last couple of sketches showed it would be better to highlight introductory material, but not intermediate and advanced articles, so when we're adding Case Studies, we'll also remove Intermediate and Advanced. Our new categories look like **Figure 10.11**.

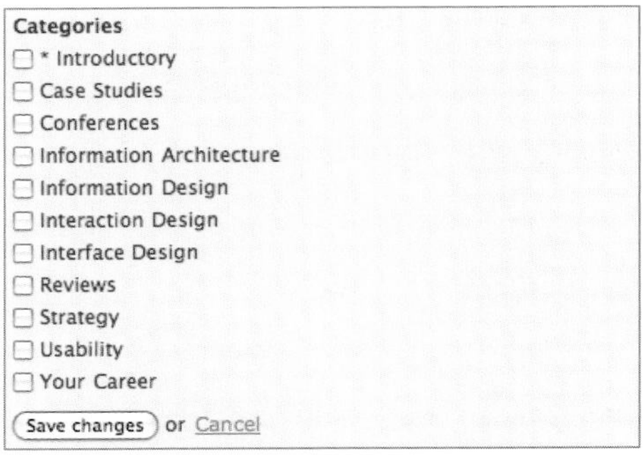

In the task analysis, both Lindsey and Phillip next choose articles to read, so the Article page will be our next stop, as well.

Categories

- ☐ * Introductory
- ☐ Case Studies
- ☐ Conferences
- ☐ Information Architecture
- ☐ Information Design
- ☐ Interaction Design
- ☐ Interface Design
- ☐ Reviews
- ☐ Strategy
- ☐ Usability
- ☐ Your Career

(Save changes) or Cancel

FIGURE 10.11 After iterating through several sketches and receiving feedback from the stakeholders, our categories have shifted slightly.

Step 9: Designing the Article Page

We're going to design the Article page the same way we designed the Keyword page: we'll jot down a quick list of all of the elements we want to make sure appear on each page:

- The article
- Article title
- Article date
- Categories
- Keywords
- Author info
- Comments and comment form

- Related articles
- Related content (events, jobs)
- Article rating
- Sharing tools (Digg, Bookmark, etc.)
- Article comment feed

That "related articles" item is deceptively singular. It's actually a form of associative navigation. In Chapter 8, The Tao of Navigation, we talk about all kinds of ways you can list "related articles." We'll brainstorm several types of related articles we can include on the B&A Article page:

- Articles in related categories—more articles about Information Architecture
- Articles with related keywords—more articles about personas and wireframes
- Articles by the same author
- Most popular articles

- New articles

- Articles with active discussions

We also wanted to promote Jobs, Events, and Forum Discussions:

- Related Jobs

- Related Events

- Related Forum Discussions

Man, that's a lot of stuff to squeeze onto one Article page. We know an Article page's primary purpose is to allow readers to consume the article. But other than that, we're not really sure what should go where. Austin does another card sort to group the different elements together. After they're grouped, he'll know what zones the page needs. Then he'll be able to start laying things out. The sorted elements are shown in **Table 10.8**.

Zone	Elements
Article metadata	Title Date Rating Categories Keywords (Synopsis)
Author metadata	Name Reputation Bio
Article	Text and images
Article tools	Rate the article Share (Digg, Facebook, etc.) Article feed
Comments & Discussion	Comments Comment form
Associated Articles	Articles from the same category Articles with the same keyword New articles
Associated discussions	Active forum discussions Active article discussions
Associated community stuff	Job posts Events
Other	Ads

TABLE 10.8 Austin's Grouping of the Article Page Elements.

Using these groupings, Austin zoned the article page for interaction (**Figure 10.12**). He ordered the zones according to what the user needs when. When the user first comes to the page, she wants to make sure this is the right article and that it's worth reading, so the article and author metadata goes at the top. Next, we see the article, and then tools for rating, sharing, and keeping up with the article (article tools). Next are the discussion tools, like comments, and finally, we show related articles.

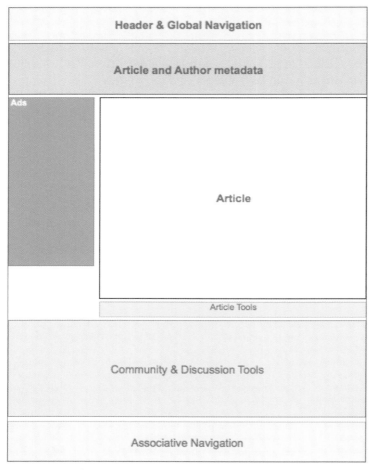

FIGURE 10.12 The B&A Article page, zoned for interaction.
Austin color-coded the zones to make them a little clearer.

Using these zones, Austin can lay out the new Article page (**Figure 10.13**).

Header and Global Navigation

Author metadata Name, photo, reputation, brief bio	Article metadata Title, date, average rating, categories, keywords
	Article
Ads	

Article tools: rate, share, feed

FIGURE 10.13 A very low-fidelity wireframe of the new Article page shows the position of the layout and not much more.

Article tools: rate, share, feed			
Events Advertised event	**Jobs** Advertised jobs		
Forum Discussions Five most active forum discussions.	**Comments** Comments and comment form		
Article discussions Five most recent or active article discussions			
Ideas Five Ideas with active discussions or needing ratings	**Related Articles - Category** Five articles from the same category or categories	**Related Articles - Keywprds** Five articles with the same keyword or keywords	**New Articles** Five most recently published articles
Footer and Global Navigation			

FIGURE 10.13 CONTINUED A very low-fidelity wireframe of the new Article page shows the position of the layout and not much more.

This first wireframe was very low-fidelity. We know where types of things go, but not where our links are. This is a good way for us to play around with the layout and make sure it really helps Phillip and Lindsey. It has all the things they need when reading an article. But to make sure it's just right, we need to add in some more detail (**Figure 10.14**).

It looks like this new Article page might help solve many of our problems from column "c." The list of related Categories and Keywords at the top allows someone like Lindsey access to all articles on a given topic. In this example, she could select "Wireframes" and be taken to the wireframe Keyword page to see introductory articles. Similarly, Phillip could take the same path to track down more advanced articles.

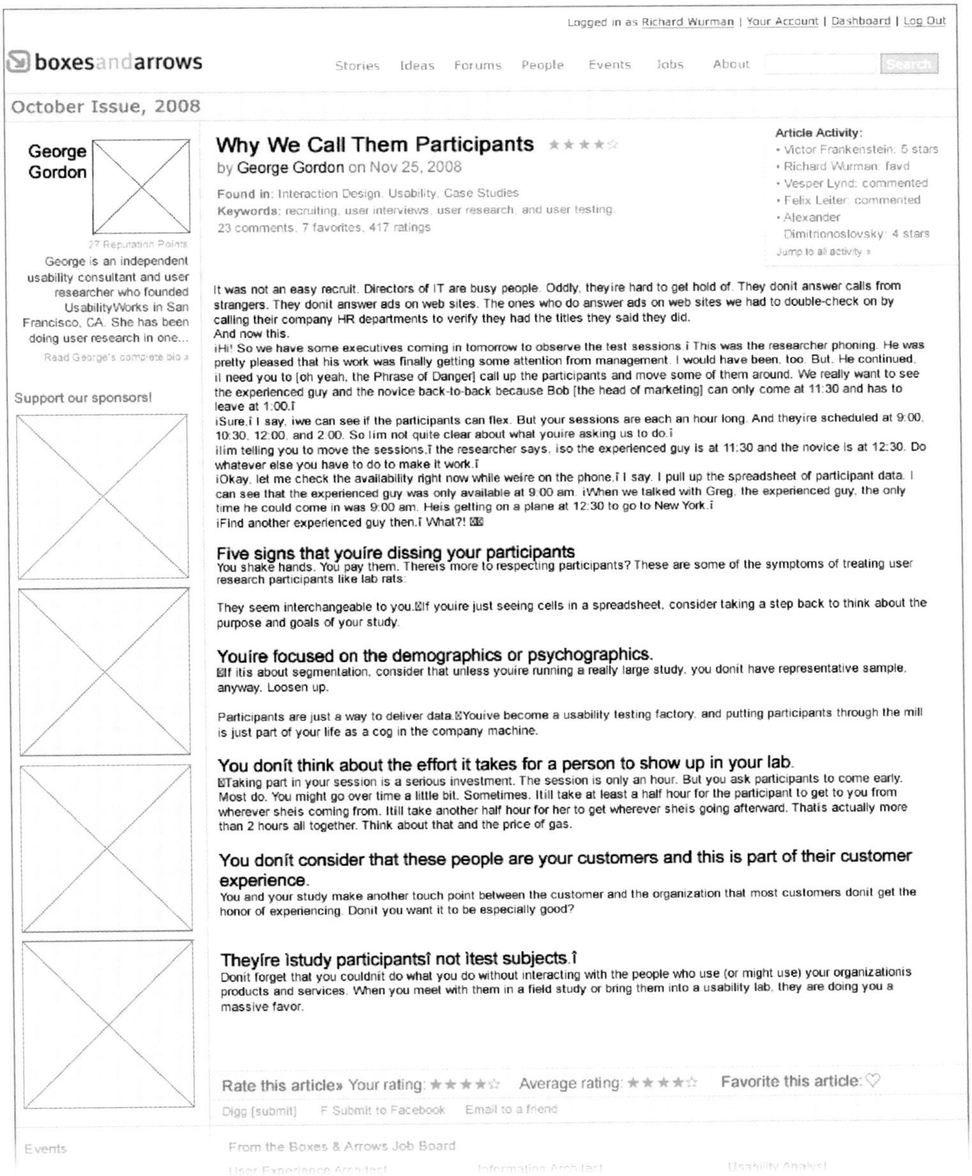

Logged in as Richard Wurman | Your Account | Dashboard | Log Out

boxesand**arrows**

Stories   Ideas   Forums   People   Events   Jobs   About   Search

October Issue, 2008

George
Gordon

27 Reputation Points

George is an independent
usability consultant and user
researcher who founded
UsabilityWorks in San
Francisco, CA. She has been
doing user research in one...

Read George's complete bio »

Support our sponsors!

Why We Call Them Participants   ★ ★ ★ ★ ☆
by George Gordon on Nov 25, 2008

Found in: Interaction Design, Usability, Case Studies
Keywords: recruiting, user interviews, user research, and user testing
23 comments, 7 favorites, 417 ratings

Article Activity:
- Victor Frankenstein: 5 stars
- Richard Wurman: favd
- Vesper Lynd: commented
- Felix Leiter: commented
- Alexander
  Dimitrionoslovsky: 4 stars

Jump to all activity »

It was not an easy recruit. Directors of IT are busy people. Oddly, theyíre hard to get hold of. They donít answer calls from strangers. They donít answer ads on web sites. The ones who do answer ads on web sites we had to double-check on by calling their company HR departments to verify they had the titles they said they did.
And now this.
íHi! So we have some executives coming in tomorrow to observe the test sessions.í This was the researcher phoning. He was pretty pleased that his work was finally getting some attention from management. I would have been, too. But. He continued, íI need you to [oh yeah, the Phrase of Danger] call up the participants and move some of them around. We really want to see the experienced guy and the novice back-to-back because Bob [the head of marketing] can only come at 11:30 and has to leave at 1:00.í
íSure,í I say, íwe can see if the participants can flex. But your sessions are each an hour long. And theyíre scheduled at 9:00, 10:30, 12:00, and 2:00. So Iím not quite clear about what youíre asking us to do.í
íIím telling you to move the sessions.í the researcher says, íso the experienced guy is at 11:30 and the novice is at 12:30. Do whatever else you have to do to make it work.í
íOkay, let me check the availability right now while weíre on the phone.í I say. I pull up the spreadsheet of participant data. I can see that the experienced guy was only available at 9:00 am. íWhen we talked with Greg, the experienced guy, the only time he could come in was 9:00 am. Heís getting on a plane at 12:30 to go to New York.í
íFind another experienced guy then.í What?! ☒☒

Five signs that youíre dissing your participants
You shake hands. You pay them. Thereís more to respecting participants? These are some of the symptoms of treating user research participants like lab rats:

They seem interchangeable to you.☒If youíre just seeing cells in a spreadsheet, consider taking a step back to think about the purpose and goals of your study.

Youíre focused on the demographics or psychographics.
☒If itís about segmentation, consider that unless youíre running a really large study, you donít have representative sample, anyway. Loosen up.

Participants are just a way to deliver data.☒Youíve become a usability testing factory, and putting participants through the mill is just part of your life as a cog in the company machine.

You donít think about the effort it takes for a person to show up in your lab.
☒Taking part in your session is a serious investment. The session is only an hour. But you ask participants to come early. Most do. You might go over time a little bit. Sometimes. Itíll take at least a half hour for the participant to get to you from wherever sheís coming from. Itíll take another half hour for her to get wherever sheís going afterward. Thatís actually more than 2 hours all together. Think about that and the price of gas.

You donít consider that these people are your customers and this is part of their customer experience.
You and your study make another touch point between the customer and the organization that most customers donít get the honor of experiencing. Donít you want it to be especially good?

Theyíre ìstudy participantsî not ìtest subjects.î
Donít forget that you couldnít do what you do without interacting with the people who use (or might use) your organizationís products and services. When you meet with them in a field study or bring them into a usability lab, they are doing you a massive favor.

Rate this article» Your rating: ★ ★ ★ ★ ☆   Average rating: ★ ★ ★ ★ ☆   Favorite this article: ♡

Digg [submit]   F Submit to Facebook   Email to a friend

Events

From the Boxes & Arrows Job Board
User Experience Architect   Information Architect   Usability Analyst

FIGURE 10.14 A more detailed wireframe.

Rate this article» Your rating ★ ★ ★ ★ ★   Average rating ★ ★ ★ ★ ★   Favorite this article »

Digg (submit)   F Submit to Facebook   Email to a friend

Events	From the Boxes & Arrows Job Board		
Dec 1 - London	**User Experience Architect**	**Information Architect**	**Usability Analyst**
Web Accessibility Training	JWT is looking for a User Experience	Jarvis Studio is looking for a Information	Zimmerman Design is looking for a
Dec 1 - Montreal	Architect in Chicago	Architect in Montpelier	Usability Analyst in Minneapolis
MontrealCHI Monthly Meeting			
			Advertise your job here »
View all events »			

Active Forum Discussions:
» Comment Votes Usability Problem
» User testing.com
» Remote usability testing
» Yahoo problem
» What do you think of our registration flow?
Jump to the forums »

	Comments	Ratings	Favorites

Stay on top of the conversation. Subscribe to the comment feed. 🔲

Active Article Discussions:
» Prototyping with XHTML and CSS
» IDEA 2008: the Chicago sessions
» Enterprise Information Architecture
» Information Architecture for Content Management Systems
» Information Architecture 3.0
Jump to the forums »

Ideas that need ratings:	More articles in Case Studies, Interaction Design, and Usability:	Related articles:	New stories posted to Boxes & Arrows:
» Prototyping with XHTML and CSS		Articles sharing all of the same keywords:	» Prototyping with XHTML and CSS
» IDEA 2008: the Chicago sessions	» Prototyping with XHTML and CSS	» recruiting + user interviews + user research + user testing	» IDEA 2008: the Chicago sessions
» Enterprise Information Architecture	» IDEA 2008: the Chicago sessions		» Enterprise Information Architecture
» Information Architecture for Content Management Systems	» Enterprise Information Architecture	**Or, browse a specific keyword:**	» Information Architecture for Content Management Systems
» Information Architecture 3.0	» Information Architecture for Content Management Systems	» recruiting	» Information Architecture 3.0
	» Information Architecture 3.0	» user interviews	
Check out more Ideas »		» user research	Check out more new stories »
	Browse all stories »	» user testing	
		Browse all keywords »	

Home	**Join the conversation**	**Browse stories**	**Recommended Topics**
About Boxes & Arrows	» Ideas	» Information Architecture	Comics, Findability, Forms, Interaction Design,
Submission Guidelines	» Forums	» Interaction Design	Personas, Prototyping, Social Media, Tagging,
		» Information Design	Usability, Wireframes, See all topics.
Your profile	**Join your peers**	» Interface Design	Browse all keywords »
» Edit your profile	» People	» Usability	
» About your reputation	» Events	» Strategy	
	» Jobs	» Your Career	**Featured Conferences**
		» Reviews	IDEA 2008, UX Week 2008.
		» Conferences	See all conferences »

FIGURE 10.14 CONTINUED   A more detailed wireframe.

The new design highlights conversations on the site, which are important for our long-term goal of engaging the reader. In addition to displaying (and encouraging) comments, we also provide links to 10 additional conversations. That's 10 more than exist on the current article page. Similarly, the horizontal row of associated navigation to articles both related and new, provides 15 additional links that users can choose after reading an article. The article page is certainly not a dead-end now.

And despite all of the links we've added, it doesn't feel busier than the old page. Because we zoned it for interaction and grouped similar functionality, the final page includes all of our design elements without overpowering the user.

Now that we've designed a solution for our main problems, we can send the article page wireframe off for comment and review.

This is what Christina said:

> "I so prefer this new categorization scheme. Makes so much more sense.
>
> I'm really looking forward to tagging. I think our users will teach us a lot about how they think of our content.
>
> We seem to have lost our topics in the global navigation. I don't mind if you want to use that space more effectively, but they belong somewhere. Sitemap on every page, perhaps?
>
> I like that you've brought in more associated navigation. Do you think you can inter-twingle it with the story in the design more? That's where people look.
>
> We have a rather long list of more stories by an author, sometimes. Do you have a sense of how that will scale?
>
> Directionally, I think this is right…when can I see the design? "

Of course, we still have a long way before the site is live. We need to address the profile problems from column b, first of all. We'll make mock-ups and test them, we'll have to code new templates in HTML and CSS, and we'll have to go through and re-categorize each article—adding keywords while we're there. But for now, we feel pretty darn good.

11

And in the End...

In which the ghosts of
information architecture
past, present, and future
visit.

> *There is a tsunami of data that is crashing onto the beaches of the civilized world. This is a tidal wave of unrelated, growing data formed in bits and bytes, coming in an unorganized, uncontrolled, incoherent cacophony of foam. None of it is easily related, none of it comes with any organization methodology.*
>
> *Now for the good news: There is a dune on the beach. There is a breakwater in the ocean that is clearly emerging in these last fleeting moments of the 20th century. The breakwater is indeed breaking up the tsunami of data and focusing it in a more oganized way to answer our questions and concerns. There is a new breed of graphic designers, exhibition designers, illustrators and photographers, whose passion it is to make the complex clear.*
>
> *I call this new breed of talented thinkers Information Architects and this book was created to help celebrate and understand the importance of their work—a work which inspires hope that as we expand our capabilities to inform and communicate that we will value, with equal enthusiasm, the design of understanding.*
>
> —*Richard Saul Wurman, from Information Architects (Watson-Guptill Publishers, 1997)*

Richard Saul Wurman wrote this in 1997. The Internet had just taken off with the general population of computer owners. Napster didn't exist. Palm Pilots were owned by a few gadget geeks, and Apple was a computer company. Hotel rooms did not have Wi-Fi (nor did most coffee shops), laptops were too heavy for your lap, and you used your cell phone only for phone calls. Yet everyone raced to put information on the Web, and throughout the late 1990s, millions of sites were added every day. There was a data-overload problem in 1997, before the dot-com boom and bust. No one knew it was just the first wave.

The Present

Today, the Web is not a novelty or a toy. It is a viable aspect of any business. Banks use it to reduce customer service calls, movies use it to sell tickets, and stores use it to expand their shopping audience beyond driving distances. For business, it's no longer a question of "Shall we build a Web site?" but rather, "When are we getting our Web site up?" Even more likely is, "Why isn't our Web site helping our business?" A disorganized intranet eats up employee time while employees try to find information they need, a disorganized external Web site prevents online shoppers from finding the items they want to purchase, and the lack of a Web site (or a badly organized one) drives the customer to the phone with basic questions like, "Where is there a store near me?" or "What is your return policy?" These calls force businesses to hire more customer service representatives.

Expensive, expensive, expensive.

Beyond the basic issue of companies losing money in missed sales and inefficient processes, disorganized Web sites do the following:

- Appear amateurish, making people less willing to hand over their credit card information.

- Annoy customers, making them vulnerable to the siren call of your competition.

- Embarrass employees, damaging morale.

The alternative is thoughtful planning and well-designed information architecture, which improves the following characteristics of your Web site:

- **Findability**—Allows customers to easily access those items they need, be they spatulas or term papers.

- **Usability**—Allows customers to wend their way to those items and accomplish the tasks they most want to accomplish.

- **Understandability**—Provides a good architectural infrastructure necessary to help people make knowledge out of information.

The most-loved brands are those brands that don't make people feel like idiots. The simple iPod is loved; the complicated Microsoft Windows is barely tolerated. Web site creators are on a cusp right now, poised between being part of the problem or part of the solution. Should we continue to throw every bit of data we've got onto the Web and "let Google sort it out?" Or do we want to start thinking about why we are putting things onto the Internet, what we want to accomplish by doing so, and how we can best accomplish those goals? Will we continue to flail about in the sea of information, or will we choose to swim?

The Future of Information Architecture

We can't even imagine what the next advance in technology will bring, any more than TV viewers in the 1950s could imagine the Internet. But every day, the line between the world of ideas and knowledge and the physical world grows thinner.

The information tsunami is growing greater with each passing day. We wrote this book for the same reason that Richard Saul Wurman wrote his: Someone will have to step up to make the complex clear. But unlike Wurman, we think it will be more than a few design specialists. Everyone in the information space will have to act as a breakwater. We wrote this book in hopes of giving you wall-building skills.

Go out and protect human beings from drowning in the sea of information. Help your company to be successful. Help a nonprofit organization make its charity more accessible to those who need it. Make your personal site a bit more useful for your friends and family.

Go make the complex clear.

Index

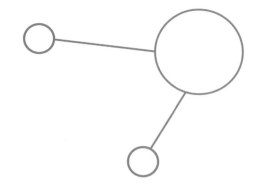

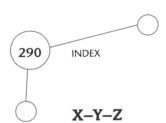

X–Y–Z